Neither Liberal nor Conservative

CHICAGO STUDIES IN AMERICAN POLITICS

A series edited by
BENJAMIN I. PAGE, SUSAN HERBST, LAWRENCE R. JACOBS, AND ADAM J. BERINSKY

Also in the series:

Additional series titles follow index

Neither Liberal nor Conservative

Ideological Innocence in the American Public

DONALD R. KINDER AND
NATHAN P. KALMOE

THE UNIVERSITY OF CHICAGO PRESS   CHICAGO AND LONDON

The University of Chicago Press, Chicago 60637
The University of Chicago Press, Ltd., London
© 2017 by The University of Chicago
Published 2017
Printed in the United States of America

26 25 24 23 22 21 20 19 18 17   1 2 3 4 5

ISBN-13: 978-0-226-45231-9 (cloth)
ISBN-13: 978-0-226-45245-6 (paper)
ISBN-13: 978-0-226-45259-3 (e-book)
DOI: 10.7208/chicago/9780226452593.001.0001

Library of Congress Control Number: 2016046170

♾ This paper meets the requirements of ANSI/NISO Z39.48-1992 (Permanence of Paper).

TO PHILIP E. CONVERSE
SCHOLAR UNSURPASSED

Contents

Preface

L ong ago and far away, Kinder had the good fortune to find himself in a seminar taught by David Sears. Sears assigned "The Nature of Belief Systems in Mass Publics" by Philip Converse. Kinder read it, and has never been quite the same since.

Kinder decided to write his seminar paper on critical reaction to Converse's essay. Turns out, there was quite a bit of it. There was so much, in fact, that Kinder had no chance to complete his paper by the end of the term (an arbitrary deadline, in any case).

Years passed. Kinder and family—Janet, Benjamin, Samuel, and Jacob—embarked on a road trip. They headed out from Ann Arbor. Their destination was Stanford, where they were to spend the academic year in blissful sabbatical. They meandered, stopping often to take in the natural wonders of the American West. Nearing the end of their journey, late on a hot summer day, they pulled in to the parking lot of a dusty diner, in what seemed like the middle of nowhere. In fact, the diner was exactly somewhere. It was in Nevada and in Utah, perfectly bisected by the state line. This meant that their table was on Mountain Time; the men's bathroom, on Pacific. The children, having been cooped up in the family station wagon for most of the day, found it fantastic, great fun, to move rapidly back and forth between the two, somehow magically gaining and losing an hour.

Kinder and Janet sat there, barely conscious, having been cooped up in the family station wagon for most of the day, and pretended the children belonged to someone else. The door of the diner swung open, and in walked Philip Converse. He was heading east to Ann Arbor, having just finished his stint as director of the Center for Advanced Study in the

Behavioral Sciences at Stanford. Kinder and Janet were delighted to see him, he was happy to see them, and he pretended not to mind their raucous children.

Years passed. Kinder decided it was time to complete his essay, to finish what he had started in the spring of 1970. He enlisted Kalmoe, then a young, splendid student, and possessed of epic patience. It took a while, but together, Kinder and Kalmoe prevailed.

*   *   *

We are delighted that our book is being published by the University of Chicago Press, and delighted as well that the publishing has been overseen by John Tryneski. John persuaded two reviewers to dig deep into our manuscript, which we had prematurely concluded was a book. The reviewers made a lot of trouble for us, but of the very best kind. We are most grateful for the time and thought they put into our work. If it is still not the book they wished we had written, it is at least much improved over what they first saw.

We thank David Sears, who started us on this journey, for that and many other things, and the University of Michigan, an extraordinary place, for stimulating colleagues and the opportunity to follow our interests wherever they might lead. Molly Reynolds deserves special thanks for helping us get to the finish line in the last year as our professional obligations multiplied and our time was divided. Leslie Keros provided superb and meticulous editing. And we thank discussants and participants at Midwest Political Science Association and American Political Science Association conferences for their helpful feedback on early versions of this work.

Philip Converse died on December 30, 2014. We had hoped to finish in time to present a copy of our book to him. Converse is gone but his work endures, and that provides some consolation. However, for those of us fortunate enough to call him friend and colleague, and who knew him not only as an extraordinary scholar but also as a humane and generous spirit, he will be sorely missed. We dedicate our book to his memory.

Introduction

Innocent of Ideology?

For those who seek to understand the structures and dynamics of
political life, the concept of ideology has proven very nearly irre-
sistible. Electoral competition, executive influence, the legislative enterprise, bureaucratic politics, judicial decisions: in all these cases and
more, political actors are assumed to be motivated, at least in part, by
ideological conviction. According to Marcel Gauchet, the prominent
French historian and philosopher, ideology has "conquered the planet."
Liberal and conservative, left and right, "have become universal political categories. They are part of the basic notions which generally inform the way contemporary societies work" (Gauchet 1992, 84, quoted
in Bobbio 1996, 92).

The American political system would seem to offer up a superb case
in point. Congress is crippled by ideological differences. The political
parties are more polarized today than at any time since the Civil War.
The courts decide First Amendment cases depending on whether it is liberal or conservative speech that is being suppressed. News organizations
abandon objectivity for ideological purity. Pundits behave badly, hurling
insults at one another. As Ronald Dworkin summarizes our situation,
"We disagree, fiercely, about almost everything. We disagree about terror and security, social justice, religion in politics, who is fit to be a judge,
and what democracy is" (2006, 1).[1]

When Dworkin says "we" he has (or should have) in mind political
elites—those whose lives are immersed in politics and who exert disproportionate influence over policy and discourse. It is a relatively small
group: the president; congressional leaders; the Supreme Court; presidential candidates; prominent journalists and editorial writers; publicists

for interest groups, corporations, and political movements; and a hand-
ful of public intellectuals. These people differ from one another in many
ways, but they have one thing in common. On the subject of politics, all
are experts.[2]

The average citizen is not. To the ongoing and perhaps increasingly
bitter ideological arguments dividing elites, most Americans are little
more than casual spectators. Parochial in interest, modest in intellect,
and burdened by the demands and obligations of everyday life, most citizens lack the wherewithal and motivation to grasp political matters in a
deep way. People are busy with more pressing things; politics is complicated and far away. Ideology is not for them.

That, at least, was the position staked out by Walter Lippmann. In
a series of influential essays written in the aftermath of World War I,
Lippmann argued that the democratic ideal of the fully informed citizen was unattainable and should be abandoned. It was unrealistic in
the same way that it was unrealistic "for a fat man to try to be a ballet
dancer" (Lippmann 1925, 39). According to Lippmann,

> The private citizen today has come to feel rather like a deaf spectator in the
> back row, who ought to keep his mind on the mystery off there, but cannot
> quite manage to keep awake. He knows he is somehow affected by what is go-
> ing on. Rules and regulations continually, taxes annually, and wars occasion-
> ally remind him he is being swept along by great drifts of circumstance.
>
> Yet these public affairs are in no convincing way his affairs. They are for
> the most part invisible. They are managed, if they are managed at all, at dis-
> tant centers, from behind the scenes, by unnamed powers. As a private per-
> son he does not know for certain what is going on, or who is doing it, or where
> he is being carried (13).

In a similar vein, Joseph Schumpeter (1942) argued against strong
forms of democracy on the grounds that the people were not up to the
task. When asked to consider matters of political importance, the average person, according to Schumpeter, "is impatient of long or complicated argument," is in possession of "weak rational processes," is "not
'all there.'" In Schumpeter's judgment, the typical citizen "drops down
to a lower level of mental performance as soon as he enters the political
field. He argues and analyzes in a way which he would readily recognize
as infantile within the sphere of his real interests. He becomes a primi-
tive again" (257, 262).

Neither Lippmann nor Schumpeter held out hope that ordinary people would be interested in big ideas. Both wrote authoritatively, but neither presented empirical proof. Schumpeter was right to say that deciding whether ordinary people possessed the means to participate fully and thoughtfully in discussions over their country's future required not "reckless assertion" but rather "laborious appraisal of a maze of conflicting evidence" (1942, 254)—but he did not undertake such an analysis himself. To be fair, in Schumpeter's time, there was hardly any evidence worth analyzing.

Which brings us, some twenty years later, to Philip Converse and his celebrated, or notorious but certainly powerful, essay on the nature of belief systems in mass publics, published in 1964. Like Lippmann and Schumpeter, Converse was motivated by an interest in how (and how well) ordinary people in democratic societies reasoned about politics. Converse enjoyed some crucial technical advantages over his predecessors, however. Most notable was the invention of the probability sample. Properly executed, probability sampling ensures that all citizens—rich and poor, young and old, men and women, of all races and faiths—are presented for study in numbers proportionate to their presence in the electorate. Probability sampling, along with advances in attitude measurement and statistical methods, meant that Converse could do what Lippmann and Schumpeter could not. Commencing with Converse, ideology became an object of scientific inquiry.

After a careful and probing analysis of a series of national election surveys carried out during the Eisenhower years, Converse concluded that the American mass public—*any* mass public, really—was incapable of following, much less actively participating in, ideological discussion. Converse found that most Americans were indifferent to or mystified by liberalism and conservatism as political ideas; that their opinions on government policy displayed little evidence of coherent organization along ideological lines; and that relatively modest proportions of the electorate were in possession of real opinions, even on matters of obvious national importance. In Converse's judgment, most Americans were innocent of ideology.[3]

Publication of Converse's essay set off a huge commotion. The blowback was fierce. Critics poked holes in Converse's argument, took exception to his methods, claimed he generalized his results recklessly, and pointed to transformations in American society that rendered his claim obsolete. But when all the evidence is considered and all the counterarguments assessed, Converse's claim of ideological innocence, taken on its own terms, stands up. So, at least, we will argue here.

Coming to grips with Converse and his critics is serious business—we spend the first part of the book on just this enterprise—but (switching metaphors) we have bigger fish to fry. Getting the Converse literature straight is important in itself, but doing that alone would be insufficient to reach a rounded assessment of the public's ideological capacity and appetite. If we were to take up Converse's claim strictly on its own terms and then declare our business complete, we would overlook a thriving and largely independent line of research that seems, on the surface at least, to suggest very nearly the opposite of what Converse was urging.

At about the time the first and most contentious round of debate over the ideological performance of the American public was beginning to subside, a new question was making its way onto the American National Election Study (ANES), the leading and longest-running study of voters and elections in the United States (and indeed the world). Beginning in 1972, and in every election study since, citizens surveyed by ANES interviewers have been asked whether they think of themselves as liberals or conservatives, and if so, to locate themselves on a seven-point scale, stretching from liberal on the left to conservative on the right.

It turns out that when asked directly in this way, many Americans describe themselves in ideological terms. Or as we will say, when asked, many Americans "identify" with an ideological point of view. *That's* surprising, if Converse is right. More surprising still, ideological identification appears to be meaningful: those who identify as liberal tend to favor redistributive policies and vote for Democratic candidates; those who identify as conservative tend to favor reductions in government spending and vote Republican.[4]

These empirical relationships are unpretentious—they are statistical tendencies, not logical imperatives—but they show up with impressive regularity. Analysis of ideological identification has become standard practice, and ideological identification itself has become part of the new conventional wisdom (see figure I.1).[5] Christopher Ellis and James Stimson go so far as to say that ideological identification is "nearly indispensable to the beliefs and choices of American citizens" (2009, 388). Ordinary people, it seems, can hardly do without it.

What does all this research activity have to say to the general claim of ideological innocence? Oddly enough, not much. With a few notable exceptions, ideological identification researchers have gone about

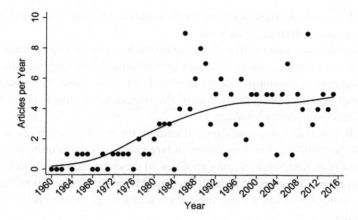

FIGURE 1.1 Research on ideological identification, 1960–2015 (count of number of articles per year in top four journals)

Note: Journals are *American Political Science Review*, *American Journal of Political Science*, *Journal of Politics*, and *Public Opinion Quarterly*.

their business without pausing to consider the larger debate on ideology. Moreover, they have gone about their business (again with important exceptions) without scrutinizing what Americans are saying—what they are *really* saying—when they describe themselves in ostensibly ideological terms.[6]

We speak to both problems here. The heart of our book reports a thorough investigation, long overdue, into the nature of ideological identification: its meaning, measurement, origins, tenacity, persistence, and consequences. That completed, we will be in a position to reconcile the evidence on ideological identification with the general claim of ideological innocence. To what extent must we reassess the ideological capacity of the American electorate, given what we know—what we are about to find out—regarding Americans' propensity to describe themselves in ideological terms?

Looking Ahead

We begin, in chapter 1, by recapitulating Converse's original argument. The need to do so may seem surprising. After all, in election and public opinion circles, Converse's essay is as famous as famous gets. Famous? Yes. Carefully read? No, not always. To make sure we start off in the right direction, we must begin with a clear account of what Converse was claiming more than fifty years ago.

Chapter 2 then takes up the scholarly storm set off by the publication of Converse's essay. Sifting through the evidence, weighing the claims pro and con, occasionally adding new findings of our own, we conclude that well into the twenty-first century, the American electorate is, by and large, *still* innocent of ideology.

This conclusion is provisional, of course, for it leaves aside the well-established finding that Americans in large numbers seem quite willing to identify as liberals or as conservatives, to describe themselves in ideological terms. To assess the challenge that this finding poses to the general conclusion of ideological innocence requires extensive and careful treatment.

We initiate this treatment in chapter 3 by stipulating what we mean by ideological identification and showing that the standard measure of ideological identification is serviceable. These matters accomplished, we then begin to explore the nature of ideological identification in the American mass public. A first finding is that ideological identification is not for everyone. When offered the opportunity, many Americans say that they do not think of themselves as liberals or as conservatives. When Americans do claim an ideological identity, furthermore, many choose moderation. These rudimentary facts begin to diminish the discrepancy between what Converse was claiming and what the evidence on ideological identification is often taken to mean.

Any theory of ideology must address how ideology arises—how it happens that ordinary people take possession of ideological ideas (insofar as they do). The purpose of chapter 4 is to explain how Americans come to see themselves in ideological terms. We show why some Americans claim an ideological identity while many others do not, investigate whether moderation should be regarded as a real ideological destination, and discover how tenaciously Americans cling to an ideological identity, once they acquire one (if they do).

In chapter 5 our analysis turns to ideological identification in the long run. We consider whether the American electorate is polarizing (it is, barely); and whether Republicans who think of themselves as liberal as well as Democrats who think of themselves as conservative are endangered species (their numbers are dwindling but extinction is still a long way off).

We come next to ideological identification's political consequences. The question of consequences is pivotal. If our purpose is to understand the opinions and choices citizens make, how vital is ideological identification to the task? In chapter 6, we provide an assessment of the effect of ideological identification on the votes Americans cast for public office, the preferences they express on the pressing issues of the day, and the "maps" they draw of political reality. We find modest and contingent effects. The ideological battles under way among American political elites show up as scattered skirmishes in the general public, if they show up at all. Insofar as ideological identification is connected to politics, it perhaps should be considered less a cause and more an effect: ideological identification as "mere summary."

In chapter 7, we summarize our results and weigh their implications. Our first responsibility is to juxtapose what we have learned about ideological identification against the broad claim of ideological innocence. As a general matter, we find little in the evidence on ideological identification to trouble the claim of innocence. On the contrary, genuine ideological identification—an abiding dispositional commitment to an ideological point of view—turns out to be rare. Real liberals and real conservatives are found in impressive numbers only among the comparatively few who are deeply and seriously engaged in political life.

The final chapter also offers commentary and conjecture on a series of significant topics that we have bumped up against in our investigation, most notably the place of ideology in politics outside the United States, the contrast between ideological identification and party identification, information inequality as a fundamental feature of modern society, and, especially important, the promise and desirability of alternatives to ideology. If, as we say, ideology remains out of reach, how *do* Americans come to judgments and decisions that, taken collectively, shape their future?

Converse and His Critics

CHAPTER ONE

Converse's Claim

A ccording to Converse, most Americans display little or no evidence of ideology in their thinking about public affairs. Of liberalism and conservatism—not to speak of more arcane political programs—Americans are largely innocent. In this chapter we retrace Converse's famous and foundational argument. If we are to make sense of the great debate over the ideological capacity of mass publics, we must begin at the beginning, with what Converse was up to back in 1964.[1]

Ideology Defined

When Converse alleges that Americans are innocent of ideology, what is it he is claiming they are missing? Innocent of what, exactly?[2]

This question is less straightforward than it may appear, for ideology has been defined in multiple ways and put to a variety of purposes. The result, predictably enough, is confusion. According to Nicholas Abercrombie, Stephen Hill, and Bryan Turner (1980, 187), "the notion of 'ideology' has given rise to more analytical and conceptual difficulties than almost any other term in the social sciences." To Giovanni Sartori (1969, 398), the growing popularity of the term "ideology" is matched only "by its growing obscurity." Jon Elster (1985, 460) warns us that the study of ideology "is fraught with dangers and difficulties, provoking resignation in some, foolhardiness in others." We could go on.

The term itself has experienced a serpentine history. It was invented by a French aristocrat who survived the Revolution to publish *Éléments d'Idéologie* (Destutt de Tracy 1801). By ideology, Count Antoine Destutt de Tracy meant those ideas drawn from competing political philosophies designed to inspire political loyalties and motivate political action (Lakoff 2011). Ideologies were "social romances"—collections of "political proposals, perhaps somewhat intellectualistic and impractical but at any rate idealistic" (Geertz 1973, 193).

By the middle of the twentieth century, the meaning of ideology had taken a sinister turn. In his essay "Ideology and Civility," published in 1958, Edward Shils offered a warning against the ideological outlooks that had "encircled and invaded public life" (450). As cases in point, Shils had in mind Italian Fascism, German National Socialism, and Russian Bolshevism. Such programs differed from one another in important ways, but they shared "the assumption that politics should be conducted from the standpoint of a coherent, comprehensive set of beliefs which must override every other consideration" (450). An odious feature of ideology, defined this way, is its imperial domination of all spheres of life. Ideology "replaces religion, provides aesthetic criteria, rules over scientific research and philosophic thought, and regulates sexual and family life" (451).

Although we acknowledge that ideology, carried to an extreme, can become the enemy of reason, Shils's conception of ideology is not ours. Nor is it what Converse had in mind. Indeed, critics who charged that Converse had underestimated the presence of ideology among the American electorate and sought to set things right believed they were doing ordinary people a favor.

The debate over the ideological capacity of mass publics began with Converse, and now more than fifty years later, it is not over yet. What has all the shouting been about? Without imagining that our conception of ideology will suit all tastes, we should at least lay our cards on the table. Here they are.

Ideology is a form of cognition. Ideology can of course refer to doctrine, as in the *Communist Manifesto*, or to practice, as in the division of labor between husbands and wives. Here, however, ideology refers to belief, or better, to configurations of beliefs. Ideology exists—if it exists—in the mind.

The subject of ideology is society, economics, and politics—as they are, and especially as they should be. That is, ideology expresses what people take to be right and proper. Opinions and actions justified in ideological terms lay claim to what *all* members of a political community should value.

The various ideas that comprise an ideology form an organized structure. Structure implies both that ideas are arranged in orderly, predictable patterns and that change in one idea requires change in others. Structure is a necessary condition for ideology. No structure, no ideology.[3]

Ideological structures are shared. "The significance of ideology," as Hans Noel has written, "is that it organizes politics for many, not just for one" (2013, 41). Rival ideologies "compete over providing and controlling plans for public policy"; they are deployed "with the aim of justifying, contesting, or changing the social and political arrangements and processes of a political community" (Freeden 2003, 32).

Finally, beliefs that constitute an ideology are held sincerely and steadfastly. Those beliefs that occupy a central position in an ideological system—insistence on equality for one person, the value of tradition for another—are especially resistant to change. For the true believer, core beliefs are prized possessions: fiercely defended, relinquished only under extraordinary circumstances.[4]

Ideology, understood in this way, supplies citizens with a stable foundation for understanding and action. Those who come to politics equipped with ideology enjoy a comparative advantage: "new political events have more meaning, retention of political information from the past is far more adequate, and political behavior increasingly approximates that of sophisticated 'rational' models, which assume relatively full information" (Converse 1964, 227).

Ideology seems, from this perspective, an altogether good thing. If Americans approached the political world with an ideology in mind, they would see that world clearly, understand it well, and form opinions and make decisions that faithfully reflect their core beliefs. Under this condition, strong democracy—government responsive to the articulated preferences of the people—seems less a sentimental dream and more a practical possibility. And so, putting our central question crudely: do Americans in fact approach the world of politics with an ideology in mind?

Argument and Evidence

We already know Converse's answer: a resounding, emphatic no. He arrived at this answer not through armchair theorizing but through painstaking empirical examination of the first round of national election studies. The studies covered the 1956, 1958, and 1960 presidential and midterm elections and were carried out to high standards by the Survey Research Center at the University of Michigan. Respondents were selected by probability sampling, which ensured that every person in the continental United States had an equal (if small) chance of being included in the sample. Professional interviewers conducted lengthy, carefully scripted conversations on politics with Americans from all walks of life: rich and poor, men and women, those vitally interested in politics and those who could scarcely care less, and more, each proportional to their actual presence in American society.[5]

Provided these rich materials, Converse embarked on his study. He began by investigating the extent to which Americans make use of ideological categories in their assessment of prominent political objects. Early on in the 1956 election study, respondents were asked what they liked and what they disliked about the Democratic and Republican parties, and in a separate set of questions, what they liked and disliked about Adlai Stevenson and Dwight Eisenhower, the Democratic and Republican candidates for president that year. Interviewers were instructed to press gently but insistently for as many as five separate answers for each question. The questions themselves were completely open ended. People could say whatever they cared to. Whatever they said was carefully recorded by the interviewers. These verbatim transcriptions were then sent back to the Survey Research Center at Michigan and pored over by Converse for evidence of ideological thinking.

Such evidence turned out to be hard to find. Converse regarded Americans to be in possession of an ideological point of view if they justified their political attachments by invoking ideological concepts. Here's an illustration of what Converse had in mind, drawn from an interview with a Chicago suburban woman. Let's call her Fran:

INTERVIEWER: Is there anything you dislike about the Democrats?

FRAN: From being raised in a notoriously Republican section—a small town downstate—there were things I didn't like. There was family influence that way.

I: What in particular was there you didn't like about the Democratic Party?

FRAN: Well, the Democratic Party tends to favor socialized medicine—and I'm being influenced in that because I came from a doctor's family.

I: Is there anything you like about the Republicans?

FRAN: Well, I think they're more middle-of-the-road—more conservative.

1: How do you mean "conservative"?

FRAN: They are not so subject to radical change.

1: Is there anything else in particular that you like about the Republican Party?

FRAN: Oh, I like their foreign policy—and the segregation business, that's a middle-of-the-road policy. You can't push it too fast. You can instigate things, but you have to let them take their course slowly. (Campbell et al. 1960, 228–29)

In these remarks, Fran does not appear to be an exceptional observer of politics. She has absorbed some of the ideological abstractions of her time, and she makes sensible use of them in justifying her political views.

In an actuarial sense, however, Fran *is* exceptional. By Converse's criteria, only 2.5 percent of the American electorate merit ideological classification. This despite the fact that respondents were graded according to their most "elevated" answer: that is, *any* evidence of ideological justification appearing in *any* portion of their commentary on the parties *or* on the candidates was sufficient to place them into the ideological category. And yet very few pass this test. Fran, it turns out, belongs to a small and select club.

Those who made use of ideological concepts but appeared neither to rely upon them heavily nor to understand them well were placed in a second category, "Near-Ideologue." Here's an example, drawn from an interview with a man living in southern California. We'll call him David:

INTERVIEWER: Is there anything you like about the Democrats?

DAVID: The Democratic Party is more for higher social security. They're more for old age pensions and better working conditions for the working man. They want a higher standard of living for all people, not just a few. The promises made by the Democrats are kept if at all possible. The facts are told to the American people.

1: Is there anything you like about the Republicans?

DAVID: I dislike everything about the Republican Party.

1: Could you explain what you mean?

DAVID: I was growing up at the time of the Hoover Administration. What a time I had, too. There was barely enough to eat. I don't think the Republicans wanted that, but they still did nothing to stop it. Not until Roosevelt came along and made things start to happen. Now the Republican Party still stands for big business, at the expense of the farmer and the

working man. Promises made are not kept—ask the poor farmer, if no one
else. (234)

Near-ideologues, who "knew some of the words but were not convincing
with the whole tune" (Converse 2006, 307), made up another 9 percent
of the public.

Insofar as Americans relied on ideological categories, they remained
orthodox. The open-ended questions could have uncovered any variety
of ideology. To be placed in the top groups, respondents had to show
only that they made more or less sensible use of an ideological idea.
Libertarianism, socialism, populism: any of these would have done the
trick. What Converse discovered, however, when he discovered any evidence of ideology at all, came almost exclusively in terms of liberalism
and conservatism.

By Converse's first test, barely one in ten Americans comes to politics
with an ideology in mind. Not surprisingly, members of this select group
of the ideologically inclined are unusual in other ways as well. They express special interest in politics. They are comparatively well educated.
They know more about current affairs. In such circles, ideology is relatively common. Outside such circles, it is exceedingly rare.

If the overwhelming majority of Americans think about the candidates and the parties without reference to ideology, what do they refer
to instead? Many appear to regard parties and candidates as agents of
group interest: as standing for (or against) the working man, or big business. Some bring up (sometimes imaginary) associations between parties and candidates, on the one hand, and the good or bad times they
seem to deliver, on the other. Still others explain their attachments as a
consequence of family tradition. A sizeable number are so disengaged
from politics that they can muster no reason at all why they might prefer
one candidate or party over another.

Unprompted use of ideology is one thing. Understanding ideology is
another. In principle, significant numbers of Americans could possess
an understanding of liberalism and conservatism despite failing to make
use of ideological concepts when justifying their own political judgments. This would be important. Those in possession of a reasonable
understanding of basic ideological terms live in a different, richer, political world from those who do not. For the former, "the single word 'conservative' used to describe a piece of proposed legislation can convey

a tremendous amount of more specific information about the bill—who probably proposed it and toward what ends, who is likely to resist it, its chances of passage, its long-term social consequences, and, most important, how the actor himself should expect to evaluate it if he were to expend further energy to look into its details" (Converse 1964, 214). For a person not so equipped, the term "conservative" simply flies by, contributing nothing to the person's understanding of political life.

The question here is what proportion of the American public can be said to understand ideological categories. To find out, Converse took advantage of a series of questions introduced into the 1960 election study. Respondents were asked whether they thought one of the parties was more conservative or more liberal than the other, then which party was the more conservative, and finally what they had in mind when they said that one party was more conservative than the other. Respondents who made it to the final stage were urged to offer multiple responses and were placed into the highest category merited by their "best" answer.

As expected, more Americans appear to understand ideological categories than make use of them on their own. Converse determined that about 17 percent of the public could both assign the terms "liberal" and "conservative" correctly to the parties and say something sensible about what the terms meant. They referred to differences between the parties over spending versus saving, social change, the virtues and limitations of capitalism, and the power of the federal government. By this test, about one in six Americans appear capable of following discussions carried out at an ideological level.

Most Americans are unfamiliar with liberal and conservative ideas, but this might mean only that they lack the ability to articulate the ideological principles that organize their political beliefs. The organization might be there nonetheless, and when push comes to shove, "it is the organization that matters, not the capacity for discourse in sophisticated language" (Converse 1964, 228).

This possibility motivated Converse to look for evidence of ideological organization. He did so by examining the structure of opinions on issues within each of two populations: a national cross section of the general public, and a smaller group made up of candidates for the U.S. House of Representatives. Both were interviewed in the fall of 1958. Both were asked their opinions on pressing domestic and foreign policy issues—aid to education, military support for countries menaced by

Communist aggression, the government's responsibility to make sure
that everyone who wants to work can find a job, and the like—issues that
were selected to represent the major political controversies of the day.

For the general public and then for the congressional candidates,
Converse calculated the correlations between opinions on each pair of
issues. Differences in the structure of opinion between the two populations revealed by this simple analysis were dramatic. Candidates' views
generally fell into predictable patterns. Across the various issues, prospective members of Congress tended to take liberal positions or they
tended to take conservative positions. Consistency was the rule. Not so
for the general public. Organization (or structure) among the opinions
expressed by ordinary citizens was almost nonexistent. The rule here
was—well, there seemed to be no rule. Citizens were unpredictable: liberal on some issues and conservative on others. Converse took this result to mean that widespread ideological innocence is not a surface
problem—a failure to articulate the foundations of belief—but a deep
one—the foundations themselves are absent. No structure, no ideology.

Perhaps. But if Americans organize their political beliefs in idiosyn-
cratic ways, then structure would be present but undetectable by Converse's analysis, which assumes that the only admissible structuring
principle is supplied by the distinction between liberalism and conservatism. Acknowledging the point, Converse proceeded to an additional
test, one unburdened by the assumption of shared ideology. If ideology—
however eccentric it might be—informs political beliefs, then those beliefs must display durability. By definition, ideological beliefs are beliefs
held with conviction.

It turns out that the policy questions included in the 1958 national
survey were posed in identical form to the same people two years earlier,
in the 1956 election study, as well as to the same people two years later,
in the 1960 study. In other words, the 1960 national election study was
the culmination of a three-wave panel. With these materials, Converse
looked for stability in political belief but found mainly change. Many
Americans took a liberal position on one occasion and a conservative
position on the next. Or they did the reverse, flipping from conservative
to liberal. Instability was rampant.

Instability was rampant despite precautions undertaken to discour-
age individuals from expressing opinions when they had no real opinions to express. Interviewers introduced the battery of policy questions
by acknowledging "different things are important to different people, so

we don't expect everyone to have an opinion about all of these (things)."
In addition, each individual policy question provided an explicit opportunity for individuals to admit (without prejudice) that they did not have
an opinion on the issue under discussion. Moreover, the issues themselves were chosen to reveal "basic and fundamental dispositions toward
questions of public policy" (Converse 1970, 170). The plan was to avoid
superficial reactions to temporary disturbances and ask instead about
major and enduring disputes.

Despite all this, among those who expressed an opinion, fewer than
two-thirds came down on the same side of a policy controversy over a
two-year period, where one-half would be expected to do so by chance
alone. Converse concluded "that signs of low constraint among belief el-
ements in the mass public are not products of well knit but highly idio-
syncratic belief systems, for these beliefs are highly labile for individuals
over time. Great instability in itself is *prima facie* evidence that the belief has extremely low centrality for the believer" (1964, 241).[6]

Instability was greatest on the issue of whether the federal government or private business should have the larger role in regulating power
and housing. Of all the policy questions, this was the most abstract and
obviously ideological, nicely capturing the debate between liberal and
conservative elites during the Great Depression and the New Deal. On
this issue, turnover of opinion was especially pronounced. In the aggregate, however, opinion moved not at all. Turnover in one direction
was almost exactly counterbalanced by turnover in the opposite direction. The combination of enormous churning at the individual level and
perfect stability at the aggregate level is peculiar. As Converse put it, it
seems most implausible that huge numbers of Americans "had shifted
their beliefs from support of creeping socialism to a defense of free enterprise, and that a corresponding large population had moved in the
opposite direction, forsaking free enterprise for advocacy of further
federal incursions into the private sector" (1970, 171). Just as curious,
turnover in opinion was no greater over four years than it was over two.
In other words, one could predict opinion on government versus free enterprise in 1960 just as well from opinion in 1956 as from the more prox-
imal 1958 opinion.

Mulling over these oddities, and translating the movement of opinion over time into Markov chains, Converse arrived at his "black and
white" model of opinion. The model proposes that on any particular
issue, the public can be partitioned into one of just two discontinuous

classes: the first made up of citizens who possess genuine opinions and hold onto them tenaciously; the second composed of citizens who are unacquainted with the issue and, when pressed, either confess their ignorance outright or, out of embarrassment or misplaced civic obligation, invent an attitude on the spot—not a real attitude, but a "non-attitude." Members of the first class never change their opinion; members of the second class either admit they have no opinion or generate an opinion randomly.

The model is elegant, but does it stand up to empirical testing? Under the black-and-white model, those who changed their views on government control of power and housing between 1956 and 1958 belong by definition to the non-attitude class. According to the model, the stability of opinion on this issue for this group going forward, given by the correlation, should be a perfect zero. The observed correlation between 1958 and 1960 turns out to be, in fact, 0.00. Again according to the model, those who expressed the same opinion on power and housing in 1956 and 1958 are a mixture of those with real attitudes and those with non-attitudes (who only appear to be stable by chance), but in known proportion. Given the known proportion, if the model is correct, the stability of opinion between 1958 and 1960 on this issue for this group, assessed by correlation, should be .47. The observed correlation turns out to be .49. In short, for the dynamics of opinion on the most ideological issue, the fit between the black-and-white model's predictions and the data is nearly perfect.

And here's the real takeaway point: the black-and-white model implies that less than 20 percent of the American electorate held real opinions on government control. The remainder, more than 80 percent, either admitted to having no opinion or (and this was the more popular option) expressed "hastily fabricated" opinions indistinguishable from random ones.

The fit between the model's predictions and opinion data on other policy questions was less exact. Converse attributed the discrepancy to the black-and-white model providing no room for the small numbers of Americans whose opinions are undergoing real change. But even in these cases, the upshot of Converse's analysis is sobering. On issues that have attracted intense and persistent attention from political elites, public opinion is not what it seems. It is a mixture of real opinions and non-opinions, with the latter often outnumbering the former.

Americans with real and stable opinions on an issue constitute what

Converse calls an issue public. Issue publics are *miniature* publics; their numbers are modest compared to the public as a whole. Moreover, membership in one issue public is no guarantee of membership in another. A person who is vitally interested in school desegregation may care not at all about farm policy. Another person preoccupied with the threat posed by Communism may have nothing to say about unemployment. And so on.

The notion of issue public brings Converse's argument full circle:

> For the truly involved citizen, the development of political sophistication means that the absorption of contextual information makes clear to him the connections of the policy area of his initial interest with policy differences in other areas; and that these broader configurations of policy positions are describable quite economically in the basic abstractions of ideology. Most members of the mass public, however, fail to proceed so far. Certain rather concrete issues may capture their respective individual attentions and lead to some politically relevant opinion formation. This engagement of attention remains narrow however: Other issue concerns that any sophisticated observer would see as "ideologically" related to the initial concern tend not to be thus associated in any breadth or number. The common citizen fails to develop more global points of view about politics. A realistic picture of political belief systems in the mass public, then, is not one that omits issues and policy demands completely nor one that presumes widespread ideological coherence; it is rather one that captures with some fidelity the fragmentation, narrowness, and diversity of these demands (1964, 247).

Innocent of Ideology

Ideology, we said at the outset, requires breadth, structure, and stability. By Converse's analysis, all three appear to be in short supply in the American electorate—not absent altogether, but rare. Dim understanding of basic ideological categories, weakly structured and unstable opinions, fragmentation of the electorate into narrow issue publics: all point in the same direction. Ideological innocence is a general condition, "not a pathology limited to a thin and disorganized bottom layer of the *lumpenproletariat*" (1964, 213).

As we will see in the next chapter, not everyone agreed.[7]

CHAPTER TWO

The Great Debate

Publication of Converse's claim of ideological innocence set off a huge commotion. Among scholars of elections and public opinion, ideology became something of an obsession. At the 1982 annual meeting of the American Political Science Association, one of us (the one alive at the time) presented an invited lecture under the exasperated and only somewhat facetious title "Enough Already about Ideology!" The lecture failed: the outpouring of articles and chapters and books on ideology continued unabated. Taken all together, the literature stimulated by Converse's original essay has reached staggering proportions. In 2014 alone, fifty years after publication, "Belief Systems" was cited nearly five hundred times.

This chapter provides a review of research relevant to the claim of ideological innocence—a *selective* review, we should hasten to add. We have no interest in attempting a comprehensive survey (the thought is soul crushing), and in any case we are sure the reader would have no interest in plowing through such a thing if we were so foolish as to produce it. Only the most significant arguments and findings are taken up here. At several points, we supply results of our own on subjects that have somehow, over the years, escaped attention. This will keep us fully occupied and, more to the point, will do the work that needs to be done.

And after the work is done, where do things stand? In our judgment, not too far from where Converse left them more than half a century ago.[1]

Ideological Innocence and Political Change

Converse toiled in a particular time and in a particular place, but he intended his conclusion to apply very widely. He called his essay "The Nature of Belief Systems in Mass Publics"—no sign of particularity there. And he concluded his essay with bold speculations on the role of abolitionist sentiment in the formation of the Republican Party in the United States in the nineteenth century and the rise of National Socialism in Germany in the 1930s.

But perhaps particularity matters. Perhaps ideological innocence has less to do with the limited capacity of ordinary citizens than with the ideological neutrality of America in the 1950s. According to this argument, the United States at that time was in political recovery from the intense ideological debates of the New Deal and from the trauma brought on by the Great Depression and the Second World War. The military conflict in Korea was drawing to a close, the economy was gathering strength, and General Dwight Eisenhower, an enormously popular and unifying figure, was president.[2]

One straightforward way to bring data to the question of particularity is by replicating Converse's analysis under different circumstances. Here we summarize the results of such efforts, organized around the four principal measures of ideological thinking investigated by Converse in his original essay.

Using Ideological Concepts

Figure 2.1 presents the proportion of the American electorate making use of ideological concepts when asked to describe what they like and don't like about presidential candidates and political parties in national surveys from 1956 to 2000. In Converse's terminology, the proportion presented in the figure includes both "ideologues" and "near-ideologues." Figure 2.1 pulls together results from teams of researchers who carefully repeated Converse's procedures (Hagner and Pierce 1982; Knight 1985; and Lewis-Beck et al. 2008). These investigations all used ANES surveys and so enable close comparison to Converse's original findings: study designs are the same; the samples are comparable; the questions that generate the raw material to be coded are identical; and

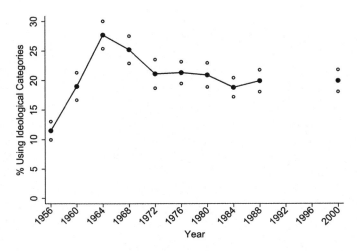

FIGURE 2.1 Use of ideological categories, 1956–2000

Source: 1956–2000 ANES.
Note: Hollow circles indicate range of 95 percent confidence intervals

the coding schemes themselves are constructed to be equivalent to Converse's. The work is laborious and grinding but worth it: in social science as in life, you get what you pay for.[3]

Perhaps the first thing to notice in figure 2.1 is that ideological thinking increases dramatically in 1964. Between 1956 and 1964, the proportion of the American electorate making some use of ideological categories more than doubles. This development must be due, as Norman Nie, Sidney Verba, and John Petrocik (1976) would say, to differences in presidential campaigns. In *The Changing American Voter*, Nie and his colleagues distinguish two presidential campaigns: the ideologically neutral contest of 1956, which was the second go-round between the incumbent and former general, Eisenhower, and the Democratic challenger, Adlai Stevenson; and the ideologically charged campaign of 1964, between President Lyndon Johnson and Senator Barry Goldwater. Nie and his colleagues suggest that if the American people are supplied with an ideologically stimulating debate, as in 1964, a sizeable fraction of them will respond in kind. Ideological thinking reflects ideological politics.[4]

Apart from the apparent rise in ideological thinking in 1964, however, the time series presented in figure 2.1 is essentially horizontal. On the whole, the level of ideological thinking in the American electorate seems quite inert. There is no sign of increased ideological thinking in response to Senator George McGovern's left-wing challenge of President Richard Nixon in 1972; no sign of diminished ideological thinking in the Carter-Ford contest four years later, as the country returned to normalcy after Watergate; and no resurgence of ideological thinking in the Reagan elections. Over this long period, those who make use of ideological categories in assessing candidates and parties remain a modest and nearly constant fraction of the electorate.

Ideological thinking fails to increase despite the fact that since World War II, the American electorate has undergone an astonishing upgrade in education. In 1950, 24.5 percent of adult Americans had completed high school; by 2010, 87.1 percent had. And whereas college graduates were hard to find among the American public in 1950 (just 6.2 percent), they were commonplace by 2010 (29.9 percent).[5]

In light of this educational transformation, one might have expected to see increases in ideological thinking. Indeed, writing in *The American Voter* with Angus Campbell, Warren Miller, and Donald Stokes, Converse himself suggested "a rising level of education might permit a slow upgrading in the level of conceptualization" (Campbell et al. 1960, 255). You'd think it would. Surprisingly, it seems not to be so.

Understanding Ideological Concepts

Converse suspected that there might be significant numbers of Americans who possess a reasonable understanding of ideological concepts despite failing to make much use of them in their own thinking—and he was right. About one in six Americans was able to muster a passable comprehension of ideological terms. The survey questions analyzed by Converse for this purpose, present for the first time in the 1960 election study, were repeated in identical form just twice more, in 1964 and in 1968, so we obviously cannot say anything about change over the long haul. But we can use them to carry out a second test of the proposition that the prominence of ideological thinking in the mass public is responsive, at least in part, to the prominence of ideology in presidential campaigns. Ideology was mostly absent from the 1960 Kennedy-Nixon contest, which was dominated by concerns over the place of Catholicism in American political life. Four years later, the ideological slugfest between Goldwater and Johnson was quite another matter. And four years after that, the intrusion of George Wallace's third-party candidacy provided an ideological jolt to the 1968 presidential election.

Attempting to replicate Converse's original analysis as closely as possible, we classified election-study respondents as understanding ideological concepts if they passed three tests: answering in the affirmative to the question of whether one of the parties was more conservative or more liberal than the other; naming the Republican Party as the more conservative; and finally, offering a sensible answer when asked what they had in mind when they claimed that the Republican Party was the more conservative.

By our analysis, 17.9 percent of the American electorate could provide a basic understanding of conservatism in 1960 (just a hair more than Converse's original estimate). The same proportion did so in 1964, at the climax of the Goldwater-Johnson campaign. In 1968, somewhat fewer Americans—14.2 percent—passed the same three tests. In other words, we find no evidence that ideologically infused presidential campaigns generate greater understanding of ideological concepts. If anything, the evidence runs the other way.[6]

Ideological Consistency

Campaigns are designed to attract and hold the electorate's attention, to overcome the demands and preoccupations of everyday life. Presidential campaigns do so with some success (e.g., Green and Gerber 2008; Lazarsfeld, Berelson, and Gaudet 1948; Rosenstone and Hansen 1993). As such, they provide, from an ideological point of view, teachable moments—opportunities for citizens to learn about liberalism and conservatism.

But on the subject of ideology, presidential candidates are generally lousy teachers. They offer their life story, criticize their opponent, embrace peace, prosperity, and the American way—but seldom spend serious time or money on articulating the ideological foundations of their program (Page 1978).

Occasionally, however, they do. In 1964, Senator Goldwater presented the American electorate with a coherent ideological program. Goldwater ran for president to reestablish conservative principles. To the senator, it was "all too clear that in spite of a Conservative revival among the people the radical ideas that were promoted by the New and Fair Deals under the guise of Liberalism still dominate the councils of our national government" (1960, 3). As a result, the nation had lost its way—it was "adrift in an uncharted and stormy sea" (quoted in Perlstein 2001, 410).

Institutions were failing. Standards were collapsing. Obscene literature was flooding into schools and libraries. Crime, divorce, addiction, and illegitimacy were spiraling out of control. All these afflictions and more, according to Goldwater, could be traced to a single underlying source: liberalism. And for the problem of liberalism, government provided no solution. On the contrary, government *was* the problem. Goldwater promised that if elected, he would sharply curtail the power and authority of the federal government, putting an end to its cancerous growth. Goldwater opposed federal aid to education, wished to repeal farm subsidies, rejected government assistance to the indigent and the elderly, and denounced the graduated income tax as confiscatory.[7]

Goldwater's opponent was Lyndon Johnson, and as president, Johnson was nothing if not a modern liberal. Johnson believed in deploying the powers of the federal government to protect and enhance human welfare. More than that, Johnson was stunningly successful in putting liberal ideas into practice. Under Johnson's direction, Congress passed major civil rights legislation, expanded spending on social welfare, and launched a fleet of new government programs intended to end poverty.

According to Converse, public opinion on policy in the 1950s, from an ideological point of view, was a mess. Views on social welfare had little to do with views on civil rights, and neither of these had much connection to preferences on foreign policy. But if ideological consistency reflects the clarity and vividness of ideological debate among elites, then we should find noticeable improvement on this score in 1964. And in fact, at the close of this unusually ideologically charged campaign, ideological consistency did increase. Associations between opinions on employment policy and civil rights and even foreign affairs tightened. Increases in ideological consistency, first detected in 1964, persisted through the elections of 1968 and 1972. These results were interpreted at the time as a sea change in public opinion (Nie and Anderson 1974; Nie, Verba, and Petrocik 1976).

Perhaps. But in 1964, coincident with the apparent sharp increase in constraint, the policy questions asked in the ANES were modified. The changes seem innocuous enough: from a format in which respondents were asked how much they agreed or disagreed with a certain policy to an arrangement in which respondents were asked to choose between a pair of opposing alternatives; and from a gentle to a somewhat more insistent invitation to admit to no opinion at all.

Could such subtle changes explain a "sea change" in the electorate's thinking? Apparently so. In an ingenious experiment, John Sullivan and his colleagues (1978) randomly assigned half their sample to be asked opinions on policy using the pre-1964 questions and the other half to be asked the new version of the policy questions. The two sets of questions produced different patterns of correlation. Moreover, and this is the critical point, these differences mimicked to a remarkably fine degree the differences that had previously been attributed to the sudden appearance of ideological candidates. Most, perhaps all, of the increase in constraint detected in 1964 is artificial, produced not by the great debate between Goldwater and Johnson but by mundane modifications in measurement.

Americans faced an unusually stark choice in 1964. Goldwater and Johnson offered the country diametrically opposed alternatives, one conservative, the other liberal. And how did this choice affect the structure of public opinion on matters of national policy? As best we can tell, not at all.

In some ways the 1964 presidential campaign signaled the beginning of a more polarized politics. Ideological differences between the parties were modest from World War II through the Eisenhower and Kennedy administrations. Polarization began increasing shortly thereafter and continued to do so up to the present. The Democratic Party has moved to the left, while the Republican Party has moved, rather more sharply, to the right.[8]

In light of ideological change in partisan elites, we might expect increasing numbers of ordinary Americans to express preferences on policy that are ideologically coherent. To see if this was so, we examined the correlations between preferences on every pair of policy questions present on the ANES from 1972 to 2012 (question wording is fixed across this period). The questions took up policy across a wide range of topics, including foreign affairs, immigration, defense, civil rights, Social Security, and abortion.

As shown in table 2.1, the average correlation between preferences on policy is, as expected, modest (Pearson $r = .16$). Of course, the real question is whether the average correlation, taken here to be a measure of ideological consistency, has increased since the Goldwater-Johnson election. It has, but ever so slightly: just .01 per decade. For many of the issue pairs, in fact, the estimated increase is indistinguishable from zero or even negative: two-thirds of the issue trends fall between −.02 and .04. In

TABLE 2.1. **Ideological constraint, 1972–2012**
(Pearson r with standard error in parentheses)

Average correlation (intercept)	.16 (.01)
Correlation trend (time in decades)	.01 (.00)
Residual standard deviations	
Intercepts	.11
Trends	.03
Data	.04
Number of observations	2,242

Source: 1972–2012 ANES.
Note: $r_{pt} = \beta_0 + \beta_p t + \varepsilon_{pt}$, where r_{pt} is the correlation between the pair of issues p in the year t, in decades.

light of the substantial ideological polarization of Democratic and Republican elites—elected officials, candidates, activists, and donors—it is striking how tiny the corresponding ideological pickup has been among the general public.[9]

Suppose for the sake of argument that ideological consistency continues to increase indefinitely at the same leisurely rate. Under this assumption, the American public's views on policy would eventually come to approximate the degree of ideological structure shown by partisan elites today. Eventually, but not anytime soon. All else equal, this achievement, if that is the right way to put it, would take place on or about 2315.

Ideological Stability

Panel studies carried out since Converse have continued to reveal instability in the ordinary citizen's preferences on policy. Wandering from one side of a policy question to the other from one sitting to the next remains common. This is so not only in the United States (e.g., Feldman 1989; Markus 1982), but also in Britain (Butler and Stokes 1969) and France (Converse and Pierce 1986). These results weigh against the argument that instability is merely a reflection of the ideological neutrality of America in the Eisenhower years.

This work is informative, but better would be an exact replication of Converse's original analysis. Such a thing, unfortunately, is unattainable. The ANES did carry out another major panel study, between 1972 and 1976, one that mimicked in design the 1956–60 ANES that furnished the raw materials for Converse's original analysis. But the comparison is compromised by changes in question format—changes that made such mischief for the analysis of opinion constraint, as discussed in the previous section.

Converse and Gregory Markus (1979) acknowledge this problem but argue that the formats are sufficiently close on several issue questions to warrant rough comparisons between the two panels. Such issues include two in the domain of foreign affairs (isolation versus intervention, and foreign aid), another on social welfare (whether government is responsible for providing employment for those who want to work), and a fourth on civil rights (school desegregation).

As shown in table 2.2, preferences on these issues were generally no more stable in the 1972–76 ANES Panel Study than in the original. On two issues, stability increased slightly; on the other two, stability decreased slightly. Table 2.2 also shows that party identification was much more stable than issue preferences in the 1972–76 ANES Panel Study, as was true in Converse's original analysis and to the same degree (despite, in the later period, the resignation of a president between the first interview and the second, which might have been expected to destabilize partisanship). Insofar as comparisons can be made, findings from the later panel closely resemble those originally reported by Converse.

Issues come and go. Some that emerged after Converse had completed his work were picked up for questioning in the 1972–76 ANES Panel Study. These issues have no counterpart in the earlier panel—they had not yet become part of the nation's political conversation—but they are of interest nevertheless.

Analysis of several of the new issues produces the familiar result: namely, unstable opinions. We see this with issues that involve dealing with urban unrest, protecting the rights of persons accused of crimes,

TABLE 2.2. **Stability of policy preferences and partisanship (Pearson r)**

	1956–60	1972–76
Isolationism	.35	.31
Employment	.46	.49
Foreign aid	.29	.26
School desegregation	.40	.41
Party identification	.84	.81

Source: 1956–60 and 1972–76 ANES.

and reforming the tax code. Preferences on these issues display, if anything, even less stability than what Converse reported on the issues ad-
dressed in the 1956–60 ANES Panel Study.

Several of the new issues, however, tell a different story. One of these
concerns busing for the purpose of desegregating the public schools.
At the time, "forced busing," as it was commonly called, was not just a
run-of-the-mill issue. Busing, as Converse and Markus (1979, 41) put it,
"probably more than any other in the civil rights area or, for that matter,
the total arena of policy debate, has had an inflammatory or polarizing
quality that has bitten deep into even relatively inattentive segments of
the public." Preferences on busing between 1972 and 1976 were unusually stable—not perfectly stable, and not as stable as partisanship, but
well above the standard result.

The same can be said for opinion on abortion. Abortion emerged
abruptly and dramatically as a public issue in January 1973, when the Supreme Court decided, in *Roe v. Wade*, that the Constitution covered a
woman's choice to have an abortion. A deeply felt and often angry conversation began, one that continues to this day. And as for public opinion? Converse and Markus found preferences on abortion between 1972
and 1976 to be unusually stable—again, not perfectly stable, not as stable
as partisanship, but well above average.[10]

Back in 1964, Converse suggested that issue publics would vary in
size. The more abstract the issue, the smaller the public, the fewer real
preferences, and the more numerous non-attitudes would be. Busing
and abortion appear to be something else again. Both draw comparatively large publics, elicit numerous real preferences, and generate fewer
non-attitudes.[11]

Citizens versus Elites

Converse was motivated to undertake his analysis at least in part on the
idea that there might exist important differences in ideational worlds between political elites and ordinary citizens. Converse suspected that such
differences, if often acknowledged in principle, were drastically underestimated in practice, and he worried that the differences might be so
great as to interfere with the ongoing discussion between elites and mass
publics so important to democracy.

From this perspective, a key finding was the dramatic contrast Con-

verse discovered between the well-organized views of candidates for
Congress and the feebly structured views of the general public. Christopher Achen took exception to this comparison, arguing that the contrast
could be explained at least in part by differences in how the policy questions were posed to the two samples. As Achen saw it, "The elite questions were more precise, the mass items diffuse. Differences in the correlations would be expected on that basis alone" (1983, 76).

Fair enough. But as things turn out, the same contrast shows up in
studies that compare the policy opinions expressed by political elites
with those expressed by mass publics using *identical* questions. Consider M. Kent Jennings's (1992) comparison of the American mass public with delegates to the Democratic and Republican national conventions. Convention delegates are "deeply committed, highly motivated,
and keenly involved partisans" (422). In this case, both convention delegates and ordinary citizens were asked about the same issues—abortion,
defense spending, the trade-off between inflation and unemployment,
and several more—in exactly the same way. And just as in Converse's
original analysis, while the preferences of the general public on major issues were, by and large, ideologically incoherent, political elites divided
neatly into those who were consistently liberal in their stated preferences
on policy and those who were consistently conservative.[12]

Non-attitudes Revisited

The most disconcerting piece of Converse's original argument is the
non-attitude thesis. If Converse is right here, then many Americans simply don't know what they want from government. "Democratic theory,"
as Achen (1975, 1227) put it, "loses its starting point."

As noted earlier, in one respect, empirical support for the idea of
non-attitude has simply mounted since the 1950s. Panel studies of national electorates have continued to reveal promiscuous instability in
policy preferences (Converse and Markus 1979; Feldman 1989; Markus
1982; Butler and Stokes 1969; Converse and Pierce 1986). But at its core,
the debate over non-attitudes is not over the fact of instability. Everyone agrees that preferences on government policy, as we measure them,
display a great deal of instability. The debate is over what to make of
instability.

Converse takes instability to be a reflection of the flimsiness of opinion. Reluctant to own up to their own ignorance, people create opinions on the spot—evanescent opinions, non-opinions—liberal on one occasion, conservative on the next. In contrast, Achen (1975) takes instability to be a reflection of shortcomings in measurement. Achen returned to the 1956–60 ANES Panel Study, correcting the over-time correlations in policy preferences for attenuation due to measurement error, on the assumption that all of the error belongs to inadequacies in instrumentation. Following these adjustments, the correlations increased dramatically, soaring toward, and in a few cases slightly above, 1.0. In other words, with measurement error removed in this way, preference is perfectly stable. Achen concludes that when citizens express an opinion on government policy, they are offering a real (and stable) opinion.[13]

Perhaps, but it seems unrealistic to attribute unreliability entirely to errors in measurement. In Converse's view, unreliability is a product not only of imperfections in instrumentation but of imperfections in citizens. Reliability varies with the amount of information a person brings to the subject, and in politics, the amount of information brought to the subject varies enormously.

This difference leads to a crucial test. If Converse is correct, then information and preference stability should be correlated: those who know a lot about politics will hold on to their opinions more determinedly than those who know little. But if instability is a product entirely of instrument unreliability, as Achen supposes, then stability should be independent of information. Consistent with Converse's interpretation, opinion stability appears to vary with the amount of information citizens bring to politics (Converse 2000; Feldman 1989; Zaller 1990; Zaller and Feldman 1992). "Crucial tests" are seldom crucial, however, and that seems to be the case here. The evidence tilts toward Converse's interpretation of opinion stability, but it is not decisive.[14]

A more straightforward test of the non-attitude thesis entails examining the stability of political beliefs among elites. Converse provided no evidence on this score, but subsequent research has filled in this gap, and in a completely unequivocal way. We now know that compared to ordinary citizens, political elites hold on to their political preferences tenaciously. Jennings (1992) shows this in his comparison between the American mass public and delegates to the Democratic and Republican national conventions. The same contrast appears in Converse and Roy Pierce's (1986) analysis of the French electorate and candidates for the National Assembly, questioned before and after the disorders that

brought France to a standstill in May 1968. Substantial differences between mass publics and political elites in preference stability cannot be
attributed to differences in instrumentation reliability, since instrumentation is held constant across populations. Rather, they reflect fundamental disparities in the richness of meaning and the crystallization of
attitude that ordinary people and political elites bring to the subject of
politics.[15]

Is it the case that people who express a non-attitude have nothing to
say on the subject? Converse (1970) comes close to this position, sug-
gesting that non-attitudes arise "from people with no real attitude on
the matter in question, but who for some reason felt obliged to try a response to the item despite our generous and repeated invitation to dis-
avow any opinion where none was felt" (175). Non-attitudes are hastily
constructed. Asked about a particular policy, many citizens "hunt and
fabricate" (177).

John Zaller and Stanley Feldman (1992) offer an alternative and perhaps more persuasive explanation. Opinion instability is common not
because citizens have no views, as Converse suggests, and not because
citizens are thrown off by poor questions, as Achen would argue, but
because citizens do not know what to think, for they cannot adjudicate
among various competing considerations. When citizens are pressed for
their opinion on some important matter, many at least can recognize the
subject and conjure up some more or less relevant considerations. But
they do not possess a well-formed and regularly rehearsed preference.
When the occasion calls for it, they must *construct* a preference on the
spot. Preferences are rickety constructions. According to this interpretation, attitudes are real, but not deeply considered.

Suppose Converse is right, *and* Zaller and Feldman are right. Then
non-attitudes are common because on any particular matter of policy
some citizens have nothing to say while others do not know what to say.[16]

Information and Ideology

Converse's argument begins with information—more precisely, with differences in information. Such differences run, in Converse's view, "from
vast treasuries of well organized information among elites interested
in the particular subject to fragments that could be measured in a few
'bits' in the technical sense. These differences are a static tribute to the

extreme imperfections in the transmission of information 'downward' through the system: Very little information 'trickles down' very far" (1964, 212). The result: huge differences in information about politics.

Information inequality plays a pivotal role in Converse's analysis. As information declines, basic comprehension of ideological systems—in the American case, almost always liberalism and conservatism—diminishes precipitously. Connections between beliefs weaken. The range of ideas taken into account contracts. Conviction gives way to vacillation and confusion. In the American mass public—in any mass public—fully formed ideological systems are few and far between.

In light of this, it is perhaps surprising to realize that in his 1964 essay, Converse provided no evidence of a connection between information and ideology. More surprising still, in the great debate over ideology that has so occupied the field for more than fifty years, nobody has seemed to be much bothered by this. You would think there would be more fuss, for the relationship between information and ideological thinking goes to the core of Converse's argument. Our purpose in this section of the chapter is to determine the strength of the connection between information and ideology that Converse insists is vital.[17]

On the measurement of information, we take instruction from John Zaller (1992), whose theory of opinion change recognizes that citizens differ from one another in the care and attention they invest in politics. Care and attention, in this scheme, entail the degree to which people pay attention to politics and understand what they have encountered, and it is measured best by tests of factual information. Such tests assess "political learning that has actually occurred—political ideas that the individual has encountered, understood, and stored" (335).[18]

ANES surveys include questions that can easily be fashioned into an overall measure of information in Zaller's terms (e.g., from the 2012 ANES, "What job or political office does John Boehner now hold?"). As a general rule, we simply count the number of correct answers and divide by the number of questions. Scales of political information in the analysis ahead are thus constrained to range in principle from 0 to 1.0 (the actual range is also 0 to 1.0; reliabilities, indicated by Cronbach's *alpha*, average about .75). With such measures in hand, we can proceed to examine the strength of the connection between political knowledge and ideological thinking. We can move rapidly here because we are covering territory that we have already explored thoroughly in chapter 1.

A principal measure of ideological thinking is the extent to which

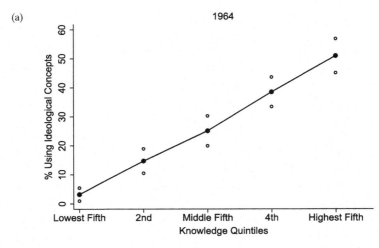

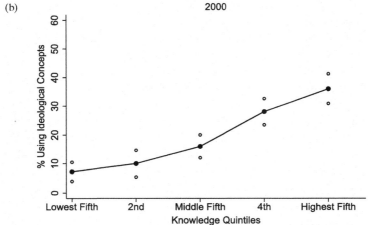

FIGURE 2.2 Political information and use of ideological concepts
Source: 1964 and 2000 ANES.
Note: Hollow circles indicate range of 95 percent confidence intervals.

citizens make use of ideological categories in their commentaries on
parties and presidential candidates. Figure 2.2 presents the relationship between political information (along the horizontal axis) and the
likelihood of justifying political attachments with ideological categories (along the vertical axis). We present results for two elections: 1964,
where the mention of ideological categories was unusually high, a reflection presumably of the ideologically charged nature of the 1964 presi-

dential campaign, and 2000, where the use of ideological categories was comparatively neither high nor low.

In both cases, we find a reasonably strong association between information and ideology. Consistent with Converse's expectation, use of ideological categories becomes more frequent as information increases. Notice also that the greater mention of ideological categories in 1964 compared to 2000 takes place entirely among the relatively well informed. The ideological themes emphasized by President Johnson and Senator Goldwater registered on the electorate in 1964, but only among those who were paying attention.[19]

More important than whether citizens rely on ideological categories to justify their own political attachments is whether they know what the terms mean and so can follow elite discussions that make use of them. Figure 2.3 displays the relationship between political information and the likelihood of success in recognizing that the Republican Party is the more conservative and in defining conservatism in reasonably sensible fashion. Once again, we present results for two elections: the ideologically rich election of 1964, and its much less ideologically laden predecessor, the 1960 contest between Kennedy and Nixon.

As before, in both instances, information and ideology are strongly associated. As information increases, so does understanding of ideological categories. The relationship is a bit stronger in 1964 than in 1960, as one would expect, though the difference is slight.[20]

Next, to ascertain the strength of connection between political information and ideological consistency, we analyze the 1992 American National Election Study. The 1992 ANES carries a good set of policy questions: on the role government should play in providing employment, the appropriate level of defense spending, the trade-off between reducing spending and expanding services, whether the government should make special efforts on behalf of black Americans, and the proper role of government in providing health care. The 1992 ANES also includes questions that allow us to construct an excellent measure of information (Cronbach's *alpha* = .80). And finally, the 1992 ANES constitutes the first wave of a panel study, so we can make use of the same questions when we take up the relationship between information and stability.

To assess ideological consistency, we simply calculate the correlation between opinions on these central matters of government policy, just as Converse did—but after first partitioning the electorate into five roughly equal groups depending on scores on the information scale. Table 2.3

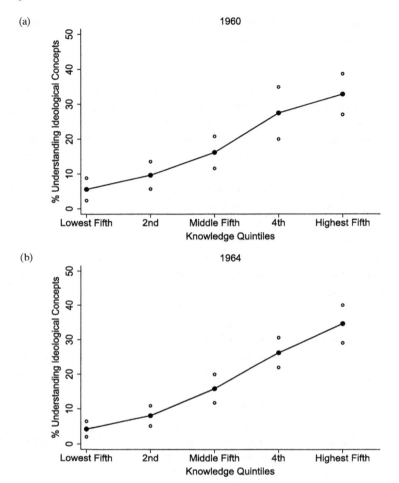

FIGURE 2.3 Political information and understanding of ideological concepts

Source: 1960 and 1964 ANES.

Note: Hollow circles indicate range of 95 percent confidence intervals.

presents a pair of correlation matrices, one (on the top) generated by the highest information group, the other (on the bottom) generated by the lowest information group.

The contrast between the two matrices is obvious. Among the relatively uninformed (bottom quintile), there is very little consistency. Opinions on defense spending are isolated from opinions on domestic policy, and even within the domestic domain, opinion shows little sign of

TABLE 2.3. **Political information and ideological consistency (Pearson *r*)**

	High information			
	Employment	Defense	Spending/ services	Aid to blacks
Defense	.21			
Spending/services	.39	.22		
Aid to blacks	.56	.28	.46	
Health insurance	.42	.33	.53	.33

	Low information			
	Employment	Defense	Spending/ services	Aid to blacks
Defense	.13			
Spending/services	.17	−.03		
Aid to blacks	.34	.02	.11	
Health insurance	.37	.12	.24	.11

Source: 1992 ANES.

being organized ideologically. The matrix arising from the relatively well informed (top quintile) is quite different. Now opinion begins to look as though it were organized; the separation between domestic and foreign policy is much less apparent; ideological coherence begins to emerge.

Comparing the median correlation across matrices provides a useful summary of the relationship between political information and consistency. Across the five groups, from the worst informed to the best informed, the median correlation marches steadily upward: from .13 among those at the bottom of the information hierarchy to .18, .22, .27 and finally, .36 among those at the top.

Respondents to the 1992 ANES were questioned again in 1996 and asked (among many other things) for their opinions on the same set of policies that appeared in the 1992 interview. This allows for a simple test of the relationship between information and opinion stability. We again partitioned the sample into five equal groups according to scores on the 1992 information measure, and then calculated correlations between opinions expressed in 1992 and in 1996, for each policy taken separately. Table 2.4 presents the results.[21]

As information increases, so does stability. The most dramatic case is provided by the trade-off between cutting back on government spend-

TABLE 2.4. **Political information and opinion stability (Pearson *r*)**

	Political information				
	Lowest		Middle		Highest
Employment	.32	.40	.37	.45	.60
Defense	.32	.41	.48	.56	.54
Spending/services	.08	.38	.37	.38	.61
Aid to blacks	.40	.46	.51	.48	.61
Health insurance	.13	.37	.49	.41	.62

Source: 1992–96 ANES Panel Study.

ing and expanding government services, perhaps the most obviously ideological of the set. On this issue, among the worst informed, the correlation barely edges above zero (.08); among the best informed, the correlation reaches a robust .61.

In short, across four key indicators of ideological sophistication, Converse's assumption that information and ideology are intimately connected is confirmed.[22]

Better Informed?

Americans are more likely to have noticed that Zsa Zsa Gabor punched a Beverly Hills police officer or, to strike a more contemporary note, that Lindsay Lohan violated her parole, than to recall anything about congressional debate over health care. Ignorance of political affairs is "the most familiar fact to arise from sample surveys in all countries" (Converse 1975, 79; Bartels 2008; Delli Carpini and Keeter 1996; Price and Zaller 1993).

That said, perhaps things have improved on the information front since Converse concluded that most Americans were innocent of ideology. The most potent predictor of political knowledge is education (e.g., Delli Carpini and Keeter 1996; but see Highton 2009), and as we noted earlier in the chapter, education levels in the United States have risen spectacularly since World War II. Surely the American public is better informed about public affairs today than it was when Converse composed his essay.

Surprisingly, it seems not to be so. Pieced together from a variety of sources, across different kinds of tests—identifying political figures, describing governmental processes, being familiar with major events, knowing basic facts of history and geography—the evidence converges on the same point: Americans are no better informed on public affairs than they were a generation or two ago (Delli Carpini and Keeter 1996; Bennett 1988, 1989; Pew Research Center 2007).

Innocence Reaffirmed

Converse began his landmark essay by acknowledging that "belief systems have never surrendered easily to empirical study or quantification" (1964, 206). If the spirited debate since the 1960s proves anything, it is that. Still, after the dust has settled, the evidence is clear: Converse's conclusion stands.

Most Americans are indifferent to or mystified by liberalism and conservatism as political ideas. Left to their own devices, only two or three in a hundred evaluate political parties and presidential candidates from an ideological point of view. More, perhaps sixteen in a hundred, appear to understand ideological terms when put before them. Everyone else—a huge majority of the public—is unable to participate in ideological discussion.

Innocence of ideology is revealed also in the political connections Americans fail to make. Ideological consistency has increased in recent decades, but at a slow, nearly imperceptible pace. As in Converse's time, few Americans today express consistently liberal or consistently conservative preferences on policy. In Robert Lane's felicitous phrase, preferences are "morselized":

> This treatment of an instance in isolation happens time and again and on matters close to home: a union demand is a single incident, not part of a more general labor-management conflict; a purchase on the installment plan is a specific debt, not part of a budgetary pattern—either one's own or society's. The items and fragments of life remain itemized and fragmented. (1962, 353)

Opinions on policy are not only unconnected to opinions on ostensibly related policies; they are also unstable over time. Non-attitudes appear to be a more or less inevitable feature of political life in mass society, a consequence of the casual and ill-informed character of much everyday political thinking.

Consistent with Converse's original diagnosis, ideological innocence and widespread ignorance of public affairs go hand in hand. Ideological thinking appears to require a serious investment in public life, an investment few care to make. And ignorance of politics—perhaps the fundamental condition underlying innocence of ideology—seems quite unchanged since "Belief Systems" was published.

Is there nothing we would now change in Converse's original indictment? We would change a few things, at the margins. First of all, it is worth noting that ideological thinking was especially uncommon in 1956. In that year, fewer than 12 percent of Americans managed at least one reference to liberalism or conservatism when describing their feelings toward political parties and presidential candidates. In retrospect, it seems unfortunate that Converse sat down to write his essay based on materials from the 1956 election. Better for the debate on ideology had 1956 turned out to be more typical. With observations taken over a long stretch of time, we can now see that on this measure, Converse underestimated somewhat the "normal" level of ideological thinking in the American public.

And although it is hard to know for sure, we suspect that the changes in question wording introduced in the 1964 ANES improved measurement. The new policy questions encourage acquiescence less, and they seem to capture ideological differences—differences between the liberal point of view and the conservative point of view—more sensitively than the questions they replaced. If so, then the American public's views on public policy are not quite so feebly structured as Converse originally reported.

By siding with Converse's interpretation of opinion instability, we don't mean to suggest that there is *nothing* to be said (or done) about instrumentation error. Questions are designed imprecisely, interviewers make mistakes, mismatches arise between citizens' views and the response categories they are presented, and so forth. When questions are posed in a way that diminishes their ambiguity, and when response alternative are clearly defined, opinion stability increases (e.g., Krosnick and Berent 1993).

And finally, we must keep in mind that from time to time issues may arise—affirmative action, abortion, immigration—that engage the attention and interest of large numbers of Americans. Under such circumstances, real preferences may come to outnumber non-attitudes—though even in such cases, we should not presume that everyone who claims to have an opinion actually possesses one.

As we see it, the argument advanced by Converse more than half a century ago requires a bit of tinkering, but little more than that. This is surprising in light of the fierce and persistent debate over its merits. It is still more surprising in light of the profound changes that have visited American society since Converse completed his analysis. Educational transformation, party polarization, revolutionary change in information dissemination, fundamental alteration in gender and race relations: impressive as these changes have been, equally impressive is how little effect they have had on how the American electorate understands politics. Ideological innocence applies nearly as well to the current state of American public opinion as it does to the public Converse analyzed. *Plus ça change, plus c'est la même chose.*

This may seem like the end of our story, but it is not. We have work to do before we can deliver a final verdict on the American public's ideological appetite. The work entails making sense of the flourishing literature devoted to ideological identification. As we are about to see, when asked directly, many Americans describe themselves in ideological terms; they say they are liberal or they say they are conservative. Moreover, they appear to do so in ways that are politically meaningful. What challenge does this pose to the general claim of ideological innocence? We commence our examination of this question in chapter 3.

The Nature of Ideological
Identification in Mass Publics

CHAPTER THREE

Meaning and Measurement
of Ideological Identification

After sorting through all the arguments and evidence generated by Converse's essay, we conclude that the American public is, by and large, still innocent of ideology. On the whole, Americans are naive in matters ideological, no less today than in the 1950s. But if this is so, what do we make of the fact that many Americans seem quite happy to describe themselves in ideological terms; that when asked directly, millions say they that are liberal or that they are conservative? Reconciling these two "truths"—ideological innocence and the widespread presence of what we call ideological identification—will fully occupy our attention, beginning here and continuing through the following four chapters.

Chapter 3 lays down the foundation for this work. First we spell out what we mean by ideological identification, describe how ideological identification is typically measured, and then show that the standard measure stands up to a series of straightforward empirical tests. With these preliminaries accomplished, we then provide a first glimpse of ideological identification in the American public. We establish three elementary but consequential facts: first, many Americans say that ideological identification is not for them; second, among those who do describe themselves in ideological terms, many seek the center; and third, among those who claim to be either liberal or conservative, conservatism wins. In the chapter's final section, we initiate a comparison that will run through much of the analysis that follows: a comparison between ideology and partisanship, between the attachments Americans form to political belief systems and those they form to political parties.

Ideological Identification Defined

Merriam-Webster's Collegiate Dictionary defines identification as a "psychological orientation of the self in regard to something (as a person or group) with a resulting feeling of close emotional association." The *Oxford English Dictionary* provides several illuminating examples:

> He . . . kept himself free from identification with either party. (Leslie Stephen, *Alexander Pope* [1880])

> Perhaps the simplest way of describing this wholeness is by saying that it is a "we"; it involves the sort of sympathy and mutual identification for which "we" is the natural expression. (Frederic Milton Thrasher, *The Gang* [1927])

> They constituted an audience so rapt and attentive, so impressionable and apparently uncritical that their identification was almost total. (Michael Thelwell, *Harder They Come* [1980])

In principle, ideological identification could encompass a close attachment to any systematic political program: socialism, libertarianism, populism, anarchism—any ism would do. In practice, for an investigation of ideological identification in the contemporary United States, the options reduce primarily to two, conservatism and liberalism.

Ideological identification is *categorical*, in that ideological programs—most notably in the American case, liberalism and conservatism—are kinds or types. Ideological identification is, at the same time, *dimensional*, in that the degree of psychological attachment varies continuously. For liberals and conservatives in full, identification constitutes a central and abiding aspect of identity. Among those who find their primary rewards in domains other than politics, attachment to liberalism or conservatism may be difficult to distinguish from no attachment at all. And there exist all shades in between.

As we noted back in chapter 1, ideologies advance normative claims. Liberalism and conservatism designate the values we should share, prescribe the actions government should take on our behalf, and point to what is good and evil in the world. For the true believer, liberalism and conservatism are moral commitments.[1]

The Standard Measure

The first attempt to assess ideological identification among the American public was carried out by the Gallup organization in 1936 (Ellis and Stimson 2012). Gallup's interest in ideology was perhaps a reaction to the New Deal, President Roosevelt's answer to the Great Depression. The president argued that the American people had a right to decent homes, productive work, and "security against the hazards and vicissitudes of life" and that these rights could be secured only through the active intervention of the national government. Putting deeds to words, Roosevelt proceeded to create the biggest public works program in American history, build new institutions designed to regulate the banks and protect organized labor, and invent a comprehensive system of unemployment and old-age insurance. In these ways and more, Roosevelt provided the country with a tutorial on the meaning of American liberalism.

Indeed, it was Roosevelt who introduced the term "liberal" into popular American discourse. The president referred to the New Deal as "liberalism," both as a way to distinguish his policies from the earlier progressive movement and as a defense against his predecessor's claim that the ideas driving his programs were un-American, "dipped from cauldrons of European fascism or socialism" (Herbert Hoover, quoted in Rotunda 1986, 72).[2] In Roosevelt's view, liberalism was simply a common-sense reaction to the dire problems confronting the nation. "Better the occasional faults of a government that lives in a spirit of charity," the president said, "than the consistent omissions of a government frozen in the ice of its own indifference" (quoted in Kennedy 1999, 280).

If Roosevelt called himself a liberal, perhaps others did as well. In May 1936, Gallup posed a simple if, to the contemporary ear, somewhat odd question to a cross section of Americans:

> If there were only two political parties in this country—Conservative and Liberal—which would you join?

As Christopher Ellis and James Stimson (2012) show, in succeeding years, Gallup, Harris, Roper, and other survey organizations developed variations on this question:

Should President Roosevelt's second administration be more liberal, more conservative, or about the same as the first?

Which of these three policies would you like to have President Truman follow: Go more to the left, by following more of the views of labor and other liberal groups; Go more to the right, by following more of the views of business and conservative groups; Follow a policy halfway between the two?

Which type of man would you prefer to have elected president in November— one who is known as a liberal, or one who is known as a conservative?

In politics, do you regard yourself as a radical, a liberal, or a conservative?

Not until 1972 did the American National Election Study try its own hand at assessing ideological identification. Since its appearance, the ANES question has become the standard way of assessing ideological identification (ANES has a way of standardizing survey measures), and it will serve as the principal workhorse for our analysis here. This is how the ANES question is worded:

We hear a lot of talk these days about liberals and conservatives. Here is a 7-point scale on which the political views that people might hold are arrayed from extremely liberal to extremely conservative. Where would you place yourself on this scale, or haven't you thought much about this?

As respondents hear the question, they are handed a card. Printed on the card is a horizontal scale. The scale marks and labels each of seven options, running from "extremely liberal" on the left through "moderate, middle of the road" in the center to "extremely conservative" on the right.

Several things are worth noting about the standard question. First of all, it supplies an explicitly political context. Liberalism and conservatism are said to refer to the political views that people hold. Second, liberalism appears on the left, conservatism on the right, preserving a spatial distinction in place since the French Revolution, when in the National Assembly the radicals sat to the left and the king's allies sat to the right (Laponce 1981). And third, the question includes an explicit invitation for respondents to admit that ideology is not for them.

Adequacy of the Standard Measure

The ANES question has become the standard—but that doesn't mean that it is good. How well does the ANES question actually work?

A measure is said to be reliable insofar as it enables repeatable observations (Nunnally 1967). We assess the reliability of the ideological identification measure through the method of retesting over brief intervals. In four ANES presidential election studies (1996, 2000, 2004, and 2008), the standard ideological identification question was asked of respondents twice, once in the preelection interview, and once in the postelection interview. Comparing what people say in the one with what they say in the other yields an estimate of reliability. Table 3.1 summarizes the results from each of the four elections. For the most part, as shown there, liberals remain liberals, moderates remain moderates, and conservatives remain conservatives.

A convenient way to summarize reliability in this context is provided by the Pearson correlation coefficient. The Pearson correlation reflects the extent to which the relative ordering of individuals is the same on one occasion as it is on another. In the case of ideological identification, the Pearson r ranges from 0.64 in 2000 (an especially turbulent and elongated postelection period) to 0.77 in 2004. These coefficients are respectable, the more so because they likely underestimate the actual reliability of the standard question. The interviews bracket the climax of a presidential campaign, the election itself, and an avalanche of political commentary— all of which might supply voters with reasons to rethink their ideological commitments. These results suggest that ideological identification is measured by the standard question with reasonable precision.[3]

A second test takes us from reliability to validity, looking for evidence that the standard question does in fact measure what it claims to measure. ANES respondents are regularly asked to name groups of people they feel particularly close to, groups who are most like them "in their ideas and interests and feelings about things." Over the years, they have been asked about their closeness to Catholics, the middle class, the elderly, and many more—including, from time to time, their closeness to liberals and to conservatives. If the standard measure is doing its job, then ideological identification should powerfully predict who feels close to conservatives and who feels close to liberals. Figure 3.1 shows that this is so. Liberals are quite likely to say that they feel close to liberals and

TABLE 3.1. **Continuity of ideological identification across presidential elections (percentage)**

Postelection	1996			
	Liberal	Moderate	Conservative	
Preelection				
Liberal	77.2	17.6	5.2	100.0
Moderate	14.7	61.7	23.6	100.0
Conservative	3.6	15.5	81.0	100.1

Note: Pearson r = 0.75

Postelection	2000			
	Liberal	Moderate	Conservative	
Preelection				
Liberal	60.5	24.0	15.5	100.0
Moderate	30.6	51.0	18.5	100.1
Conservative	4.8	20.8	74.4	100.0

Note: Pearson r = 0.64

Postelection	2004			
	Liberal	Moderate	Conservative	
Preelection				
Liberal	83.2	12.9	4.0	100.1
Moderate	18.5	63.9	17.6	100.0
Conservative	3.0	13.6	83.5	100.1

Note: Pearson r = 0.77

Postelection	2008			
	Liberal	Moderate	Conservative	
Preelection				
Liberal	75.6	17.3	7.0	99.9
Moderate	18.5	58.4	23.1	100.0
Conservative	3.5	13.2	83.4	100.1

Note: Pearson r = 0.75
Source: 1996, 2000, 2004, 2008 ANES.

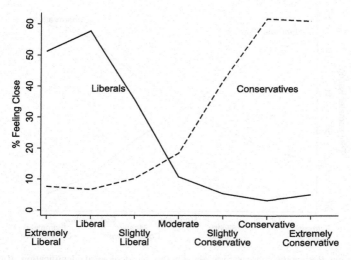

FIGURE 3.1 Feeling close to conservatives and liberals by ideological identification

Source: 1972, 1976, 1980, 1984, 1988, 1992, 1996, and 2000 ANES.

very unlikely to say they feel close to conservatives. Conservatives display the same tendency, run in reverse.[4]

In our third and final test, we take advantage of the fact that in every presidential year since 1972, ANES respondents have been asked to express their feelings toward a wide array of social and political groups. Ratings are assessed through the so-called thermometer scale, ranging from very cold and highly unfavorable (0 degrees) to very warm and highly favorable (100 degrees). Conveniently for our purpose, among the groups regularly rated on the ANES thermometer scale are "liberals" and "conservatives." The simple test of measurement quality here requires that ideological identification be closely associated with ratings of ideological groups.

Figure 3.2 shows that the standard measure of ideological identification passes this test as well. Self-identified liberals evaluate liberals warmly and conservatives coolly. Self-identified conservatives return the favor, and more.[5]

In sum, across elementary but crucial tests, the standard measure performs quite well. Taken all around, the results provide assurance that the standard measure can do what we want it to do: namely, enable an investigation into the nature of ideological identification in the American electorate.[6]

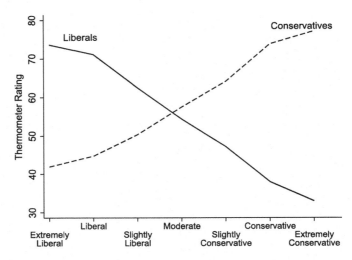

FIGURE 3.2 Ratings of conservatives and liberals by ideological identification. Ratings range from 0 ("very cold") to 100 ("very warm").

Source: 1972–2012 ANES (weighted and combined).

Ideological Identification in the American Electorate: Three Simple Lessons

Table 3.2 presents the distribution of ideological identification in the American public, based on combining results from the ANES surveys from 1972 to 2012. A first and important lesson we should take from table 3.2 is that ideological identification is not for everyone. When offered the opportunity, many Americans say that they do not think of themselves as liberals or conservatives: in all, 27.5 percent decline to identify themselves in ideological terms. (The percentage diminishes slightly over this period, from roughly one-third at the beginning to roughly one-quarter at the end.) Many Americans say no to ideology, even though the survey setting encourages the expression of opinion. When attitudes are asked for, people generally oblige—perhaps more than we would like them to.

Moreover, when Americans do claim an ideological identity, many choose moderation. This is the second lesson. Figure 3.3 displays the distribution of ideological identification in the American public from 1972 to 2012, excluding the nearly 30 percent who said that they didn't know or hadn't thought about themselves in ideological ways. As shown

TABLE 3.2. **Distribution of ideological identification in the American public, 1972–2012**

Identification	Percentage	N
Extremely liberal	1.8	626
Liberal	7.8	2,706
Slightly liberal	9.1	3,153
Moderate, middle of the road	24.5	8,522
Slightly conservative	13.6	4,742
Conservative	13.3	4,613
Extremely conservative	2.4	844
Don't know (DK)/Haven't thought much about it (HTMA)	27.5	9,568
Total	100.0	34,774

Source: 1972–2012 ANES Cumulative Data File.

there, ideological identification generally follows a bell-shaped distribution. Many Americans choose the ideological middle: exactly one-third (33.3 percent) of those who claimed some acquaintance with ideological terms selected the midpoint of the scale, labeled "moderate, middle of the road." This percentage fluctuates over the period but not very much. Should moderation be considered an ideological position? We don't think so, for reasons spelled out in chapter 4.

The third lesson is conservative advantage. More Americans describe themselves as conservative than describe themselves as liberal. As figure 3.3 shows, the distribution of ideological identification is displaced to the right. This is true on average, and it is true, as far as we can tell, whenever measurements have been taken.

As we noted earlier, questions intended to capture something resembling ideological identification have been asked of samples of the American electorate beginning in the 1930s. Over time, the questions differ, and one hard-earned lesson about public opinion is that apparently small differences in question wording and format can make a large difference in what opinion seems to be. Stimson (1991) developed a method that renders responses to these various questions comparable. The result is an estimate of the American public's average ideological identification from 1937 to 2012, which we display in figure 3.4.[7]

As shown there, over the last three-quarters of a century, conservatives have *always* outnumbered liberals. Liberals were a distinct minority during the Eisenhower administration and the Reagan years, unsur-

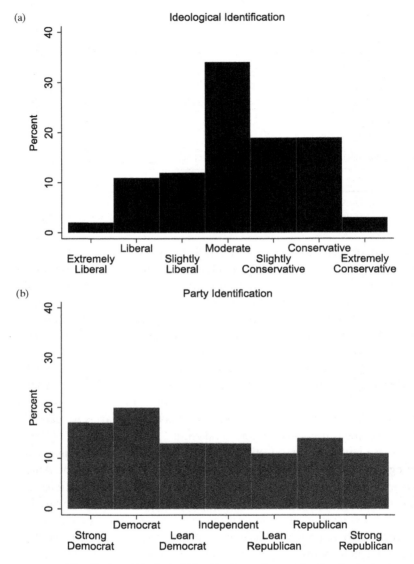

FIGURE 3.3 Distribution of ideological identification and party identification in the American electorate

Source: 1972–2012 ANES (weighted).

FIGURE 3.4 Ideological identification over the long haul, 1937–2012

Source: Ellis and Stimson 2012.
Note: Percentage conservative = % conservative/[(% liberal + % conservative)] × 100.

prisingly. But they were also outnumbered when we might reasonably
have expected the opposite: throughout the Roosevelt presidency and
the New Deal; as Lyndon Johnson was putting in place a Great Society;
and as Barack Obama was offering the nation a "liberal vision" (Baker
2013, 1).

We see no evidence here of ideological eras: long, slow political cycles, when a taste for liberal experimentation in politics runs its course
and is replaced by a taste for conservative caution and consolidation,
which in turn generates an appetite for a new round of experimentation,
and so on (Schlesinger 1986). On the contrary, ideological identification
seems largely inert. Whatever changes are taking place in society and
politics, Americans, on balance, continue to lean to the right.[8]

Ideological Identification and Party Identification

Political parties are vital to American politics. Parties nominate candidates and wage campaigns in the hope of gaining control over the ma-
chinery and resources of government. Parties are crucial to the structuring of legislative action: setting agendas, proposing alternatives, and
voting for or against legislation. One might say—E. E. Schattschneider

has said it—that modern democratic government is "unthinkable save in terms of parties" (1942, 1).

The centrality of political parties to politics has direct implications for how citizens make sense of the candidates and policies put before them. In *The American Voter*, Campbell et al. (1960) define party identification as a persistent attachment to one of the two major political parties. Party identification is more than a temporary infatuation: it is an enduring part of a person's identity, a "sense of belonging which is abiding" (Converse and Pierce 1985, 146). And it is consequential:

> To the average person the affairs of government are remote and complex, and yet the average citizen is asked periodically to formulate opinions about these affairs. At the very least he has to decide how he will vote, what choice he will make between candidates offering different programs and very different versions of contemporary political events. In this dilemma, having the party symbol stamped on certain candidates, certain issue positions, certain interpretations of political reality is of great psychological convenience. (Stokes 1966, 126–27)

At a conceptual level, party identification bears a clear resemblance to ideological identification. Both are aspects of political identity. Both, by definition at least, entail an abiding commitment. And both are presumed to be consequential in shaping what Americans believe and what they do in politics. On each of these points, the evidence on behalf of party identification is massive. As for ideological identification, we have yet to see. Moving forward, it will prove instructive to compare the two—the attachments Americans form to political parties with those they form to ideological groups.[9]

Sharp differences arise immediately. First of all, if close to one-third of Americans have failed to develop a taste for ideological identification, the same cannot be said for partisanship. In response to the canonical question on party identification, only a small percentage of Americans admit that they do not think of themselves in partisan terms. Just 4.9 percent did so, in presidential election surveys carried out by ANES between 1972 and 2012, as against the 27.5 percent of the electorate who, over the same period, declined to claim an ideological identity.[10]

Moreover, when it comes to partisanship, Americans do not flock to the middle as they do when asked about ideology. Figure 3.3 displays the distributions of ideological identification and party identification together. The contrast between the two is stark. Extreme liberals and extreme conservatives are rare; by comparison, strong Democrats and strong Republicans are abundant.[11]

And while Americans are, on balance, conservative in their ideological identification, they are, on balance, Democratic in their party identification. Party identification, as figure 3.3 shows, is displaced to the *left*. At each step away from the independent center, Democrats outnumber Republicans.

That the "average" American is both Democratic and conservative does not mean that partisanship and ideological identification are uncorrelated. On the contrary, Democrats tend to claim liberalism as their ideological home, while Republicans are inclined, rather more disproportionately, toward conservatism. On the idea that American political parties offer, to some degree at least, ideological alternatives (Gerring 1998; Poole and Rosenthal 1984), it would be disconcerting if we did not find ideological identification and party identification to be correlated. Figure 3.5 shows that they are.[12]

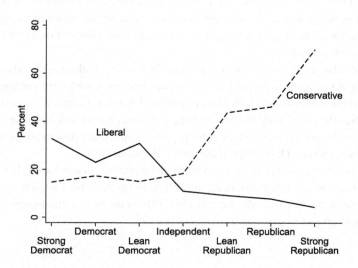

FIGURE 3.5 Ideological identification by partisanship in the American electorate

Source: 1972–2012 ANES (weighted).

Conclusion

Americans identify with all kinds of things: baseball teams, hometowns, schools, religions, political parties, and more. The question we grapple with here is the extent to which Americans also identify with ideological programs—that is, feel a strong and abiding attachment to liberalism or to conservatism.

The first step in this quest is the development of adequate instrumentation. This requires us to move from conceptualization to operationalization, and in the social sciences, the road between the two is not always smooth or straightforward. But after running a series of empirical tests, we concluded that a measure intended to assess ideological identification, introduced into the 1972 ANES and in widespread use since, fulfills its intended purpose well.

With this validated measure in hand, we began to explore the nature of ideological identification in the American mass public. We discovered that a majority of Americans appear indifferent to liberalism and conservatism: either they say that they do not think of themselves in these terms or, when push comes to shove, claim ideological moderation. These are simple facts, but important ones, and should be kept in mind as we proceed. They begin to soften the contrast between the general claim of ideological innocence and the assumed importance of ideological identification.

We also commenced a comparison between ideology—the attachments Americans form to political belief systems—and partisanship—the attachments Americans form to political parties. Contrasts are striking. Nearly all Americans are willing to embrace partisan labels, many claim to be strong supporters of their party, and while conservatives outnumber liberals, Democrats outnumber Republicans.

As we have seen here, some Americans describe themselves as liberal or conservative; many others do not. Explaining how this happens—how it is that some become ideological while others do not—is the business of the next chapter.

CHAPTER FOUR

Becoming Ideological

According to Elster (1985), the first obligation of a theory of ideology is to explain how ideology arises—how it happens that ordinary people come to take possession of ideological ideas (insofar as they do). We know surprisingly little about this. In all the outpouring of empirical research on the nature of ideology, its correlates, and its consequences, the question of the origins of ideology—and more specifically, the question of the origins of ideological identification—has been largely passed over.

Our principal purpose here is to explain how Americans come to an ideological point of view (insofar as they do). By the time they are eligible to vote, many Americans lay claim to an ideological identity. Millions describe themselves as liberals. Millions more describe themselves as conservatives. How does this happen? Once it happens, how resolutely do Americans hold on to their ideological identity? And what does this all mean for the claim of ideological innocence?

Information and Identification

Politics is a hard subject, and not everyone cares to study it. Converse argued that differences in command of political information have profound consequences for differences in political thinking, and that ideological thinking was common only among the very best informed. Consistent with this, in chapter 2 we reported strong associations between measures of information and standard measures of ideological sophistication. Here we propose that differences in political information are also essential for distinguishing between those who claim an ideological identity and those who do not.

To test this proposition, we make use of the remarkable study of political socialization created by Jennings, the Youth-Parent Socialization Panel Study. In the spring of 1965, under Jennings's direction, a national sample of high school seniors was interviewed on a wide range of political subjects. Members of the class of 1965 (as we will refer to them) were questioned again in 1973, and the 1973 interview included the standard ideological identification question: i.e., whether respondents thought of themselves as liberals or conservatives, and if they did, where they would place themselves on a seven-point scale, stretching from extreme liberal to extreme conservative.[1]

Figure 4.1 displays the results, which will look familiar. As we saw for the American public as a whole, members of the class of 1965 tend to occupy the ideological middle ground. Extreme categories, on the left or on the right, are undersubscribed, and nearly one-third (31.5 percent) of those who claim some acquaintance with ideological terms select the midpoint of the scale, labeled "moderate, middle of the road." And just as we found earlier for the entire public, so too for the class of 1965: not everyone chooses an ideological identification. Among the class of 1965,

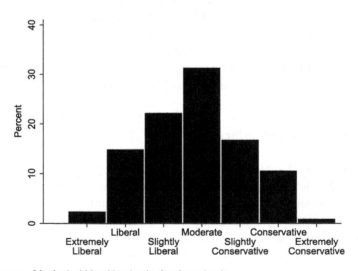

FIGURE 4.1 Ideological identification in the class of 1965

Source: 1965–1973 Youth-Parent Socialization Panel Study (N = 1,153).

almost one in seven—13.9 percent, to be exact—said that they did not think of themselves in ideological terms.[2]

This is a sizable percentage, though not as sizable as the more than 25 percent of the general public who fail to claim an ideological identification. The difference between the two is accounted for by the fact that the Jennings study excluded those who dropped out of school before the spring of what would have been their senior year (roughly 27 percent of the cohort), and those with less than a high school education are prodigiously overrepresented among those who admit that they never think of themselves in ideological terms. When we combined the 1972 and 1974 ANES studies and examined only those respondents who were between twenty and thirty years of age and who had completed high school, we found that 15.7 percent of this group admitted that they did not think of themselves in ideological terms—a figure close to the 13.9 percent of the class of 1965 who said no to ideological terminology in interviews carried out in 1973.

By our reasoning, those who claimed an ideological identification in 1973 should be distinguished from their former classmates by their greater knowledge of politics. Conveniently for our purposes, high school seniors were asked six factual questions about public affairs in the spring of 1965, and then asked the same questions in 1973. On both occasions they were requested to name the governor of their state; the length of term for US senators; the country that had many concentration camps during World War II; the party affiliation of Franklin Delano Roosevelt; the number of justices serving on the US Supreme Court; and the country led by Marshall Tito. To create a scale of political information, we simply counted the number of correct answers.[3]

As expected, information powerfully predicts who claims an ideological identity and who does not. Among the most knowledgeable of the class of 1965—those who answered all twelve test items correctly—ideological identification was virtually certain: 99.8 percent claimed some form of ideological identity. Among the least knowledgeable—those who answered no more than two information items correctly—just 55.1 percent claimed an ideological position as their own.

These percentages treat moderation as an ideological destination. Suppose instead that the only legitimate ideological categories are liberal and conservative. (We argue for this later in the chapter.) Then, among the most knowledgeable of the class of 1965 (again, those who answered all twelve information questions correctly), 85.2 percent claimed an ideological identity. And among the least knowledgeable (as before, those who answered no more than two questions correctly), just 24.5 percent claimed to be either a liberal or a conservative.

Just 24.5 percent? Keep in mind that these are people who did not know who served as the governor of their state, who could not name Germany as the country during World War II responsible for concentration camps, who were unable to identify Franklin Delano Roosevelt as a Democrat, who were unable to specify the length of term for US senators, who could not say how many justices served on the Supreme Court, and who did not know that Marshall Tito was the leader of Yugoslavia. They did not know any of this in 1965, and none of it again in 1973. That one-quarter of high school graduates completely in the dark as far as political affairs goes nevertheless claim an ideological identity may be disconcerting. It suggests that not everyone chooses an ideological identification for what might reasonably be regarded as ideological reasons.[4]

The relationship between information and identification is summarized statistically in the first column of table 4.1. In this analysis, the dependent variable is coded 0 or 1, where 1 means that the person claims some ideological identification (liberal, moderate, or conservative) and 0 means not; and information is represented by the twelve-item scale, scored 0 (0 correct) to 1.0 (12 correct). As table 4.1 indicates, information has a significant and strong association with the likelihood of claiming an ideological identification.

TABLE 4.1. **Information and ideological identification (probit coefficients with standard errors in parentheses)**

	Model I	Model II
Political information	1.37 (.19)	.61 (.23)
Political involvement		.49 (.21)
Some college		.37 (.12)
College graduate		.65 (.14)
Family income		.23 (.18)
Parent education		−.06 (.18)
Female		−.23 (.10)
White		.28 (.16)
Constant	.34 (.11)	−.05 (.22)
Pseudo R^2	−.06	.10
N	1,218	1,218

Source: 1965–73 Youth-Parent Socialization Panel Study.

Information clearly matters, but what else? On this question, the rich literature on political participation offers up some clear advice, under the assumption that identifying with an ideological position can be considered a (mild) form of taking part in politics.

The first recommendation concerns resources. Taking part in politics eats up time, money, and opportunity. Because prospective participants count costs (or act as if they do), those with the greatest resources are most likely to take part. In the current case, the implication is that those who come from affluent, well-educated families should be more likely to describe themselves in ideological terms. Theories of participation also emphasize skills. Politics, we keep saying, is a complicated and difficult subject. People are drawn to it, or drift away, partly as a consequence of the analytical skills they can bring to bear upon it. We measure such skills crudely, by distinguishing among those in the class of 1965 whose formal education ended with high school, those who went on to college but failed to complete a degree, and those who earned a four-year college degree. People take part in politics, or not, also as a consequence of taste. Some people find politics fascinating; many others do not. We measure involvement in politics by how closely members of the class of 1965 said they followed government and public affairs and paid attention to political news on television, in newspapers, and on the radio. A final class of explanatory variables concerns social identity. The class of 1965 came of age just as restrictions on African American voting were being lifted in the South and just before the second wave of the feminist movement would challenge the traditional idea that the world of politics belonged to men. As a result, whites more than blacks, and men more than women, may be more likely to describe themselves in ideological terms.[5]

The results of this analysis, also shown in table 4.1, indicate that choosing an ideological identification is a product primarily of information, involvement, and skill (education). The effects of all three are statistically significant and substantial. Moreover, once the effects due to information, involvement, and skill are taken into account, everything else pretty much washes away. Among the class of 1965, those who came from affluent or well-educated families were no more likely to enlist in an ideological camp than those who did not. Whites were no more likely than blacks to do so. And men were only slightly more likely than women to take up an ideological identity.

In many ways, the Youth-Parent Socialization Panel Study is ideally suited to our interest in the formation of ideological identification. But it

TABLE 4.2. **Information and ideological identification in the American public (probit coefficients with standard errors in parentheses)**

Political information	1.28 (.08)
Political involvement	.49 (.06)
High school graduate	.29 (.04)
Some college	.68 (.05)
College graduate	.91 (.06)
Family income	.47 (.06)
Female	−.13 (.03)
White	.19 (.04)
Constant	−1.04 (.06)
N	9,845

Source: 1972–2008 ANES.

is of course just a single study, based on a particular sample, at a particular time. To test the generality of our results, we carried out a separate and independent test, running essentially the same model, this time on ANES surveys from 1972 to 2008.

The results, summarized in table 4.2, are reassuring on this score. Once again we see that crossing the threshold to an ideological identity is a consequence primarily of information, involvement, and skill. If anything, the importance of information is even greater here.

We conclude that Americans take possession of an ideological identification insofar as they are intrigued by politics, possess the intellectual wherewithal to make sense of this difficult subject, and command a basic working knowledge of how politics works.[6]

Campaigns and Identification

Is that the whole story? Perhaps not. Research on political participation points to the importance of mobilization: "the process by which candidates, parties, activists, and groups induce other people to participate" (Rosenstone and Hansen 1993, 25–26). People participate in politics in part because they are asked to do so. One regular and important way that mobilization takes place is through campaigns. The modern presidential campaign in particular is a noisy, shiny, expensive affair, designed— with some success—to mobilize voters' interest and attention (e.g., Gerber and Green 2000; Green and Gerber 2008; Lazarsfeld, Berelson, and Gaudet 1948; Rosenstone and Hansen 1993; Sears and Valentino 1997).

With this in mind, we might expect to observe increases in ideological identification over the course of presidential campaigns. We might expect this especially when the campaign highlights ideological differences between the parties, as in the case of 1980, when Ronald Reagan ran as a crusading conservative. If campaigns encourage people to enlist under one ideological banner or another, 1980 would seem to present an excellent case in point.

As it happens, we can test this proposition well, for the standard ideological identification question was included on each of three independent cross-sectional studies carried out by ANES across the 1980 campaign. By this evidence, ideological identification did *not* increase over the campaign: 64.9 percent of Americans claimed an ideological identification in February; 65.5 percent did so in April; and slightly fewer, 64.1 percent, did so in September. We see nothing here to suggest that the ideologically charged 1980 presidential campaign persuaded many Americans to think of themselves in ideological terms.

If the 1980 campaign, which placed the iconic figure of twentieth-century American conservatism in the White House, failed to generate much in the way of ideological identification in the electorate, what should we expect of other campaigns? Not much—which is what we find. In ANES presidential election studies from 1976 to 2008, the ideological identification question appears in the preelection interview, and in such studies, preelection interviewing commences immediately after Labor Day and finishes on the eve of Election Day. This design allows us to see whether, in the two-month run-up to the election, ideological identification increases. Combining studies to enhance statistical power, we estimated the relationship between likelihood of identifying with an ideological group—liberal, moderate, or conservative—and time to Election Day.

We find no evidence of rising ideological identification as the presidential campaign reaches its climax. Table 4.3 shows large and precisely estimated effects of information, involvement, and education but no effect of proximity to the election. If anything, ideological identification *declines* as the election nears, though the effect is not significant. This is so for the entire electorate (as shown in the table); it also holds among the young, who might be thought poised to declare an ideological affiliation.[7]

Presidential campaigns mobilize attention and motivate learning. But they do so, at least on the evidence presented here, without stimulating citizens to think of themselves as ideological.

TABLE 4.3. **Campaigns and identification: Time to Election Day and likelihood of ideological identification (probit coefficients with standard errors in parentheses)**

Time (days to election/67)	.07 (.06)
Political information	1.56 (.07)
Political involvement	.51 (.06)
Some college	.54 (.04)
College graduate	.82 (.05)
Constant	−.81 (.06)
N	9,648

Source: 1976–2008 ANES (pooled).

Experience and Identification

Campaigns intrude on everyday life only temporarily. A month or two of sound and fury, and they are gone. What about the longer haul? Perhaps Americans become more likely to think of themselves as liberals or conservatives as they progress through their adult lives, accumulating political experience as they go.

We know something like this takes place for party identification. In *The American Voter*, Campbell et al. (1960) discovered a substantial relationship between age and partisanship. Older Americans were much more likely to think of themselves as strong Democrats or strong Republicans, and much less likely to think of themselves as independents, than the young. Subsequent investigations have found the same pattern, and more detailed analysis has provided support for a single and elegant explanation for it. Older Americans are more likely to be strong partisans than are younger Americans as a consequence of a lifetime's acquisition of electoral experience. The gradual strengthening of partisan loyalty over the life cycle is a product of a person's "continuing experience with the party system" (Converse 1969, 148; see Converse 1976).[8]

Does the same process govern ideological identification? Over the span of life, as people begin to follow politics, participate in political discussions, take positions, vote for or against candidates, and so on, do they become more likely to think of themselves in ideological terms?

Apparently not. Figure 4.2 displays the simple relationship between age and ideological identification, and for comparison purposes, between age and strength of partisanship. The results come from combin-

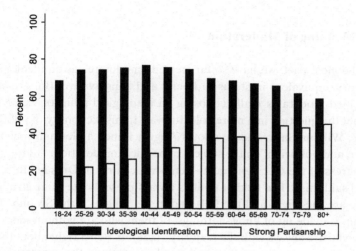

FIGURE 4.2 Ideological identification and partisan strength by age

Source: 1972–2012 ANES (weighted), presidential election years.
Note: "Ideological identification" means liberal, moderate, or conservative; "strong partisanship" means strong Democrat or strong Republican

ing ANES presidential election studies carried out between 1972 and 2012. As expected, figure 4.2 shows that strength of partisanship increases across the life span. The proportion of the American electorate that identifies either as a strong Democrat or as a strong Republican marches upward from early adulthood to the end of life. Age and partisan strength are positively correlated, and the correlation is likely a result of the lifelong accumulation of political—and especially electoral—experience.[9]

The relationship between age and ideological identification is different. As figure 4.2 reveals, the likelihood of identifying with an ideological group—liberal, moderate, or conservative—increases slightly through early adulthood, levels off in middle age, and then declines. In short, the elegant explanation for the lifelong intensification of partisanship does *not* apply to ideology. The gradual accumulation of electoral experience over the course of life strengthens partisanship but appears to have little or no bearing on the likelihood of claiming an ideological identity.[10]

The Meaning of Moderation

For the most part, we have so far treated "moderate" as an ideological category, equivalent in status to liberal and conservative. But are self-described moderates really choosing an ideological point of view? We can put the question in a more colorful way. In his dictionary of political terms, William Safire (2008) quotes August Bebel, a German socialist, writer, and politician, on the subject of political moderation. Addressing a congress of the German Social-Democratic party in Dresden in 1903, Bebel said this: "The field of politics always presents the same struggle. There are the Right and the Left and in the middle is the Swamp. The Swamp is made up of know-nothings, of them who are without ideas, of them who are always with the majority" (428). Is Bebel right about those who occupy the center of the ideological spectrum in the contemporary United States?

To find out, we returned to the Jennings study, this time categorizing members of the class of 1965 into one of *three* groups: those who described themselves either as liberal or as conservative; those who described themselves as moderate; and those who said they never thought of themselves as liberal, conservative, or moderate (this last group serves as the omitted category). Our statistical model takes into account the same explanatory variables as before—information, involvement, education, as well as family social class, parents' education, gender, and race—and is estimated this time with multinomial probit.

The results, presented in table 4.4, suggest that it may be best *not* to treat moderate as an ideological category. As shown there, information, involvement, and education powerfully distinguish between those who identify as a liberal or conservative from those who say they never think of themselves in ideological terms. But neither information nor involvement nor education distinguishes between those who "identify" as a moderate from those, again, who say they never think of themselves in ideological terms. In the latter case, the coefficients run in the predicted direction, but none reaches statistical significance (information comes closest).

To pursue this question further, we compared moderates to those who rejected ideological terms on several standard measures of ideological sophistication. With respect to the consistency of opinion on pressing matters of public policy, the two groups are indistinguishable. The

TABLE 4.4. **Ideological moderation as a consequence of information, involvement, and education (probit coefficients with standard errors in parentheses)**

	Liberal or conservative	Moderate
Political information	1.02 (.32)	.47 (.33)
Political involvement	.99 (.30)	.17 (.31)
Some college	.74 (.17)	.14 (.18)
College graduate	1.20 (.19)	.27 (.20)
Family income	.24 (.25)	.35 (.26)
Parent education	.04 (.25)	−.25 (.26)
Female	−.43 (.14)	−.11 (.14)
White	.45 (.24)	.21 (.24)
Constant	−1.01 (.32)	−.13 (.32)
N	1,218	

Source: 1965–73 Youth-Parent Socialization Panel Study.

same can be said for opinion stability: moderates are no more likely to express stable opinions on policy than are their peers who reject ideological terms altogether. We do find moderates somewhat more likely to use ideological categories when discussing what they liked and disliked about the presidential candidates and the political parties than those who say ideology is not for them—though both groups were much less likely to use ideological categories than either liberals or conservatives.[11]

All things considered, the "moderate" category seems less an ideological destination than a refuge for the innocent and confused.

Persistence

Some Americans cross over the threshold and become liberals or conservatives. Then what? Is this their ultimate destination, or merely the first stop on an ideological journey? In the final section of this chapter, we take up the persistence of ideological identification once acquired.

On the idea that ideological identification is, in fact, identification—that is, a strong and persistent psychological attachment—then liberal and conservative self-descriptions, once adopted, should be more or less fixed. To use Robert Abelson's (1986) metaphor—core beliefs are like cherished material possessions—adult Americans should take *ownership* of their ideological identity.

This section is made up of three distinct but related parts. First, we consider the staying power of ideological identification among those who describe themselves as liberal or conservative, assessed in periods of political turbulence. Second, we track stability and change in ideological identification from early adulthood to late middle age. Third, we show that ideological tenacity is apparent only among Americans seriously engaged in political affairs.

Ideological Perseverance and Political Disorder

Here we examine the durability of identification as a liberal or a conservative during periods of political upheaval, looking for stability in the face of forces pushing for change. At each point, we compare the stability of ideological identification against the stability displayed by partisanship. Our expectations for party identification are clear. To the authors of *The American Voter*, party identification was a "durable attachment, not readily disturbed by passing events and personalities" (Campbell et al. 1960, 151), and so it seems to be (Converse and Markus 1979; Green, Palmquist, and Schickler 2002). As for ideological identification, much less has been said and almost no evidence presented, so let's take a look.

REAGAN COUNTRY   Ronald Reagan's victory in the 1980 presidential election was widely interpreted as a triumph of modern conservatism. Claiming an ideological mandate, Reagan proceeded to cut taxes, slow down spending on social programs, lighten government regulations, and pour money into national defense. To assess stability and change in ideological identification over the 1980 campaign, we draw on the 1980 ANES Panel Study. There, a representative sample of the American electorate was questioned face-to-face in February 1980, interviewed again in June, and then again in September. Each interview included the standard ANES ideological identification question.

We assess stability and change here and throughout this section with the Pearson product-moment coefficient (r). Pearson r captures stability and change in relative positioning. Insofar as individuals are ordered the same way from one occasion to the next, Pearson r will approach 1.0. Insofar as the ordering of individuals on one occasion reveals nothing about how they are ordered at the next, Pearson r will return a value of 0. As table 4.5 reveals, by this measure, ideological identification is reasonably stable across the 1980 presidential campaign (Pearson $r = .66$), but not nearly as stable as party identification (Pearson $r = .86$).

TABLE 4.5. **Stability and change of ideological identification and party identification (Pearson r)**

	Ideological identification	Party identification
Conservative triumph		
February 1980–September 1980	.66	.86
Watergate		
1972–74	.60	.79
1974–76	.62	.81
September 11		
2000–2002	.65	.80

Source: 1980, 1972–76, and 2000–2002 ANES Panel Studies.

Party identification's superiority over ideological identification in this respect is actually greater than the simple comparison in table 4.5 suggests. The calculation of Pearson r for party identification sets aside those who do not think of themselves in partisan terms, just as the parallel calculation for ideological identification sets aside those who do not think of themselves in ideological terms. The rule is the same, but as a practical matter, it carries dramatically different consequences for the two cases. More than 40 percent of the ANES Panel sample disappears in the case of ideological identification (missing on either the first interview or the second), compared to about 2 percent in the case of party identification.[12]

One way to take into account this difference is to think of the stability of an attitude as the weighted average of the observed stability among the fraction of the electorate who "possess" the attitude and an assigned value of zero among the fraction of the electorate who do not. Applying this correction to the stability of ideology and partisanship from the beginning of the 1980 presidential campaign to near the end yields a synthetic correlation of .38 for ideological identification and .84 for party identification—a huge difference.

WATERGATE   The 1972–1974–1976 ANES Panel Study brackets an especially tumultuous political period. It encompasses Richard Nixon's landslide reelection, the deepening Watergate scandal, the eventual resignation of the president, Gerald Ford's elevation to the presidency (having been appointed vice president after Spiro Agnew's resignation), and Ford's narrow loss to Jimmy Carter in the 1976 presidential election.

Watergate was trouble for the country but a political nightmare for the Republican leadership and the party's rank and file. Perhaps under these circumstances, party identification would surrender its advantage over ideology when it comes to stability.

Not really. The results, also shown in table 4.5, indicate that ideological identification is moderately stable across this remarkable portion of American political history, but party identification is substantially more so. Applying the same correction to the observed Pearson correlations as we did in our analysis of the 1980 ANES Panel yields (synthetic) Pearson two-year correlations of .39 and .38 for ideological identification and .77 and .80 for party identification.

SEPTEMBER 11   Respondents comprising a representative national sample of Americans of voting age were interviewed by ANES during the 2000 presidential election and then again in the fall of 2002 during the midterm elections. The 2000 interviews were carried out before 9/11—before the collapse of the twin towers, the dark gash into the Pentagon, the transformation of US policy, and the declaration of indefinite war on terrorism. The 2002 interviews were carried out after 9/11 and in an entirely altered context: as domestic security alerts issued by the Department of Homeland Security had become routine, after American-led forces had swept the Taliban regime out of power in Afghanistan, and in the midst of planning for war with Iraq.

The events of 9/11 changed politics and policy, but without disturbing the sharp contrast we have been seeing between ideological identification and party identification. The pattern remains the same. Once again, ideological identification is reasonably stable (Pearson $r = .65$), but not as stable as party identification (Pearson $r = .80$). Corrected, the synthetic correlations are .44 for ideology and .79 for party.

Ideological Persistence over the Life Span

Again, ideological identification is—or is supposed to be—an *abiding* psychological attachment to an ideological group. It is durable, not easily shaken. An identification stays with you. That's what it means to be identified. It is a conviction, an enduring commitment.

With the Jennings socialization data, we can calculate a summary measure of the stability of ideological identification over the long haul, from 1973, as the erstwhile high school seniors were beginning to settle down—marry, finish school, start a family, launch a career—to 1997, their late middle ages. Over this twenty-four-year period, ideological identification is reasonably stable (Pearson $r = .45$), though not as stable as party identification (Pearson $r = .60$).

Once again, party identification's advantage here is greater than it seems, since the correlation calculation sets aside those who do not think of themselves in ideological terms (in the first case) or in partisan terms (in the second). More than one-third of the sample disappears on ideological identification (37.3 percent) compared to less than 2 percent on party identification. This yields, by our standard correction, synthetic correlations of .28 and .59.

Persistence and Information

The correlations we presented in previous sections are average figures; they summarize stability and change for the class of 1965 or for the electorate as a whole. For an overall comparison between ideological and partisan identification, they provide exactly what we want.

At the same time, average figures can be deceiving. Average figures ignore the many ways that Americans differ from one another. In particular, averages overlook a basic fact of political life: namely, that the individuals who comprise mass publics differ enormously in how much they know about politics. We take this to be the principal lesson of Converse's essay, and it should certainly apply here. Persistence should depend on information. We expect ideological identification—*real* ideological identification—to show up only among Americans who know a lot about politics.

To see if this is so, we estimated the stability of ideological identification conditional on information, where information is based on performance on factual test items, or, in one instance, on interviewer ratings. We ran the model on each of five panel studies: the ANES 1980 presidential campaign study; the 1972–74 ANES; the 1974–76 ANES; the ANES 9/11 panel study; and the 1973–97 class of 1965 study. For purposes of comparison, we estimated the stability of party identification conditional on information in each instance as well.[13]

The results, summarized in table 4.6, show that information makes a *huge* difference to the stability of ideological identification. The table gives predicted values for the stability of ideological identification (and separately for party identification) at three levels of information: for peo-

TABLE 4.6. **Stability of ideological identification (I) and party identification (P) by information (Pearson r)**

	1973–97		1972–74		1974–76		1980 campaign		2000–2002	
Information	I	P	I	P	I	P	I	P	I	P
5th percentile	.20	.68	.15	.68	.27	.76	.34	.77	.28	.70
50th percentile	.38	.57	.47	.78	.49	.80	.54	.86	.63	.84
95th percentile	.55	.50	.73	.87	.72	.84	.74	.96	.91	.95

Source: 1965–97 Youth-Parent Socialization Panel Study; 1980, 1972–1974–1976, and 2000–2002 ANES Panel Studies.

ple scoring at the fifth percentile of information, the fiftieth percentile, and the ninety-fifth percentile. As shown in the table, ideological identification is much more stable among Americans who are well informed than among those who are poorly informed. The differences associated with information are enormous.

Information also makes a perceptible difference to the stability of party identification in three of the five surveys, but the differences here are much less conspicuous than in the case of ideological identification. Even among the poorly informed, party identification is impressively stable. In fact, the estimated stability of party identification among the *least* informed is roughly equivalent to the estimated stability of ideological identification among the *best* informed.

Ideology for the Few

Becoming ideological arises from engagement in public affairs. Absent real involvement in political life, absent the intellectual capacity required to master complexity and manipulate abstraction, absent knowledge of how politics works, the ordinary person will see little reason and have little basis for internalizing an ideological point of view. Together, involvement, ability, and information set a high threshold for identification. If moderates are regarded as nonideological, which we believe they should be, then the proportion of those who fail to claim an ideological identification constitutes a majority of the American electorate. Ideological identification is not for everyone, just as politics is not, and for the same reasons.

Once acquired, is ideological identification a permanent part of identity? Not by the evidence presented here. In periods of political turbulence, Americans are much more likely to retain their partisanship than their ideological identification. We see this in Reagan's rise to power, in the wake of the Watergate scandal, and in the aftermath of 9/11. On each occasion, Americans were bombarded by events and appeals that might have been expected to induce a re-thinking of political commitments. Insofar as this happened, it occurred much more for ideology than for party.[14] The same is true across the disturbances and vicissitudes of life: from early adulthood to late middle age, Americans tend to be more steadfast in their partisanship than in their ideology. Once again, and much as Converse would have expected, in these respects ideological identification depends crucially on information. Taking real ownership of ideology, like becoming ideological in the first place, is a political accomplishment limited for the most part to the well informed.

CHAPTER FIVE

In the Long Run

" *In the long run*," John Maynard Keynes reminds us, "we are all dead" (1924, 80). Conceding Keynes his melancholy point, ideology in the long run is our subject here. In the first section we consider whether the American electorate is becoming more ideological, whether we are heading toward a society polarized by ideological differences. And in the second we take up whether, over the long haul, "liberal" and "conservative" are becoming synonymous with "Democrat" and "Republican"; in other words, whether ideology and partisanship are consolidating into a single predisposition.[1]

Polarizing?

The United States today is deeply divided, or so we are told. We live in red states—bastions of conservatism—or in blue states—hotbeds of liberalism. We disagree, sharply and acrimoniously, over guns and abortion and immigration, over taxes and terrorism, over practically everything. According to John Jost, the nation is "sharply divided along ideological lines" (2006, 658). Going further, James Davison Hunter argues that we have descended into a "culture war," an apocalyptic struggle for America's soul (1992, 1994; Hunter and Wolfe 2006).

No. Red states and blue states are not so different (Fiorina, Abrams, and Pope 2011). On matters of policy, most Americans take moderate positions (DiMaggio, Evans, and Bryson 1996; Hetherington 2009; Fiorina and Abrams 2008). And as we have reported here, on the standard ANES question, Americans tend to occupy the ideological middle ground. Extreme categories, on the left or on the right, are underpopulated; nearly one-third of those who claim some acquaintance with ideological terms select the center; and substantial numbers decline to choose any ideological identification at all.

Figure 5.1 portrays, in the top panel, an imaginary electorate experiencing ideological polarization. There, no one fails to choose an ideological position; hardly anyone occupies the center; practically everyone stacks up either at the extreme left or at the extreme right. It is easy

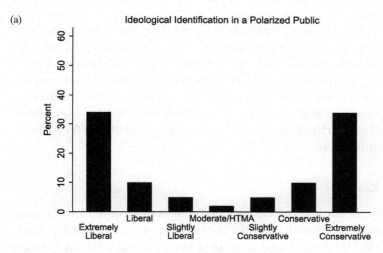

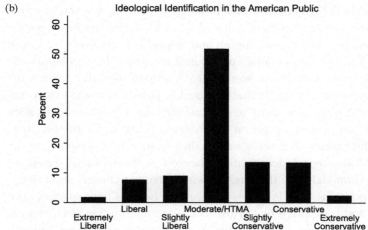

FIGURE 5.1 Ideological polarization: hypothetical and real

Source: On the bottom, the 2012 ANES (face-to-face sample, weighted).

enough to imagine that life in such a place would be unpleasant—rather like Congress these days—and perhaps even dangerous. In the bottom panel of figure 5.1 is displayed the actual distribution of ideological identification in the American electorate, based on pooling ANES presidential election studies from 1972 to 2012. The one distribution is a near perfect inversion of the other: an ideologically divided society is a topsy-turvy version of the one Americans currently inhabit. Assessed in terms of ideological identification, the American electorate is very far from polarized.[2]

But it could be that the electorate is *polarizing*; that is, becoming more polarized, more ideological. The question here is trajectory: whether the American electorate is moving toward ideological polarization, even if it has a long way to go. The question is important, and we will pursue it from multiple angles, but we do not expect to turn up much. Innocence of ideology is a general condition, not much disturbed by rising education or by polarizing parties. We assume the same will hold for ideological identification.

Rival Camps?

To what extent is the American electorate moving toward two opposing camps, one liberal, the other conservative? One way to get at this is simply to fold the standard measure of ideological identification around its center, and then examine how it changes over time. For this purpose, moderates and those who said that ideological identification was not for them are scored 0; "slight" liberals and "slight" conservatives are scored .33; liberals and conservatives are scored .67; and extreme liberals and extreme conservatives are scored 1.0. A second indicator reflects the idea that ideology "can be characterized as polarized to the extent that opinion is diverse, 'far apart' in content, and relatively balanced between ends of the opinion spectrum" (DiMaggio, Evans, and Bryson 1996, 694). This feature is captured well by the variance (s^2) of response to the standard ideological identification question. A third measure refers directly to bimodality, or the extent to which ideology clusters into two opposing positions, with locations between the two positions sparsely populated, and is captured by kurtosis (k). If the distribution of ideology is single peaked, kurtosis is positive; as the distribution flattens, kurtosis becomes negative.[3]

Figure 5.2 reveals that the American electorate *is* polarizing. Since the 1970s, the ideological center has shrunk; variance has increased; and kurtosis has declined. Perhaps more to the point, on each of the three indicators, the movement is slight. Americans, one could say, are *inching* their way toward an ideologically divided society.[4]

If we break down the movement of ideological identification into its component parts, two trends stand out. First is a gentle but steady decline in the proportion of those who either describe themselves as mod-

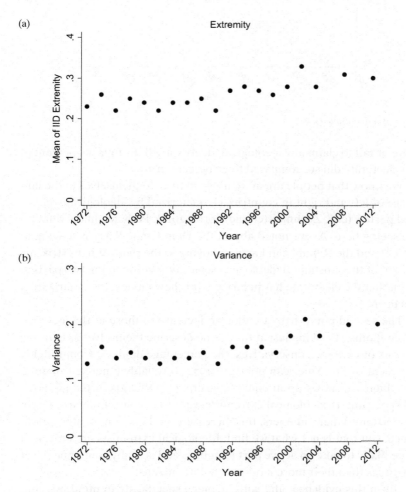

FIGURE 5.2 Distribution of ideological identification in three aspects, 1972–2012

Source: 1972–2012 ANES.
Note: "IID" means ideological identification.

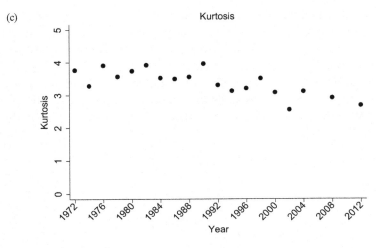

FIGURE 5.2 (*continued*)

erate or fail to claim any ideological identity at all. In 1972, 55 percent of the electorate did so, compared to 47 percent in 2012.

We know that people are more likely to refer to themselves in the language of left and right in countries characterized by ideologically polarized parties (e.g., Zechmeister and Corral 2012). Perhaps that is what we are seeing here. As we noted above, the Democratic Party is moving to the left and the Republican Party is moving to the right. What's striking, in light of the substantial ideological separation between the two parties, is not that the electorate has polarized. It is how modest the polarization has been.

The second noteworthy trend is an increase in those at the ideological endpoints. Looking just at those who describe themselves as extreme liberals or extreme conservatives, the percentage doubles, from roughly 3 percent of the American public in 1972 to roughly 6 percent in 2012. This increase shows up in equal measure at both ends of the ideological spectrum. If ideological extremists were to exercise influence out of proportion to their numbers, this increase would take on greater significance. But that is not what we find. Ideological extremists are only a bit more likely to take an active part in politics and actually command fewer resources than their more moderate fellow citizens.

Given this evidence, and with ideology specifically in mind, we conclude that the American electorate is very far from polarized. Nor will it be polarized anytime soon. On the current trajectory, Americans will have to wait a very long time before they find themselves in a society divided by ideology.[5]

Increasing Disagreement?

That said, perhaps liberals and conservatives disagree with each other more ardently today than they used to. If that turned out to be true, arguments over policy—over how best to move the country forward— might be more heated; compromise further out of reach.

We know that *partisan* differences have been increasing. Democrats and Republicans disagree more sharply with each other than they used to, clashing over domestic policy, international affairs, and the president's performance, among other matters (e.g., DiMaggio, Evans and Bryson 1996; Baldassarri and Gelman 2008; Hetherington 2009; Jacobson 2008; Levendusky 2009). But what about ideology? Are liberals and conservatives disagreeing with each other now more than before?

To answer these questions, we calculated correlations between ideological identification and opinion on every policy question present on the ANES from 1972 to 2012. We then estimated a model that allows the average correlation and the time trend to vary by issue. The results, summarized in table 5.1, indicate that the association between ideological identification and opinion on policy is not increasing. Nor, for that matter, is it decreasing. As shown in table 5.1, since the 1970s the average correlation between ideological identification and opinion on policy has not moved at all.[6]

Table 5.1 also presents the results from a parallel analysis, this time of

TABLE 5.1. **Ideological and partisan differences over policy, 1972–2012 (Pearson *r* with standard errors in parentheses)**

	Ideology and preference	Partisanship and preference
Average correlation	.23 (.01)	.18 (.02)
Time (decades)	.01 (.01)	.04 (.01)
Residual standard deviations		
Average correlation	.08	.09
Time	.02	.03
Data	.05	.04
N	268	268

Source: 1972–2012 ANES.

the relationship between opinions on policy and party identification. In this case, the average correlation *is* increasing. Since the 1970s, the correlation between partisanship and opinion on policy has increased, on average, .04 per decade.

In short, taking disagreement as an expression of polarization, we find no evidence of ideological polarization and substantial evidence of partisan polarization. Democrats and Republicans are disagreeing more; liberals and conservatives are not.[7]

Increasing Animosity?

Although liberals and conservatives do not disagree with each other more than before, maybe they just *dislike* each other more. Perhaps ideological animosity is on the increase.

Animosity between partisans is rising. Since at least the 1980s, Democrats have been expressing increasing hostility toward Republicans. Over the same period, Republicans have been returning the favor, expressing increasing hostility toward Democrats (Iyengar, Sood, and Lelkes 2012; Iyengar and Westwood 2014). Figure 5.3 summarizes thermometer scale ratings given to Democrats and to Republicans by ANES respondents from 1980 to 2012, separately by party identification.[8] As shown there, across this period, both Democrats and Republicans felt quite positive about their own party. Naturally enough, Democrats were much warmer toward the Democratic Party than they were toward the Republican Party, and the same holds, just as naturally, but in reverse, for Republicans. The interesting point here is this: while Democrats maintain their positive feelings toward their own party, their feelings for the Republican Party, not all that positive to begin with, turn substantially more negative. Republicans show the same tendency, if not quite so dramatically. In 2012, Congress, illegal immigrants, even atheists were more popular among the American public than Republicans were with Democrats and Democrats were with Republicans.[9]

Do we see the same pattern of increasing animosity between liberals and conservatives? Not really. These results are also presented in figure 5.3. The format follows that for partisanship. Summarized this time are average thermometer ratings given to liberals and conservatives by ANES respondents from 1972 to 2012, separately by ideological identification.[10] As expected, liberals were much more favorable toward their own ideological soulmates than they were toward their ideological adversaries. Conservatives show the same pattern. What is different about ideological animosity is that until recently, it showed no signs of an increase. Liberals are not exactly wild about conservatives, but their feelings have not grown more negative. Likewise, conservatives are on average quite cool toward liberals, but their feelings have not grown cooler. This is so, as figure 5.3 shows, up until 2012. In 2012, liberals and con-

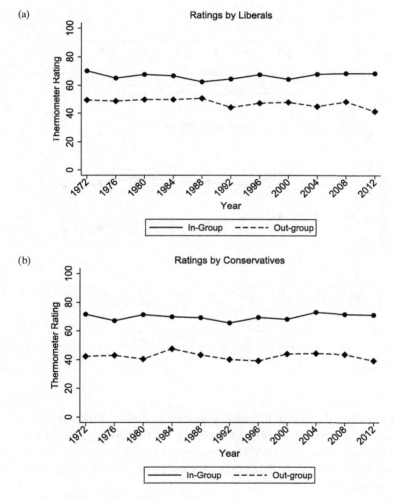

FIGURE 5.3 Ideological and partisan animosity

Source: For ideological animosity, 1972–2012 ANES; for partisan animosity, 1980–2012 ANES.

(c)

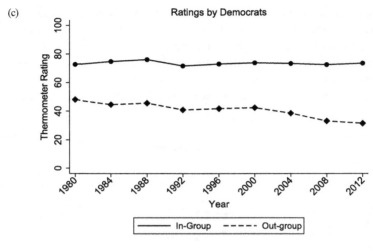

(d)

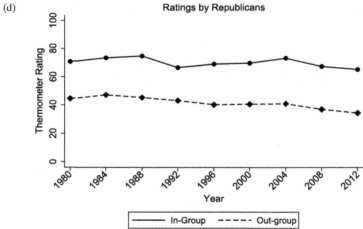

FIGURE 5.3 (*continued*)

servatives both display an increase in mutual irritation. Whether this is
the start of a trend or merely a temporary fluctuation, we cannot say.
What we can say is that while Democrats and Republicans have grown
steadily and increasingly unhappy with each other, liberals and conservatives have not.

All things considered, then, the American public shows little indication of growing more ideological. Liberals and conservatives are outnumbered by moderates and those who reject ideological terminology altogether. The proportion of the electorate claiming an ideological identity is rising, but at a glacial pace. Liberals and conservatives disagree somewhat over policy, but no more than they used to. And, until 2012, liberals and conservatives displayed no more ill will toward each other than before. In these respects, as in others, the American public today remains nearly as innocent of ideology as it was a generation or two ago.

Partisan-Ideological Fusion?

In the previous section and throughout our analysis more generally, we have looked for change and found very little of it. For the most part, our investigation of ideology has turned up results that fit comfortably with what Converse was reporting decades ago. In this section, at last, we find something different. Here is evidence of substantial change.

As we know, Democrats tend to claim liberalism as their ideological home, while Republicans, in greater proportion, claim conservatism. What draws our attention here is not that ideological identification and party identification are associated—it would be peculiar if they were not—but that the association between the two has increased substantially over the last four decades. Today, much more so than before, Democrats identify as liberals and Republicans identify as conservatives.[11]

To capture the association between partisan and ideological identification, we have created a measure called "ideological-partisan consistency," which distinguishes between those whose partisan and ideological identities are consistent (by standard assumption) from those whose identities are inconsistent (by standard assumption). Here is how the measure works in operational terms:

Ideological-partisan consistency is 1 if the person is a Democrat and a liberal *or* if the person is a Republican and a conservative.

Ideological-partisan consistency is −1 if the person is a Democrat and a conservative *or* if the person is a Republican and a liberal.

Ideological-partisan consistency is 0 otherwise (moderates, independents, those who reject partisanship, and those who reject ideological identification)

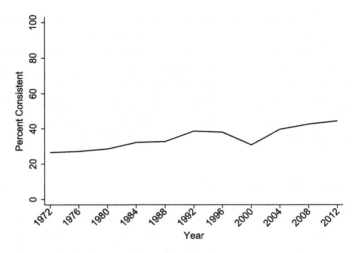

FIGURE 5.4 Consistency between party identification and ideological identification, 1972 to 2012. Share of the American public whose ideological and partisan identifications match

Source: 1972–2012 ANES.

Figure 5.4 displays the movement of this measure over time. There we see a gradual, nearly monotonic increase in consistency between 1972 and 2012. The percentage of Americans who think of themselves as Democrats and as liberals, or as Republicans and as conservatives, grows from 26.5 percent of the electorate in 1972 to 44.3 percent in 2012. This increase takes place within both partisan camps, though it is more pronounced among Republicans.[12]

Ideological-partisan consistency is rising in the American electorate, and the question is, why? Like Marc Hetherington (2001) and Matthew Levendusky (2009), we propose that the increasing consistency since the 1970s is a consequence of the sizable and persistent changes that have taken place in the positions of the political parties over the same period. The parties have traveled in opposite directions, the Democratic Party moving to the left, the Republican Party moving to the right (McCarty, Poole, and Rosenthal 2006). As the parties diverged, they presented certain segments of the American electorate with what Abelson (1959) long ago described as a "belief dilemma." Republicans who heretofore had thought of themselves as liberals might have become concerned, if they were paying attention, that their party was shifting to the right on abortion or race or on some other matter of importance to them. In symmetrical fashion, Democrats who heretofore had thought of themselves as conservatives might have become concerned, if they were paying attention, that their party was moving to the left on abortion or race or on some other matter of importance to them. To resolve this dilemma, citizens could either alter their partisanship or modify their ideological position. Cognitive consistency theory stipulates that the less psychologically central attitude will be the one to change (Abelson 1968; Festinger 1957). For abundant reasons spelled out over the previous chapters, we would expect Americans to resolve their dilemma by modifying their ideological identity. When push came to shove, Americans would adjust their ideology to fit their partisanship.[13]

Such adjustments have come about, according to our account, because of changes in the party system. As polarization of the political parties has increased, Americans have become more likely to adopt partisan and ideological identifications that match. But even when the parties are polarizing over matters of importance, we cannot take for granted that Americans will notice, for they are immersed in private affairs. Set against the more compelling claims of family, work, and leisure, politics will often seem far away and unimportant. With this in mind, we propose that the effect of party polarization on ideological-partisan consistency will be limited to Americans engaged enough in public affairs to notice what the parties are up to, and engaged enough as well to take seriously the implications of what they see for their own political identity.

We measured party polarization by party differences on roll-call votes in Congress (Poole 1998). We took congressional voting to represent the broader set of cues that reach citizens on where the parties stand. The evidence for party polarization over this period is abundant: it shows up in party platforms, presidential candidates' stump speeches, presidential appointments, as well as votes cast in Congress (e.g., Rohde 1991; Sanbonmatsu 2002; Wolbrecht 2000). We combined ANES presidential election studies from 1972 to 2012 and estimated the effects of party polarization, political information, and their interaction with ordinary least squares regression. Table 5.2 displays the results.[14]

The first thing to notice there is the first-order importance of information. The well informed are much more likely to display consistency in their partisanship and ideological identification than are the poorly informed—additional evidence, not that we needed it, on the vital importance for ideology of distinguishing between those who are engaged in political life from those who are not. We also find a statistically significant and substantial interaction between party polarization and politi-

TABLE 5.2. **Effect of party polarization on ideological-partisan congruence, 1972–2012 (OLS regression coefficients with standard errors in parentheses)**

Party polarization	.04 (.05)
Political knowledge	.29 (.06)
Political polarization × political knowledge	.36 (.08)
Constant	−.10 (.03)
N	20,903
R^2	.07

Source: 1972–2012 ANES.

cal information. Among the least informed, the effect of party polarization is virtually zero. For them, it matters not whether the two parties are ideologically far apart or ideologically inseparable. Among the well informed, however, the effect of polarization is large. Those who pay attention to politics are generally much more likely to express ideological-partisan consistency, a tendency considerably accentuated when the party system offers clear and distinct ideological alternatives.[15]

Ideological Identification in the Long Run

Ideological identification over the long haul has been our subject here. First we considered whether the American electorate is becoming more ideological. Not really, is our answer. Americans are only slightly more separated by ideology today than they were in the 1970s; liberals and conservatives disagree with each other over policy no more today than they did before; and only recently have liberals and conservatives expressed more animosity toward each other than they did in the past. Taken all around, a society divided by ideology lies off in the far distance, supposing it exists there at all. If we are divided, if we are beset by anger and resentment, it is not over ideological principles. We need to look for alternative measures and methods to diagnose our troubles.[16]

A second aspect of long-term change we examined here has to do with the increasing association between partisanship and ideological identification. Today, Democrats tend to identify as liberals and Republicans tend to identify as conservatives, and both these tendencies are stronger than in Converse's time. We explained increasing consistency as a product of the large and persistent changes in the party system taking place over this period. As the political parties polarized, Americans—well-informed Americans—altered their ideological identification to correspond with their partisanship. In consequence, each party's supporters have more in common with each other than they did in the 1970s, and less in common with the other side. No doubt this has contributed in some measure to the increase we have seen in partisan animosity (Levendusky 2009; Hetherington and Rudolph 2015).

Consistency has increased, but we should be careful not to exaggerate this trend. In *The Reputational Premium*, Paul Sniderman and Edward Stiglitz (2012) argue that there is no longer any reason to distinguish between partisanship and ideology in the American electorate; that the two have become amalgamated into a single predisposition. Ideological identification and party identification are "locked together" (94). To fail to recognize the "fusion of ideology and party," Sniderman and Stiglitz write, "is to miss the temper of contemporary American politics" (94).[17]

We disagree. Liberal Republicans and conservative Democrats are less abundant on the American political landscape than they were a generation or two ago, but ideological identification and party identification are not "locked together," nor have they been "fused" into a single disposition. In 2012, after forty years of party polarization, liberal Democrats and conservative Republicans, taken together, comprised less than a majority of the American electorate. Partisanship and ideology are not the same: not in conception, not in distribution, not in formation, and not in tenacity. Nor, as we are about to see in the next chapter, are they the same in their consequences.

CHAPTER SIX

Consequences?

So far we have considered the nature, origins, persistence, and long-term dynamics of ideological identification. This brings us to the meat of the matter, to ideological identification's consequences. When offered the opportunity, many Americans describe themselves as liberals or conservatives. What, if anything, follows from that? To what extent does ideological identification motivate thinking and action? If, as we contend, ideological innocence is a general condition, then we should have a hard time turning up evidence of ideological identification's influence. If, however, the evidence runs the other way, then we will have reason to reevaluate the American appetite for ideology.

The proof of the pudding is in the eating; let's get on with the meal. We consider, in turn, the effect of ideological identification on the votes Americans cast for elected office, the preferences they express on important issues of the day, and the beliefs they develop about the nature of their society. In the final empirical section of the chapter, we reverse field, and consider the possibility that ideological identification should be considered not a cause but an effect of participation in political life: ideological identification as "mere summary."

Liberals, Conservatives, and the Vote

Elections are widely regarded as *the* democratic moment. They are the "critical technique," as Robert Dahl (1956) once put it, for ensuring that leaders take into account the interests and aspirations of voters. Through participating in elections, voters can register their approval or disapproval with the governing party, return or remove elected public

officials accordingly, and thereby, perhaps, effect alterations in government policy.[1]

Ideology and Voting for President

In 2012, Barack Obama and Mitt Romney together spent roughly $1.5 bil-
lion making appeals to the American electorate. If information and interest are obstacles standing in the way of ideological voting, it seems
reasonable to think those obstacles will be lower and easier to overcome
in the case of presidential elections.

Self-described liberals do indeed tend to vote for Democratic presidential candidates, just as self-described conservatives tend to vote Republican. Table 6.1 displays the association between ideology and the
vote for each presidential election from 1972 through 2012. Over this period, liberals have generally voted Democratic; conservatives have generally voted Republican. The relationship between ideological identification and presidential vote is impressive and appears to be increasing.

Based on evidence very much like that arrayed in table 6.1, Jost
(2006) concludes that ideological identification tells us all we need to
know about presidential voting. Ideology explains presidential elections.
It's as simple as that.

It's not. For one thing, substantial numbers of the voting public—in
excess of 20 percent—are simply missing from table 6.1, tossed over-
board because they failed to describe themselves in ideological terms.
Whatever is driving their presidential votes, it cannot be ideological
identification.[2]

For another, the American electorate is, of course, awash in moderates. And while liberals are strongly inclined to vote for Democratic
presidential candidates and conservatives are likewise strongly inclined to vote for Republican candidates, moderates—the many, many
moderates—vote conservative on some occasions and liberal on others.
Moderates voted decisively for Nixon and Reagan, *and* they voted decisively for Clinton and Obama. Moderation may have its virtues, but ideological consistency is not among them.

And for a third, correlations—even strong correlations—are insufficient to establish causality. Outside of true experimental designs, es-
tablishing causality is always problematic. However, as the economist
Robert Solow once remarked, just because a germ-free environment is
unattainable does not mean that we might as well conduct surgery in a

TABLE 6.1. **Ideological identification and the presidential vote, 1972–2012 (percentage)**

		Extremely Liberal	Liberal	Slightly liberal	Moderate	Slightly conservative	Conservative	Extremely conservative
1972	McGovern	83.3	82.7	56.3	31.1	15.4	10.4	5.0
r =.47	Nixon	16.7	17.3	43.7	68.9	84.6	89.6	95.0
1976	Carter	88.4	83.5	73.1	52.5	26.5	19.0	14.3
r =.44	Ford	11.6	16.5	26.9	47.5	73.6	81.1	85.7
1980	Carter	90.9	92.3	59.5	39.4	30.0	15.9	27.3
r =.42	Reagan	9.1	7.7	40.5	60.6	70.0	84.1	72.7
1984	Mondale	91.3	74.6	66.9	45.0	22.3	13.7	23.1
r =.44	Reagan	8.7	25.4	33.1	55.0	77.7	86.3	77.0
1988	Dukakis	94.7	88.6	76.7	51.3	32.9	14.1	17.5
r =.48	Bush	5.6	11.4	23.3	48.7	67.1	85.9	82.5
1992	Clinton	100.0	93.8	87.3	61.2	36.8	16.8	28.0
r =.54	Bush	0.0	6.2	12.7	38.8	63.2	83.2	72.0
1996	Clinton	100.0	98.8	89.2	66.3	36.8	17.4	29.9
r =.59	Dole	0.0	1.2	10.8	33.7	63.2	82.6	70.1
2000	Gore	100.0	85.3	81.7	59.9	36.2	17.0	4.3
r =.55	Bush	0.0	14.7	18.3	40.1	63.8	83.0	95.7
2004	Kerry	100.0	95.6	87.6	58.3	29.2	12.1	7.3
r =.61	Bush	0.0	4.4	12.4	41.7	70.8	87.9	92.7
2008	Obama	98.8	94.8	80.6	61.4	10.9	10.9	10.2
r =.63	McCain	1.2	5.2	19.4	38.6	89.1	89.1	89.8
2012	Obama	97.3	97.6	86.1	60.6	26.3	11.6	6.1
r = .65	Romney	2.7	2.4	13.9	39.4	73.7	88.4	93.9
Total	Democrat	95.1	90.1	75.6	52.2	28.2	14.1	15.2
r = .52	Republican	5.0	9.9	24.4	47.8	71.8	85.9	84.8

Source: 1972–2012 ANES Cumulative Data File.
Note: N = 12,843. Third-party votes excluded.

sewer. When it comes to causal inference from observational data, we can do better, and we can do worse.

Doing better means, first of all, confronting the problem of alternative explanations. The extensive literature on voting and elections nominates three plausible alternatives to ideological voting: normal vote theory, which portrays voters as motivated to affirm their partisanship (Campbell et al. 1960; Converse 1966a); spatial theory, which portrays voters as motivated to advance their policy positions (Downs 1957; Jessee 2012; Poole and Rosenthal 1984); and retrospective voting theory, which portrays voters as motivated to reward or punish the governing party for its performance in office (Fiorina 1981; Hibbs 2000; Kramer 1971). We will estimate the effect of ideological identification on the vote while holding constant the effects produced by these three factors.[3]

And we will do so with panel data, thereby acknowledging the imperative of temporal precedence: that (in our universe) cause precedes effect. With contemporaneous correlations, causality is especially hard to sort out (Bartels 2000; Lenz 2013). We will predict the vote as reported shortly after the election from ideological identification (and other political predispositions) observed before the election.

The requirement that we estimate the effect of ideological identification on the vote with panel data while holding constant effects due to alternative causal factors means that we have at our disposal a half-dozen cases—presidential elections bracketed by high-quality panel studies: Carter versus Ford in 1976, Reagan versus Carter in 1980, Clinton versus George H. Bush in 1992, Dole versus Clinton in 1996, Kerry versus George W. Bush in 2004, and McCain versus Obama in 2008. In all six, the vote was measured immediately after the election. In the 1976, 1992, 1996, and 2004 contests, ideological identification was assessed two years before, during the midterm elections; in the 1980 and 2008 cases, ideological identification was assessed in January of the election year, as the primary season was getting under way. Probit regression results are presented in table 6.2.

Much of what appears in table 6.2 is familiar. (It would be troubling if it were otherwise.) We see a large effect of party identification, consistent with normal vote theory; a significant effect of opinion on policy, consistent with spatial theory; and a significant effect of economic assessments, such that voters who see economic conditions improving tend to support the incumbent, consistent with retrospective voting theory.

Over and above these standard and expected effects, does ideological

TABLE 6.2. **Estimated effect of ideological identification on presidential vote
(probit coefficients with standard errors in parentheses)**

	Carter v. Ford	Carter v. Reagan	Clinton v. Bush	Clinton v. Dole	Kerry v. Bush	Obama v. McCain
Ideological identification	.48 (.13)	−.29 (.20)	1.02 (.20)	−.57 (.19)	.76 (.16)	.91 (.12)
Party identification	1.00 (.07)	−1.29 (.11)	1.05 (.09)	−1.36 (.11)	1.27 (.11)	1.36 (.09)
Economic performance	.33 (.05)	.02 (.16)	.84 (.13)	.91 (.15)	.68 (.16)	1.07 (.43)
Views on policy	−.35 (.10)	1.00 (.23)	−1.42 (.25)	.93 (.21)	−.45 (.17)	−.38 (.11)
Intercept	−.02 (.05)	−.23 (.16)	.24 (.09)	.38 (.08)	.21 (.12)	−.20 (.07)
Pseudo R^2	.29	.35	.09	.53	.48	.57
N	1,081	496	733	824	686	2,013
Percent predicted	76.7	79.4	82.7	86.3	86.0	87.8

Source: 1972–76 ANES Panel, 1980 ANES Panel, 1990–92 ANES Panel, 1992–96 ANES Panel, 2002–4 ANES Panel, and 2008–9 ANES Panel.
Note: Each column is a separate probit equation. Outcome is vote for incumbent party candidate.

identification have a role to play in presidential voting? Yes. The coefficient indexing the impact of ideological identification is properly signed in all six cases and is statistically significant in all but one. These results are consistent with the conclusion that presidential voting is motivated, in part, by ideology.

It could be argued that our model underestimates the real effect of ideological identification. In particular, controlling on the effect of opinions on policy could be seen as unfair. Insofar as ideological identification influences the positions Americans take on the issues of the day— government spending on domestic programs, environmental policy, gay marriage, whatever the case may be—then including policy preferences in the model leads us to underestimate the effect (direct and indirect) of ideology.

We will take up the relationship between ideological identification and opinion on policy in the next section of the chapter. For now, suppose we simply exclude policy preferences from the vote model. Under this alternative specification, the estimated effect of ideological identification does increase, and in all six instances. In no instance, however, is the increase large. Excluding preferences on policy from the vote model (a mistake, in our judgment) has no material consequence for our conclusion so far: namely, that ideological identification has a modest effect on the presidential vote.

It is perhaps easier to argue that our model exaggerates the effect of ideological identification. Keep in mind that the model includes the 20 percent or so of voters who claim no ideological identification and whose votes therefore cannot be accounted for by ideology. You might think that those without any ideological identification would turn out to be haphazard in their electoral choices. That would be incorrect. Their choice cannot be explained by their ideological identification, as they have none, but their choice can be explained—and quite successfully—by the standard account of voting, with party identification doing most of the work.[4]

Ideological versus Partisan Voting

The probit coefficients presented in table 6.2 provide an estimate of the amount of change in the probability of an incumbent vote that results from a change in one unit in ideological identification, say from extreme liberal to moderate, or from moderate to extreme conservative (with partisanship, views on policy, and assessments of the economy held constant). Likewise, the coefficient on party identification provides an estimate of the amount of change in the probability of an incumbent vote that results from a change in one unit in partisanship, say from strong Democrat to independent, or from independent to strong Republican (again with other variables held constant). This is all well and good, but in interpreting effects, we must remain mindful of distributional difference: while strong partisans are abundant on the American political landscape, extreme ideologues are rare. This difference needs to be taken into account in assessing the relative importance of ideological and partisan voting.

To do so, we made use of a procedure developed by Larry Bartels (2000) that permits us to estimate the magnitude of ideological and partisan voting in a way that incorporates both the effect on voting of distinct types of ideological identification and partisanship and the relative size of each type.

The first step in the procedure was to code ideological identification into three variables: extreme (–1 for extreme liberal, +1 for extreme conservative, and 0 for all other voters), average (–1 for average liberal, +1 for average conservative, and 0 for all other voters), and slight (–1 for slight liberal, +1 for slight conservative, and 0 for all other voters). In each instance, those coded as 0 included moderates and those who claimed no ideological identification. We did the same for partisanship. Strong partisanship was coded –1 for strong Democrats, +1 for strong Republicans, and 0 for all others; weak partisanship was coded −1 for weak Democrats, +1 for weak Republicans, and 0 for all others; and leaning partisanship was coded −1 for leaning Democrats, +1 for leaning Republicans, and 0 for all voters. To parallel ideological voting, those coded 0 included pure independents as well as those few who claimed no partisan identification at all.

Then we included both sets of variables—one representing ideological voting, the other representing partisan voting—in our model of the vote, with all other variables measured and coded as before, and with coefficients estimated once again by probit. The coefficients for extreme ideological identification, average ideological identification, and slight ideological identification reflected the degree to which the choices of voters with these types of ideological commitments departed from the baseline vote (that is, the voter who was neither partisan nor ideological, who saw neither improvement nor decline in the economy, and who occupied the exact center of disputes over policy). Likewise for strong, weak, and leaning partisans.[5]

To summarize the overall effect of ideological identification, we calculated the average of the estimated effects—one for extreme liberals and conservatives, one for average liberals and conservatives, and one for slight liberals and conservatives—weighting each by the proportion of the electorate taken by the corresponding ideological type. For the effect of partisan identification, the calculation followed in exactly the same way. Estimates of ideological and partisan voting, calculated in this manner, are presented in table 6.3.

The results show that, for the six presidential elections we are able to examine, partisan voting is always large and ideological voting is generally small. Partisanship dominates ideology for two reasons. The first has to do with the greater potency of partisanship: identifying with a po-

TABLE 6.3. **Ideological and partisan voting in American presidential elections (weighted average probit coefficients)**

	1976	1980	1992	1996	2004	2008
Ideological voting	.12	−.05	.23	−.15	.25	.51
Partisan voting	.59	−.74	.64	−.87	.88	1.03

Source: 1972–76 ANES Panel, 1980 ANES Panel, 1990–92 ANES Panel, 1992–96 ANES Panel, 2002–4 ANES Panel, and 2008–9 ANES Panel.
Note: Equation also included measures of opinions on policy and assessments of national economic conditions (estimates not shown).

litical party is a more consequential commitment than is identifying with an ideological point of view. The second has to do with differences in distribution: the American public is both strongly partisan and moderately ideological. These two facts in combination mean that elections are contests over partisanship much more than they are contests over ideology. Borrowing military metaphors, presidential campaigns consist of major partisan battles and occasional ideological skirmishes.

Information and Ideological Voting

Mass publics are characterized by huge inequalities in political information, and as we have seen time and again, these inequalities matter. We expect the same to be true here: that the strength of ideological voting will depend on the voter's cognitive command of public affairs (cf. Jacoby 1991; Knight 1985; Sniderman, Brody, and Tetlock 1991).

To find out if this is so, we added a new set of variables to our vote model: a term to represent the main effect of information, and then a set of multiplicative terms to represent the interaction between information and each explanatory variable.[6] The results of this analysis are summarized in table 6.4.

Notice first that party identification is a powerful determinant of presidential voting without regard to information. It is powerful for the

TABLE 6.4. **Ideological and partisan voting in presidential elections by political information (probit coefficients with standard errors in parentheses)**

	1976	1980	1992	1996	2004	2008
Ideological identification	.00 (.37)	.93 (.64)	−.17 (.63)	.44 (.52)	.86 (.26)	.17 (.42)
Ideological identification × political information	.78 (.55)	−1.79 (.93)	1.84 (.94)	−1.64 (.82)	−.02 (.42)	.98 (.64)
Party identification	1.17 (.20)	−1.16 (.33)	.78 (.24)	−1.07 (.11)	1.41 (.17)	1.69 (.27)
Party identification × political information	−.32 (.31)	−.24 (.52)	.44 (.38)	−.41 (.47)	−.47 (.27)	−.29 (.43)
Political information	.43 (.21)	.16 (.68)	.23 (.39)	−.54 (.33)	−.41 (.22)	−1.06 (.37)
Intercept	−.29 (.13)	−.32 (.42)	.12 (.24)	.69 (.21)	.21 (.13)	.31 (.23)
N	1069	496	733	802	674	856
Pseudo R^2	.30	.36	.45	.54	.54	.62

Source: 1972–76 ANES Panel, 1980 ANES Panel, 1990–92 ANES Panel, 1992-1996 ANES Panel, 2002–4 ANES Panel, and 2008–9 ANES Panel.
Note: The model also includes measures of policy preferences, retrospective judgments of the economy, and interaction between each of these and political information (effects not shown).

poorly informed, for the well informed, and for those in between. Voters don't have to be experts to know about the Democratic and Republican Parties; they are regularly reminded of the place of partisanship in American politics.

Things are very different for ideology. The effect of ideological identification on the presidential vote depends critically on information. In five of six cases, the interaction between ideological identification and political information is significant. Ideological identification has no effect on presidential voting among the poorly informed, and only a modest effect among the average informed (if indeed there is any effect at all). Ideological identification contributes appreciably to presidential voting only among the well informed. According to these results, ideological voting requires a certain level of engagement in politics, a threshold many voters fail to cross.[7]

An implication of this result is that ideological voting, modest in presidential elections, might disappear entirely in lower-profile contests. By comparison to presidential elections, House elections are carried out largely in darkness: voters tend to be ill informed and to make lightly considered decisions, and party and incumbency generally carry the day (Stokes and Miller 1962; Cover and Mayhew 1977; Mann and Wolfinger 1980). Under such circumstances, it would be surprising if we turned up much in the way of ideological voting here—and we don't.

Applying the requirement of panel data gave us four sets of House elections to analyze: those carried out in 1976, 1992, 1996, and 2004. The results of a simple vote model are summarized in table 6.5. For convenience, the table presents, for each election year, results from House and presidential elections side-by-side (with estimates based on ANES respondents who reported voting for both offices).

As expected, the estimated effect of ideological identification diminishes from presidential to House elections. It diminishes in all four cases, precipitously so in three. Ideological voting appears to be negligible, or nearly so, in elections for Congress.[8]

Liberals, Conservatives, and Preferences on Policy

In this section of the chapter we take up the relationship between ideological identification and preferences on government policy. Such preferences assume a privileged place in democratic theory. From a democratic

TABLE 6.5. **Effect of ideological identification on voting in presidential (P) and House (H) elections (probit coefficients with standard errors in parentheses)**

	1976		1992		1996		2004	
	P	H	P	H	P	H	P	H
Ideological identification	.43 (.14)	.19 (.13)	1.16 (.23)	.35 (.18)	-.77 (.20)	.12 (.17)	.66 (.19)	.57 (.18)
Party identification	1.04 (.08)	.85 (.07)	1.14 (.10)	.88 (.09)	-1.37 (.12)	1.12 (.11)	1.28 (.13)	1.16 (.13)
Views on policy	-.41 (.11)	-.26 (.10)	-1.42 (.28)	-.55 (.23)	.87 (.23)	-.77 (.20)	-.63 (.19)	-.55 (.18)
Constant	.07 (.05)	-.14 (.05)	-.18 (.07)	-.20 (.06)	.53 (.09)	.01 (.07)	-.63 (.19)	-.23 (.09)
Pseudo R^2	.27	.18	.43	.24	.52	.37	.47	.41
N	884	884	559	559	620	620	475	475

Source: 1972–76, 1990–92, 1992–96, and 2002–4 ANES Panel Studies.

point of view, what the people want—on immigration or Social Security or affirmative action—must influence what the government actually
does. Insofar as this holds, opinion becomes the drive wheel of politics.[9]

Liberals generally favor spending more on education; they want to
keep abortion legal; they support measures designed to protect the environment. Conservatives generally favor spending more on defense;
they support the death penalty for capital crimes; they oppose government regulation of business. The correlation between ideological identification and preference on policy is modest on average but is reliably
present.[10]

The question is not whether ideological identification and preferences
on government policy are correlated. The question, rather, is whether the
correlation should be interpreted in causal terms. To what extent does
ideological identification determine the positions Americans take on important matters of public policy? We take three independent cracks at
answering this question.

Panel Test

The first effort resembles what we did for ideological voting. As in the
case of our analysis of voting, and for the same reason, we relied here
on panel data, where ideological identification is measured prior to policy preferences. And as in the case of our analysis of voting, and for the
same reason, our analysis took into account plausible determinants of
preferences in addition to ideological identification: in the case of policy,
these were party identification (partisanship should matter insofar as
the party symbol is "stamped" on a particular policy) and a pair of core
American political values, equal opportunity and limited government.

Values refer to beliefs that certain modes of conduct or certain end
states are desirable. Values transcend particular objects and specific sit-
uations; they are relatively abstract and durable claims about virtue and
the good society (Stoker 1992). We concentrated here on limited government and equal opportunity because each has played a central role in
American political development (e.g., Lipset 1967; Myrdal 1944; Verba
and Orren 1985); each has been shown to play an important role in motivating preferences on policy (e.g., Feldman 1988, 2003; Goren 2001;
Kinder and Sanders 1996; McCann 1997; Sears, Henry, and Kosterman
2000); and each has divided liberal and conservative thinkers from the
French Revolution onward (Levin 2014).

For purpose of estimation, we concentrated on the 1992–96 ANES Panel Study, which offers a rich array of questions on policy. We also dipped into the 2000–2002 and 2008–9 ANES Panel Studies, partly for purposes of replication but more to extend the analysis to important policy domains that did not become prominent until the turn of the new century: most notably, the major tax reforms proposed by President Bush in his first term, and the bundle of new policies directed at terrorism, initiated by the attack on the World Trade Center and the Pentagon on 9/11. We took up each policy separately, and we estimated parameters with ordered probit.[11]

Although we took up policies one-by-one, we were looking for general effects. A defining feature of ideology is its broad scope, its wide range. Ideology encompasses "a system of ideas and ideals forming the basis of an economic or political theory." The effects of ideological identification should show up across the board.

They do not. Results of the analysis are summarized in table 6.6. As shown there, the effect of ideological identification comes and goes. We find not general effects, but domain-specific ones.

The clearest, strongest effects show up in two places: in policies dealing with women's issues, especially abortion; and in policies arising from the emergence of the gay rights movement, including employment discrimination, military service, and marriage. Ideological identification also appears to influence opinion on environmental protection and on efforts to reform welfare during President Clinton's first term, though not as strongly.

Elsewhere, however, the effects of ideological identification are either small or absent. And elsewhere covers a vast territory. Ideological differences have little influence over opinion on immigration, affirmative action, capital punishment, gun control, Social Security, health insurance, the deficit, foreign aid, tax reform, and the war on terrorism.

Women's issues and gay rights, where ideological identification appears to leave a mark, are the exceptions. We wondered whether these results, which stand out so starkly against a background of negligible returns, would survive additional controls. Perhaps we overlooked a variable correlated with ideology that was actually doing the explanatory work.

One such variable might be religion. For many Americans, abortion and same-sex marriage raise moral questions. It would not be surprising if faith played a role in shaping preferences on these matters. The second

TABLE 6.6. **Impact of ideological identification on policy preferences (ordered probit coefficients with standard errors in parentheses)**

Welfare	
Employment	.08 (.16)
Services/spending	.36 (.16)
Health care	.22 (.14)
Social Security	−.08 (.16)
Welfare programs	.48 (.17)
Food stamps	.35 (.16)
Homeless	.16 (.15)
Income inequality	.17 (.13)
Taxes	
Taxes vs. deficit	.10 (.16)
Inheritance tax	.29 (.18)
Tax cut	.32 (.14)
Race	
Assistance to blacks	.20 (.15)
Affirmative action	.14 (.15)
Gender	
Abortion	.72 (.15)
Child care	.43 (.17)
Gay rights	
Prohibit discrimination	.67 (.16)
Military service	.62 (.15)
Crime	
Spending on crime	.08 (.15)
Capital punishment	.07 (.14)
Gun control	.19 (.16)
Environment	
Spending	.65 (.16)
Environment vs. jobs	.37 (.13)
Government regulation	.32 (.13)
War on terror	
Afghanistan war	.28 (.27)
Iraq war	.34 (.17)
Homeland security	.09 (.42)
Immigration	
Increase/decrease	.14 (.14)
Protect borders	.14 (.14)
Government assistance	.42 (.19)
Defense	
Spending	.27 (.12)
Foreign policy	
Isolationism	−.24 (.17)
Foreign aid	.10 (.14)

Source: 1992–96 ANES Panel Study and (for opinions on the inheritance tax, President Bush's 2001 tax cut, and the war on terror) the 2000–2002 ANES Panel Study.
Note: Each row is a separate equation. Each equation includes, in addition to ideological identification, measures of partisanship, limited government, equal opportunity, and race (effects not shown).

takes seriously the proposal that public opinion on policy is group-centric: that is, determined to a large extent by the sentiments citizens feel toward the social groups implicated in the policy.[12] For abortion, this means sentiments toward the women's movement and feminists; for same-sex marriage, it means sentiments toward gays and lesbians.

To see what difference this might make, we took another go at preferences on abortion and gay rights. We reestimated the effect of ideological identification, after first adding measures of faith, religiosity (the degree to which Americans take their faith seriously), and group sentiments to the model. It turns out that taking these additional considerations into account erases the effect our simpler analysis had assigned to ideology. On abortion and gay rights, as on matters of policy generally, ideology plays a minor role.

Right Shift?

Questions intended to capture something like ideological identification have been asked of samples of the American electorate beginning in the 1930s. As we noted earlier, Stimson (1991) developed a method that renders responses to the various questions comparable. The result is an estimate of the American public's average ideological identification from 1937 to 2012, which we presented back in figure 3.4.

A close look at this time series reveals something remarkable. In 1964 liberals in large numbers began to vanish from the American electorate. Over the next several years, this hemorrhaging accelerated. By 1967, the proportion of the American public claiming to be liberal had declined by nearly one-third. In the view of Ellis and Stimson, the Johnson presidency "marked the end of 'liberalism' as a competitive ideological force" (2009, 396).[13]

How can this precipitous decline of liberals be explained? Ellis and Stimson (2012) set out several possibilities: liberal excess under Johnson and a Democratic Congress; the "Great Society" reaching beyond Franklin D. Roosevelt's "common man" to provide material assistance and political voice to the American underclass; the collapse of civil order in American cities; and liberalism being defined as programmatic sympathy for black Americans, who responded not with gratitude but with "demands, riots, and protests" (83).

However this rapid change in ideological identification should be explained, it offers us a second opportunity for a sharp test of the power of

TABLE 6.7. **Shift in opinion on policy following the abrupt decline of liberal identification, 1964–68 (percent supporting liberal option)**

Policy	1964	1968
Health care	50	52
Employment	31	31
School integration	41	38
Open housing	57	68
Fair employment	39	38
School prayer	15	13

Source: ANES Cumulative Data File.

ideology to shape opinion on policy. If ideological identification drives opinion on policy, then we should see in this period a corresponding shift away from liberalism on matters of policy. Do we?

We do not. Six policy questions are asked in identical form in the 1964 and 1968 ANES. The questions cover government health care, school prayer, fair employment, school integration, open housing, and whether the government should be obliged to provide employment and a decent standard of living for those determined to work. On five of the six, as shown in table 6.7, the public shifts neither to the right nor to the left. On the sixth—open housing—the public moves in the liberal direction, against expectations. In short, there is nothing here to support the proposition that Americans alter their preferences on policy as a consequence of change in their ideological identification.

Ideology Primed?

Our third and final try examines whether the effect of ideological identification on policy preferences increases when ideology is primed. Priming assumes that when people are asked for their opinions on complex political questions such as affirmative action or health care, they do not undertake a comprehensive and exhaustive review of everything they know. Rather, opinion depends on those bits and pieces of memory that come to mind (Tversky and Kahneman 1973). When political circumstances change, news stories and elite rhetoric shift, and what floats to consciousness changes accordingly. The more attention media pay to a particular aspect of political life—the more frequently that aspect is *primed*—the more people will incorporate what they know about it into their opinions. Defined this way, priming has received strong and consistent support, in experimental and observational studies alike (e.g., Iyengar and Kinder 1987; Jacobs and Shapiro 1994; Krosnick and Kinder 1990; Lenz 2013; Mendelberg 2001; Tesler 2015; Valentino, Hutchings, and White 2002).

The change in political circumstance that we focus on here is Reagan's rise to prominence. Between the beginning of 1980 and the following fall, Reagan was first candidate, then nominee, and finally president. With his ascendance came a corresponding rise in the salience of conservative discourse. Reagan called himself a conservative, ran on conservative principles, and presented the country with conservative policy proposals. As a consequence, Americans should have come to think about government policy with their ideological identity more prominently in mind.

We test for priming by following the logic and method spelled out by Gabriel Lenz (2013). Lenz's method requires a three-wave panel, supplied in our case by the 1980 ANES Panel Study. Face-to-face interviews were carried out with a representative sample of Americans in January, June, and September 1980. A second requirement is that over the course of the three waves, something happens—a war erupts, a recession begins—that increases the importance of the putative causal factor, in this case, ideological identification. Here, it is Reagan who "happened."

The 1980 ANES Panel Study included questions on five policies in each of the three waves of interviewing: spending on defense, the tradeoff between cutting government spending and expanding government services, managing relations with the Soviet Union, producing energy versus protecting the environment, and fighting inflation versus fighting unemployment. We take up each one separately. Results are presented in table 6.8.[14]

For each policy, the table presents three values. In the left-hand col-

TABLE 6.8. **Impact of ideological identification on policy preferences before and after Reagan's rise (OLS coefficients)**

Policy	Before Reagan	After Reagan	Difference
Defense	.06	.11	.05
Soviet Union	−.02	.08	.10
Services/savings	.16	.09	−.07
Environment	.14	.01	−.13
Inflation/unemployment	.04	.07	.03

Source: 1980 ANES Panel Study.
Note: OLS coefficients give the impact of ideological identification on change in policy preference. None of the differences (third column) is statistically significant by adjusted Wald test (p values range from .28 to .51).

umn is the estimated impact of ideological identification as assessed in January on change in opinion between January and June; in the middle column is the estimated impact of ideological identification as assessed in June on change in opinion between June and September; and in the right-hand column is the difference between the two estimates. A significant difference—more precisely, a significant increase—indicates support for ideological priming.

As shown there, the results provide no support for priming. The estimated effect of ideological identification increases in three of the five cases, but in no case does the increase approach statistical significance ($p > .25$ in all three instances). Averaging across the five policies, the estimated priming effect is a perfect 0.00. We take this as evidence not against priming—priming's empirical support is abundant—but against the idea that ideological identification drives policy preferences.

Liberals, Conservatives, and the Ideological Construction of Reality

Politics is a complicated business, and it takes place, for the most part, far away. The average person pays attention only intermittently and casually. Under these circumstances, many citizens may feel free to construct a picture of the political world that reinforces their predispositions.

This has long been suspected in the case of partisanship. As Campbell et al. (1960) suggested in *The American Voter*, "Identification with a party raises a perceptual screen through which the individual tends to see what is favorable to his partisan orientation. The stronger the party bond, the more exaggerated the process of selection and perceptual distortion will be" (133). In *Elections and the Political Order*, Donald Stokes (1966) pushed the point harder: "for most people the tie between party identification and voting behavior involves subtle processes of perceptual adjustment by which the individual assembles an image of current politics consistent with his partisan allegiance. . . . The capacity of party identification to color perceptions holds the key to understanding why the unfolding of new events, the emergence of new issues, the appearance of new political figures fail to produce wider swings of party fortune. To a remarkable extent these swings are damped by processes of selective perception" (127).

All this was mostly conjecture at the time, but the claim of partisan bias has stood up well to empirical testing. Party identification indeed appears to be, as Bartels put it, "a pervasive dynamic force shaping citizens' perceptions of, and reactions to, the political world" (2002, 138; see Gerber, Huber, and Washington 2010; Jacobson 2008; Berinsky 2009; Gaines et al. 2007).

Can the same be said for ideological identification? Michael Freeden (2003) suggests that the answer is yes, that we should be able to turn up evidence for the ideological construction of reality. "Political facts," Freeden begins, "never speak for themselves" (2). They speak, he continues, only when they are interpreted, and the work of interpretation is done by ideology:

> Through our diverse ideologies, we provide competing interpretations of what the facts might mean. Every interpretation, each ideology, is one such instance of imposing a pattern—some form of structure or organization—on how we read (and misread) political facts, events, occurrences, actions, on how we see images and hear voices. (2–3)

In this section of the chapter we will test whether ideological identification works this way. In a series of cases, we will see whether liberals and conservatives differ over matters of fact. Do liberals and conservatives fashion a picture of politics that conforms to their predispositions, as Democrats and Republicans seem to?

In our analysis of this question, we consider only well-established facts; where the right answer is clear; where experts agree; where, to put it in an old-fashioned way, the truth is known. Of course, consensus among experts is not infallible; at some point in the future, it could be altered or even reversed. Acknowledging this as a possibility, here we examine facts as defined by the relevant expert community. And finally, we consider only consequential matters: in particular, we look for ideological bias in views of the economy.

Ideology and the Economy

At least since FDR and the Great Depression, economic performance has been the primary engine driving political change in the United States. National election outcomes, presidential popularity, and support for the political parties all hinge on economic conditions. When the economy is booming, incumbents are rewarded; when the economy struggles, incumbents are removed (e.g., Achen and Bartels 2016; Erikson, MacKuen, and Stimson 2002; Green, Palmquist, and Schickler 2002; Hibbs 2000; Kramer 1971; Rosenstone 1983).

One way to explain this association is through self-interest: citizens examine their own economic circumstances and make political decisions accordingly, supporting presidents and parties and policies insofar as they are seen to advance their own economic interests. This is part of the story, but only part. Voters pay at least as much attention to the problems of the country as they do to their own. "Sociotropic" voters ask, in effect, what have you done for the *nation*? What have you done for *us*? (Kinder and Kiewiet 1981).[15]

The sociotropic result raises the question of how voters figure out how the economy is faring. They know what has happened in their own families, but judgments of the nation's well-being do not have the same grounding in personal experience. Moreover, the economy has many parts: unemployment, income, prices, interest rates, stocks and bonds. Faced with such complexity and uncertainty, how is the average person, preoccupied with the trials and tribulations of everyday life, able to decide whether things are going well or poorly in the country? Under such circumstances, perhaps liberals and conservatives come to view the economy in a way that reinforces their ideological commitments. Let's see.

We start with a pair of parallel tests. The first is based on the 1972–76 ANES Panel Study, the second on the 1992–96 ANES Panel Study. In both cases, predispositions—both party identification and ideological identification—are assessed in the first interview; judgments of change in the national economy are assessed in the second. (And so the latter cannot be a cause of the former.) Conveniently for our analysis, economic conditions were improving and at roughly the same rate in the two cases. Equally conveniently, the sitting president was Republican (Gerald Ford) in one case and Democratic (Bill Clinton) in the other.[16]

Table 6.9 summarizes the results of a simple model designed to estimate partisan and ideological bias. The model assumes that assessments of the national economy are subject to two forms of bias: partisan and ideological. Assessments of the national economy is each person's judgment of change in the national economy over the past year, coded −1 if much worse, 0 if unchanged, and +1 if much better. The coding of ideological identification and party identification is contingent upon the party affiliation of the incumbent president. Party identification is

TABLE 6.9. **Ideological and partisan bias in judgments of national economic conditions (OLS regression coefficients with standard errors in parentheses)**

	1976 economy	1996 economy
Ideological identification	.01 (.07)	.06 (.05)
Party identification	.26 (.04)	.16 (.04)
Constant	.30 (.03)	.20 (.02)
N	957	463
R^2	.04	.08

Source: 1972–76 and 1992–96 ANES Panel Studies.

scored −1 if the person strongly identifies with the party opposing the president, 0 if independent, and +1 if the person strongly identifies with the president's party. Likewise, ideological identification is scored −1 if the person strongly opposes the president's ideology, 0 if moderate, and +1 if the person strongly favors the president's ideology, with those who claim no ideological identification treated as missing.

The results are clear. In 1976 and 1996, we find a substantial effect of party identification and no effect at all of ideological identification. Democrats and Republicans disagree sharply over how the economy is going, depending on whether the leader of their party happens to be the president. Liberals and conservatives do not. Partisan bias? Yes. Ideological bias? No.

When we reestimated the model summarized in table 6.9, this time with partisanship and ideological identification measured contemporaneously with judgments of the economy (that is, with economic assessments measured in 1976 and 1996, respectively), we found essentially the same result: a substantial effect of partisanship and no effect of ideology. This suggests that we might safely expand our analysis of partisan and ideological bias in judgments of the economy to cross-sectional analysis.[17]

In every ANES presidential election study from 1972 to 2012, respondents have been asked whether economic conditions have improved, worsened, or stayed the same over the past year.[18] Combining studies, we first looked to see how faithfully citizens take into account the actual state of the economy in making this judgment. We expected that judgments of the economy would be responsive to real changes in economic conditions, and this would be true particularly among the well informed. The results, presented in the first column in table 6.10, show this

TABLE 6.10. **Ideology, partisanship, and assessments of national economic conditions, 1972–2012 (OLS regression coefficients with standard errors in parentheses)**

Change in economic conditions	.13 (.003)	.13 (.003)
Political information	−.03 (.02)	−.03 (.02)
Change in economic conditions × political information	.05 (.004)	.04 (.01)
Ideological identification	—	.032 (.016)
Party identification	—	.28 (.01)
Constant	−.52 (.01)	−.51 (.01)
N	20,045	13,639
R^2	.12	.18

Source: 1972–2012 ANES.

to be true. As economic conditions improve, citizens are more inclined to say that things are getting better, especially insofar as they are well informed.[19]

The key question for us is whether assessments of national economic conditions display evidence of political bias. To find out, we added two new variables to the model: party identification and ideological identification, coded as before. The results, presented in column two of table 6.10, do indeed indicate evidence of bias. *Partisan* bias, we should say. Democrats and Republicans differ sharply on the economy depending on which party holds the White House. Liberals and conservatives do not.[20]

Ideology and the Deficit

For some time now, the federal budget deficit has been a bone of contention between the two parties. During campaigns and in between, Republicans complain about runaway federal spending and uncontrolled growth of government, characterizing their opponents as "tax and spend" liberals unwilling to make the hard choices necessary to bring the budget into balance. Democrats do their best to ignore the issue.

In the 1996 ANES, the electorate was asked whether the budget deficit had increased or diminished over Bill Clinton's time as president. (By referring explicitly to Clinton, the question may augment bias arising from partisanship.) On average, Americans believed that the budget deficit had increased somewhat over Clinton's time in office. In fact, the federal budget deficit had shrunk very substantially: from $429 billion in 1992 to $144 billion in 1996—a decline of nearly two-thirds.[21]

Did Democrats and Republicans differ over the deficit? They did, and

TABLE 6.11. **Ideology, partisanship, and the deficit (OLS regression coefficients with standard errors in parentheses)**

Ideological identification	.04 (.07)
Party identification	.21 (.05)
Constant	−.06 (.03)
N	453
R^2	.06

Source: 1992–96 ANES Panel Study.

in the expected manner. Republicans were much more likely to say that the deficit grew during Clinton's first term than Democrats were. Did liberals and conservatives differ over the deficit? They did not. These results are shown in table 6.11. Once again, Democrats and Republicans, but not liberals and conservatives, appear to construct a world they wish to see.

Ideology and Unemployment

In its intricacies and complexities, the economy is—let's face it—nearly impossible to understand. It is hard even to summarize. Likewise, the federal budget traffics in numbers beyond human comprehension. Let's move on to a less obscure and better-grounded aspect of economic reality: unemployment. Beginning in 1988, respondents in ANES presidential election studies have been asked to say whether, over the past year, the level of unemployment in the country had improved or worsened. Unemployment varied substantially over these years, ranging from a 1.3 percentage point increase between 2007 and 2008, as the country headed into the Great Recession, to a 1.0 percentage point decline between 2011 and 2012, as the country began to crawl out of it.[22]

Combining observations across the ANES presidential election studies, we estimated our standard model, treating judgments of change in unemployment as a product of ideological identification and partisanship.[23] The results, on display in table 6.12, tell a familiar tale: a strong effect of party and a negligible effect of ideology. Democrats and Republicans assessed unemployment in the country differently, just as they did the budget deficit and the economy as a whole, depending on which party held the presidency. And once again, whether a Democrat or Republican occupied the White House left virtually no impression on economic judgments made by liberals and conservatives.

TABLE 6.12. **Ideology, partisanship, and unemployment**
(OLS regression coefficients with standard errors in parentheses)

Ideological identification	.04 (.02)
Party identification	.25 (.01)
Constant	−.32 (.01)
N	7,024
R^2	.11

Source: 1988–2012 ANES presidential election studies.

Ideological Identification as Mere Summary

In the literature on ideological identification and political choice, the reigning assumption is that causality runs from the former to the latter: ideological identification is the predisposing cause, and policy preference or vote the resulting effect (e.g., Banaji and Heiphetz 2010; Bartels 2008; Jacoby 1991; Jost, Federico, and Napier 2009; Kinder and Sears 1981; Lewis-Beck et al. 2008; Sears 1993; Sniderman, Brody, and Kuklinski 1984). In our analysis so far, we have followed this practice—with rather unimpressive results.

Perhaps it was a mistake to treat ideological identification as motivating. Perhaps ideological identification is primarily an effect, not a cause, of a person's political views.

This is the clear implication of research on ideology—left and right—carried on outside the United States. According to Dieter Fuchs and Hans-Dieter Klingemann (1990), the liberal-conservative distinction in the United States and the left-right distinction everywhere else can be considered "functional equivalents." Insofar as that is true, it is striking that the extensive literature on left and right, which is almost without exception ignored by scholars of American ideology, makes precisely the *opposite* assumption than the standard one we have been making here: that far from being a cause of preference and choice, ideological identification is a *product* of preference and choice. According to this literature, the French and the Germans, the Costa Ricans and the Venezuelans, all come to think of themselves as left or right as a consequence of the positions they take on their nation's most pressing problems (e.g., Sani and Sartori 1983; deVries, Hakhverdian, and Lancee 2013; Converse and Pierce 1986; Inglehart 1990; Inglehart and Klingemann 1976; Zechmeister and Corral 2012).

And so, in this last section of the chapter, we consider the proposition that for many Americans, ideological identification is no more than a rough summary of their political experience. We explore this possibility in three distinct settings. Each represents a serendipitous meeting between an intuition about how this might work, on the one hand, and high-grade data available to test it, on the other. Our analysis is opportunistic, not comprehensive. We offer, as illustrations, ideological identification as influenced by votes cast for an ideological candidate; as a reflection of group identity; and as a product of a generation's encounter with historic events.

Ideological Identification as a Product of Voting for an Ideological Candidate

Our hypothesis here derives from Daryl Bem's (1965, 1972) theory of self-perception. According to Bem, people *infer* what their attitudes and attachments must be from observing their own behavior. Actions freely chosen are revelations about private predispositions. As Bem would have it, when people are asked whether or not they like brown bread, they infer that they do when they notice that they are eating it all the time, and they infer that they do not when they notice that they never eat it. Turning to politics, when people are asked whether they are liberal or conservative, some may answer by reflecting on what they have recently said and done. Having just voted for Reagan, they may come to the realization, insofar as they understand Reagan to be conservative, that they are conservative, too. They infer what their ideological identity must be, in light of what they have freely chosen to do.

We can bring our hypothesis to data by analyzing the Jennings study of political socialization. Remember that members of the class of 1965 were interviewed first in the spring of 1965, as they were about to graduate, and then again in 1973 and 1982. On both of the latter occasions, they were asked the standard ideological identification question. The 1973–82 panel brackets two presidential elections: Carter's victory over Ford in 1976, and Reagan's successful challenge of Carter in 1980. The latter is the more interesting of the two. Carter and Ford were both moderates, and they were running ideologically quiet campaigns in the shadow of President Richard Nixon's resignation. In 1980, Reagan ran as a representative of the conservative wing of the Republican Party, proud successor to Goldwater, and he aimed to restore conserva-

TABLE 6.13. **Effect of presidential voting on change in ideological identification (ordered probit coefficients with standard errors in parentheses)**

	Ideological identification in 1982
Ideological identification in 1973	1.23 (.15)
Vote for Reagan in 1980	.70 (.14)
Vote for Carter in 1980	−.44 (.15)
Vote for Ford in 1976	.10 (.17)
Vote for Carter in 1976	.04 (.17)
N	445
Pseudo R^2	.15

Source: Youth-Parent Socialization Panel Study.
Note: The equation also included measures of parental partisanship, parental social class, religion, region, and race (effects not shown).

tive principles. A vote for Reagan might be the sort of action, freely chosen, that would lead young voters to the inference that they, themselves, were conservative.

With this in mind, we estimated the impact of votes cast in 1976 and 1980 on change in ideological identification between 1973 and 1982. The results, presented in table 6.13, indicate that voting in ideological contests does appear to have consequences for how young Americans think of themselves in ideological terms. A vote for Reagan pushed young voters to the right; a vote for Carter nudged young voters to the left. By contrast, and as expected, participation in the ideologically bland contest of 1976 seemed to have no consequence for ideological adjustment.[24]

Ideological Identification as a Product of Social Group Identity

What one thinks about politics depends, in part, on one's place in society. Rich or poor, Christian or Jewish, black or white: these categorical social distinctions matter for politics. They generate differences in interests and priorities, which lead to differences in political preferences and perhaps, ultimately, to differences in ideology. Here we test whether membership in social groupings plays an influential role in ideological identification.

To do so we combine ANES presidential election studies from 1972 to 2012 and estimate the effect of group membership on ideological identification. Group membership is represented in this analysis by income

TABLE 6.14. **Ideological identification as a reflection of social group membership (OLS regression coefficients with standard errors in parentheses)**

	Conservative identification
Income	.15 (.01)
Union member	−.05 (.01)
Race (black)	−.14 (.01)
Gender (female)	−.04 (.01)
Age	.00 (.00)
No religion	−.18 (.01)
Jewish	−.34 (.03)
Catholic	−.07 (.01)
Liberal Protestant	−.04 (.01)
Conservative Protestant	.02 (.01)
Other religion	−.05 (.02)
N	18,586
R^2	.08

Source: 1972–2012 ANES.
Note: The equation also included measures of education and region (effects not shown).

(rich and poor), race (black and white), gender (men and women), age (young and old), union membership (members and not), and varieties of religious faith (as well as secularists). Table 6.14 presents the results.[25]

Turns out, ideological identification is connected to membership in social groupings. Income, race, and religion have the most substantial effects. The rich are more likely to identify as conservative than are the poor. Blacks are liberal; whites are conservative. Jews and secularists lean to the left; Protestants to the right. Gender and age leave fainter traces on ideology: women are a bit more likely than men to identify as liberal; the old are a bit more likely to identify as conservative than are the young.

We repeated the analysis summarized in table 6.14, this time taking up each election year survey separately, looking for evidence that the relationship between membership in social groupings and ideological identification would change over time. We found little of it. Apart from a modest increase in the effect due to income, the emergence of the modern gender gap (early in the series, women were a bit more likely than men to call themselves conservative), and a decline in the racial divide, the effect of group membership on ideological identification appears nearly constant.

The results presented here resemble quite closely what is found in European publics. There, too, researchers uncover the enduring importance of social structure. In Europe, class and religion supply the major lines of ideological conflict. In the United States, class and religion and race do (Dalton 2010; deVries, Hakhverdian, and Lancee 2013; Inglehart and Klingemann 1976; Inglehart 1990).

Ideological Identification as a Product of a
Generation's Encounter with History

According to Karl Mannheim ([1928] 1952), political generations are created by the conjunction of individual development and historical change. The formation of a distinctive generational perspective comes out of the openness of early adulthood and the presence of galvanizing events. Under these circumstances, a generation will enter politics "imprinted" with a long-lasting commitment to a particular point of view.[26]

That's the theory. We can test its applicability to ideological identification by returning one last time to Jennings's Youth-Parent Socialization Panel Study. The class of 1965 entered adulthood at a time of great racial turmoil: acts of civil disobedience carried out by thousands of ordinary men and women; scores of sit-ins, marches, freedom rides, and voter registration drives; landmark federal legislation; devastating assassinations; and epidemics of violence and disorder in hundreds of American cities. This dramatic sequence of events captured the nation's attention and, perhaps, made racial concerns a more central aspect of what it meant to be a liberal and what it meant to be a conservative.[27]

As part of the Jennings study, high school seniors were asked in 1965 for their opinion on school integration, and also for their feelings toward whites and (in the vernacular of the time) Negroes. In 1973, the same people, now settling into adult roles, were asked the same questions plus two more: on busing for the purpose of school desegregation, and on whether government should provide special assistance to blacks and other minorities. The question here is whether reaction to the racial crisis taking place in early adulthood, as captured by responses to these questions, has consequences for ideological identification later, in late middle age.[28]

The answer is a resounding yes. As shown in table 6.15, views on race expressed in 1965 and 1973 powerfully predict ideological identification

TABLE 6.15. **Reaction to the racial crisis circa 1965 and ideological identification circa 1997 (Generalized Least Squares coefficients with standard errors in parentheses)**

Views on race	.72 (.09)	−.15 (.24)
Political information	−	.78 (.18)
Views on race × political information	−	1.37 (.35)
Constant	−.10 (.07)	.39 (.13)
N	844	844
Number of clusters (schools)	97	97

Source: Youth-Parent Socialization Panel Study.
Note: Families are treated as nested within schools and variances are adjusted for clustering. Both equations also include measures of race, gender, religion, region, and (parental) social class, all as measured in 1965 (effects not shown).

in 1997. For this particular generation, those who were liberal on race as young adults were quite likely to call themselves liberal at age fifty, while those who were conservative on race as young adults were quite likely to call themselves conservative at fifty.[29]

This is a strong effect. We thought it might be stronger still among those who were paying attention to the remarkable run of events unfolding as they were coming of age. Not everyone paid attention, and even those who did might not have possessed the interest or the wherewithal to draw a conclusion about their own ideological identity. The results in the second column of table 6.15 show that the impact of reaction to the racial crisis is dramatically augmented by political information. For those near the bottom of the information scale, reactions to the crisis had no bearing at all on later ideological identification. In contrast, among those near the top of the information scale, the crisis taking place during the formative years left a deep imprint on ideological self-description later on.

Cause or Effect?

In this chapter, we took up the question of ideological identification's political consequences. We searched for effects but discovered rather little. Ideological voting? Some, but not too much. Properly estimated, ideological identification has a small effect on the presidential vote and practically no effect in contests further down the ballot. On matters of policy, we turned up little evidence of ideological identification's influence. And if many Americans seem motivated to construct a picture of the political world that reinforces their predispositions, such bias arises from partisanship, not ideology.

In the final section of the chapter we explored the possibility that ideological identification might be less a cause than an effect of participation in political life, offering three illustrations. First, consistent with Bem's theory of self-perception, some young Americans drawn to Reagan's candidacy came to think of themselves as conservatives. Second, much as we see elsewhere in the world, liberal and conservative identification in the United States reflects, to some degree, social identity. Differences in income, race, and religion give rise to differences in ideological outlook. Third, crises of historic magnitude can leave a long-lasting mark on the ideological identification of those who experience the crisis as young adults (insofar as they were paying attention as the crisis progressed). In these three respects, at least, ideological identification appears to be a reasonable response, a sensible summary, of political experience. Ideological identification may be meaningful, at least for some Americans, but it is not, by the analysis we have undertaken here, consequential.

All in all, the results reported in this chapter seem quite consistent with the general claim of ideological innocence. Now that we have completed our investigation of ideological identification, it is time for a general reckoning. For that we turn to our next and final chapter.

Conclusion

CHAPTER SEVEN

Findings and Implications

Philosophy? Philosophy? I am a Christian and a Democrat—that's all.

Franklin Delano Roosevelt

In this final chapter, we review our findings and draw out their implications. We begin, naturally enough, with the question that gave rise to our endeavor in the first place: whether the broad claim of ideological innocence must be modified—or even upended, as some have argued—in light of the new findings on ideological identification. If you have read this far, you know that our answer is no. *Our* answer is no, but, of course, not everyone sees things the same way we do. In the next section of the chapter, we examine three influential perspectives on ideology that run crossways, or appear to run crossways, to the position we advance here. Then, in quick succession, we consider the role played by ideology in political life outside the United States; bring to completion the comparison between ideology and partisanship; and argue for the essential importance of information and information inequality in understanding the politics of mass publics. Finally, in the last section of this last chapter, we sketch out a promising way forward, a way to approach the question that the enormous literature on ideology fails to answer. If ideological reasoning is beyond most people's capacity and interest, how *do* they form judgments and make decisions on political matters that, taken collectively, shape their society's future?

Ideological or Not?

By the standards of human history, American society is remarkably affluent, extraordinarily well educated, and awash in news of politics. Not-
withstanding these advantages, Americans (most Americans) glance at
the political world mystified by its abstractions and ignorant of its par-
ticulars. They have no acquaintance with and little interest in liberalism
and conservatism as political programs. Their opinions are ideologically
incoherent: some are liberal, some conservative, and some, when examined closely, seem not to be opinions at all. Most know little about what
is happening in politics and even less about why. So it was, according to
Converse, in the middle of the twentieth century. So, by and large, it is
today.

This summary is fine as far as it goes, but it doesn't go far enough.
It fails to consider the flourishing literature on ideological identification
since Converse completed his essay. A large fraction of our effort here
has gone to determining how much the broad claim of innocence must
be modified in light of these new findings. Our conclusion: not much.

More than one-quarter of Americans simply reject the invitation to
describe themselves in ideological terms. Ideological identification is not
for everyone, just as politics is not. Another quarter picks the middle of
the road as a destination—more out of confusion than principle. Even
when Americans claim an ideological identity, they are quite likely to
change their mind, to flip from one side to the other. And while there are
many ways to describe the contemporary American electorate, ideologically polarized is not one of them.

As for the consequences of ideological identification, we have been
hard pressed to find any. When estimated properly, the effects of ideological identification are small on presidential voting and disappear altogether in elections where stakes are lower and information scarcer. Ideological identification and preferences on policy are correlated, but we
find little evidence of an underlying causal relationship. While Americans show every sign of constructing their view of the nation's economic
health to protect their partisanship, their willingness to do so to protect
their ideological commitments is notably absent. If anything, ideological
identification seems more a reflection of political decisions than a cause:
ideological identification as mere summary.

Taken all around, the evidence on ideological identification presented here fits comfortably with the broad conclusion of ideological innocence. Based on these results, we see no reason to reopen the case. To the contrary, the results fortify the original verdict. By and large, Americans come to politics without ideology in mind.

That's how things are today. That's how things have been. And that is how they are likely to be for some time to come. Americans are no better informed about politics than they were fifty years ago. Today we have more and ready access to politics, that's for sure, but we have more and ready access to everything. We can watch and listen to whatever we care to whenever we wish. Given choice, most Americans opt for drama or comedy or sports or celebrity or pornography or music or whatever—any of these, for most of us, before politics.

Alternatives

Not everyone shares our view. Here we take up notable challenges—or what seem like notable challenges—to our argument from Robert Lane, John Jost, and James Stimson.

Ideology Reconceived?

Participants in the great debate over ideology that has so occupied the field since Converse generally share a common framework. However much they disagree over findings and interpretations, however much they lend support to or dissent from the conclusion of innocence, they are all working off the basic terms and methods established in Converse's original analysis.

Not Robert Lane. In a series of influential studies (1962, 1969, 1973), Lane develops an alternative approach. Lane is interested less in what Americans have to say about employment policy or the presidential candidates than he is in their views on broader political matters: notions of "fair play and due process, rights of others, sharing of power, the proper distribution of goods in society (equality), uses and abuses of authority" (1962, 15). In *Political Ideology*, Lane (1962) reports the results of his extended and wide-ranging conversations with fifteen working-class men of New Haven, Connecticut, on such topics, concluding that "the common man has a set of emotionally-charged political beliefs, a critique of alternative proposals, and some modest programs of reform" (15).

Lane's results are often read as making trouble for the claim of ideological innocence. Read closely, they do not. When Lane and Converse write on the same subject, their findings converge (Kinder 1983).

Lane distinguishes between two opposite modes of thought: "contextualizing," or thinking that places political issues and events in topical, temporal, and historical context; and "morselizing," or thinking that considers issues and events in isolation. Lane concluded that with an occasional exception, morselizing dominated the common man's political thinking:

> This treatment of an instance in isolation happens time and again and on matters close to home: a union demand is a single incident, not part of a more general labor-management conflict; a purchase on the installment plan is a specific debt, not part of a budgetary pattern—either one's own or society's. The items and fragments of life remain itemized and fragmented.
>
> Now, the very morselizing tendency that prevents these men from discovering the pattern and significance of an event prevents them from ideologizing. While they do not place events in the context of a pattern of history or policy, neither do they place them in the context of some . . . forensic ideology. (1962, 353)

One can almost feel Lane's irritation with the "common man's" failure to make connections, to grasp relationships between ideas and events that are so obvious to him. Such failures are pervasive and they persist even in the face of Lane's resorting, by his own admission, late in his conversations, to "rather invasive coaching" (quoted in Converse 2006, 302).

The End of the End of Ideology?

"The end of ideology was declared more than a generation ago by sociologists and political scientists who—after the titanic struggle between the ideological extremes of fascism and communism in the middle of the 20th century—were more than glad to see it go." So John Jost begins his widely cited essay published in the *American Psychologist* in 2006. The principal "end-of-ideologists" were, in Jost's reading of intellectual history, Edward Shils, Raymond Aron, Seymour Martin Lipset, Daniel Bell, and one Philip Converse.[1]

Converse's membership in this group is peculiar. No doubt Converse was aware of the debate over the end of ideology carried out among a small number of prominent public intellectuals, but no sign of it appears in his 1964 essay. Converse cites neither Shils nor Aron nor Lipset nor Bell, and he takes no notice of their observations or conclusions. The argument over the end of ideology took place among elites and it was, for the most part, *about* elites. Converse, of course, was making an argument about the ideological capacity of ordinary people. Moreover, Converse was not arguing for the *end* of ideology; he was claiming that in mass societies, ideology has *always* been out of reach of the average citizen.

In Jost's view, the end-of-ideologists, again including Converse, were persuasive. They were so persuasive, in fact, that research on ideology was promptly abandoned. Were it so! In fact, stimulated by Converse's essay, research on ideology in political science, and in the social sciences more broadly, exploded. For decades, Converse's argument remained a center—perhaps *the* center—of empirical work on public opinion.

If Jost's command of the history of his subject leaves something to be desired, we still need to confront his principal claim: namely, that in direct contradiction to Converse and the small mountain of evidence reviewed and reported here, "ideology is very much a part of most people's lives" (2006, 655). How does Jost arrive at this conclusion?

Early in his *American Psychologist* essay, Jost writes "even casual observers of today's headlines, newscasts, and late night talk shows cannot escape the feeling that ideology is everywhere" (652). But the question is not whether ideology permeates headlines, newscasts, and late-night talk shows (a claim Jost advances without evidence). The question is whether ideology exists in the minds of everyday citizens. To establish that this is really so, Jost draws heavily on the standard measure of ideological identification. Referring to ideological identification, he asserts that a "large majority of the American public knows whether they usually prefer liberal or conservative ideas" (656). This is not true. He asserts further that "most Americans are able to place themselves on a liberal-conservative dimension" (656). This is true, but only if moderation is counted as constituting an ideological program, which we have reason to doubt. Jost claims that "public opinion polls show the nation to be sharply divided along ideological lines" (658). No, they don't. They show the opposite. Jost points to increasing polarization between red states and blue states as providing "vivid evidence that ideology exists and matters" (Jost, Nosek, and Gosling 2008, 134). He is mistaken. Fiorina, Abrams, and Pope (2011) show that Americans living in red states and Americans living in blue states are not so different from one another on matters of politics; that on ideological identification in particular, they are practically indistinguishable; and that the evidence of increasing polarization is negligible.

Jost soldiers on. He claims ideology is motivating, the engine of action. Ideological identification, according to Jost, "helps to explain why people do what they do; it organizes their values and beliefs and leads to political behavior" (653). To support this thesis, Jost points to the strong correlation between ideological identification and presidential voting, concluding that ideological identification explains virtually all of the variance in postwar presidential voting. In chapter 6, we show that ideological identification has a small effect on presidential voting and a still smaller effect on voting in lesser contests.

We have spent this much time on Jost out of alarm that his argument may be becoming the conventional wisdom in psychology. The *American Psychologist*, where his article on the end of the end of ideology appeared, is psychology's flagship journal. His essay on the nature and consequences of ideology was published a few years later in the prestigious *Annual Review of Psychology* (Jost, Federico, and Napier 2009). In the *Handbook of Social Psychology*, the principal reference work in social psychology, Banaji and Heiphetz (2010) provide an admiring summary of Jost's work, concluding that it overturns Converse and "establishes the presence of ideology in everyday life" (376). Evidently, the debate over ideology is over and Converse lost. Exactly backward, in our view.[2]

Liberal and *Conservative?*

In *Issue Evolution, The Macro Polity*, and *Tides of Consent*, not to mention in a series of influential papers, James Stimson has made major contributions to the field of public opinion. In *Ideology in America* (2012), written with Christopher Ellis, Stimson turns his attention to ideology. Acknowledging that most Americans are ideologically unsophisticated, Ellis and Stimson want to know whether those in possession of some ideological inclination, however partial or rudimentary, lean predominantly to the left or predominantly to the right. Is the American electorate fundamentally liberal? Or is it essentially conservative?

Ellis and Stimson's answer is: both. Americans are liberal *and* they are conservative. By this they mean that Americans are, on average, sincerely inclined to support liberal policy initiatives—Social Security, spending on environmental problems, government subsidies for child care, and so on—and at the same time, Americans are, on average, sincerely inclined to describe themselves as conservative. Ellis and Stimson call this misalignment a paradox, show that it is "an enduring feature of American public opinion" (98), and do their best to explain it.

We are of course especially interested in what they have to say about ideological identification—what Ellis and Stimson prefer to call symbolic ideology.[3] At first it seems they have little to say. They seem to be in close contact with the good reasons for skepticism on this front: "we know from a wealth of research that citizens quite often do not understand the political meanings of the terms 'liberal' and 'conservative.' Citizens may use such terms, but it is clearly at odds with the facts, known since at least Converse (1964), to say that the American public thinks about politics in explicitly ideological ways, or in ways that exhibit deep familiarity with what ideological terms mean" (16). Nevertheless, they proceed on the assumption that symbolic ideology (ideological identification) is meaningful to those who claim it. In the end, they conclude that "Americans are both liberal *and* conservative and both conceptions of ideology matter" (193).

They *say* both conceptions of ideology matter, but they do not convince us that ideological identification matters. It is not even clear that they have persuaded themselves on this point. Late in the book, they seem to assign to ideological identification a purely expressive function. Referring to symbolic ideology, or as we would prefer, ideological identification, they write: "The real power of ideology for many may not be its role in structuring political choice or its ability to help understand how one's own beliefs correspond with that of political elites. Rather, at least for some, it is the label itself that matters" (174).

That Americans are, on average, inclined to support liberal policy initiatives while being, on average, predisposed to think of themselves as conservative, is fascinating, and Ellis and Stimson have intriguing things to say about how this odd state of affairs could come to pass. They are also quick to acknowledge that they were not the first to notice this apparent contradiction in American public opinion. They say that this honor belongs to Lloyd Free and Hadley Cantril (1967).

But Free and Cantril were actually making a different point: that Americans tend to be operationally liberal and ideologically conservative. By operationally liberal, Free and Cantril mean, much like Ellis

and Stimson, a preference for government programs that accomplish social objectives. But by ideological conservatism, Free and Cantril mean,
unlike Ellis and Stimson, a preference for conservative values: individualism, self-reliance, a government limited in scope and power. Free
and Cantril are making a claim about the simultaneous appeal of liberal
policies and conservative values in American public opinion. Ideological identification—whether Americans think of themselves as liberal or
conservative—plays no role in their argument.

Free and Cantril (1967) do take up ideological identification (again,
what Ellis and Stimson call symbolic ideology) in a separate and brief
chapter. They included in their surveys a question asking respondents
how they would describe themselves, with the presented options running from very liberal to very conservative. Free and Cantril found
most Americans confused about the meaning of ideological terms.
"Conservatives"—that is, those who described themselves as conservative—often supported liberal policy initiatives (the misalignment that
Ellis and Stimson analyze). Meanwhile, "liberals"—that is, those who
described themselves as liberal—often embraced conservative principles. They found, moreover, near majorities to be mistaken about the
ideological positions staked out by Goldwater and Johnson in 1964, who
were at the time offering the American electorate the clearest ideological choice in a generation. Free and Cantril concluded that ideological
identification was "relatively meaningless" and went on about their business—to undertake a comprehensive study of American public opinion—without saying anything more about it.

Ideology Elsewhere

Converse viewed innocence of ideology as a general condition. Although
relying exclusively on evidence from mid-twentieth century United
States, Converse was not afraid to speculate about other times and other
places, under the assumption that ideological indifference is a universal
feature of modern mass politics. Is this so?

Not according to Marcel Gauchet, the prominent French historian and philosopher, whom we met in the introduction. Recall that in
Gauchet's view, liberal and conservative, left and right, "have become
universal political categories. They are part of the basic notions which

generally inform the way contemporary societies work" (Gauchet 1992, 84, quoted in Bobbio 1996, 92).[4]

Gauchet is correct in one very important respect. Surveys of political experts, party programs, and election platforms around the world all reveal the same thing: among elites, left-right is the dominant language of politics (e.g., Huber and Inglehart 1995; Castles and Mair 1984; Hooghe, Marks, and Wilson 2002; Benoit and Laver 2006; Budge, Robertson, and Hearl 1987; Laver and Budge 1992; Budge *et al.* 2001; Noel and Therien 2008).

But we are interested, as Converse was, in ideological thinking among ordinary people. And insofar as researchers elsewhere have posed the same questions to mass publics as Converse did to the American public, they have received very much the same answers. On comprehension of ideological categories, on ideological coherence of beliefs on government policy, on the presence of non-attitudes, on the crucial importance of information, and on the dramatic contrast between citizens and elites: in all these respects, what Converse found to be true in the United States, others have found to be true elsewhere (e.g., Butler and Stokes 1969; Converse and Pierce 1986; Fuchs and Klingemann 1990; Inglehart 1990; Klingemann 1979; Putnam, Leonardi, and Nanetti 1979).

Likewise for ideological identification. What we have found in the United States matches up well with what others have reported from other places (Dalton 2010; Zechmeister and Corral 2012).[5] Citizens are more likely to claim an ideological identity insofar as they are comparatively well educated, interested in politics, and know a great deal about public life—wherever they happen to live (e.g., Zechmeister and Corral 2012). Everywhere, extreme categories on the left or the right are underpopulated, while huge numbers of citizens claim the center. Measured by ideological identification, all the established democracies, including the United States, are ideologically moderate (e.g., Converse and Pierce 1986; Dalton 2010; Huber 1989; Inglehart and Klingemann 1976).[6]

Can we not find a single place where the verdict of ideological innocence is reversed? What about France? The vocabulary for describing the landscape of politics in ideological terms was created there, and left and right remain today embedded in French political culture.

Mindful of this, Converse, working with Roy Pierce (1986), wondered whether ideological identification might be more highly developed among French voters than their American counterparts. They surveyed the French electorate and candidates for the French National Assembly before and after the disorders of the spring of 1968. At this charged moment in French political history, the party system was in flux. In this place and under these circumstances, ideological identification might "provide an efficient if abstract shorthand for organizing a very wide variety of more concrete political information" and "greatly increase the capacity to make sense of incoming political information and hence to organize it cognitively and to retain it more effectively in accessible memory" (Converse and Pierce 1986, 234).[7]

It might have, but it didn't. In matters ideological, France resembles the United States. The French public's mastery of ideological terminology appears to be about as modest as the American public's. Left-right identification among the French is none too stable, of little use in organizing preferences, and largely irrelevant to the vote. If this is how things were in France in the spring of 1968, then we are inclined to conclude that ideological innocence is an endemic feature of mass politics.

The Primacy of Partisanship

Running through much of our analysis has been a comparison between ideology and party. At every juncture, we have turned up sharp contrasts between the two. Americans generally think of themselves as Republicans or Democrats. Such identifications are durable, and they strengthen over time. Party identification influences vote choice powerfully, for voters who are deeply engaged in political life as for those who could barely care less. In all these respects, party identification really seems to be identification. And in all these respects, ideological identification suffers by comparison.

The same contrast shows up in a distinctly different style of analysis than the one carried out here: in aggregate time series, where the dynamics of ideological identification turn out to be sharply different from the dynamics of partisanship—and different in ways that are consistent with our characterization of the average American as ideologically innocent. In aggregate analysis, ideology is less persistent than partisanship (Box-Steffensmeier, Knight, and Sigelman 1998). When perturbed by some shock, aggregate ideological identification returns to equilibrium more rapidly than does aggregate party identification. Moreover, the two series—one for ideological identification, the other for party identification—are generally uncorrelated. This suggests that fluctuations in party fortunes should not be interpreted in ideological terms. A swing toward the Democratic Party does not mean liberalism is on the rise. Movement toward the Republican Party says nothing about conservatism gaining ground. Shifts in aggregate partisanship and shifts in aggregate ideology are independent.[8]

Differences between ideology and partisanship are a reflection, we suggest, of how the world of politics is typically organized, in the United States and in many places around the world. We have in mind most of all the presence of political parties. Parties are vital to politics. They are, as E. E. Schattschneider once put it, not "merely appendages of modern government; they are in the center of it and play a determinative and creative role in it" (1942, 1). Political parties command resources, buildings, workers, and huge megaphones. Parties nominate candidates, run campaigns, host and run conventions, organize legislative assemblies, and make law. The language of partisanship pervades political discourse. And for their part, citizens are regularly offered the opportunity to *act* on their partisanship: to vote, argue, work on a campaign, give money, register, show up at a rally, and more. Such behavioral commitments reinforce and strengthen partisanship (Converse 1969; Markus and Converse 1979; Jennings and Markus 1984).

There is nothing like this for ideology. Even if so inclined, voters cannot cast a ballot for the Liberal Party or the Conservative Party (except from occasional precincts in upstate New York). Parties are material realities in a way that ideologies are not. Liberalism and conservatism belong to the realm of ideas and to those who practice politics as a vocation. This makes liberalism and conservatism fair game for intellectual historians and political theorists but rather less helpful to ordinary people trying to follow, not all that determinedly, what is going on in political life.

Information Inequality

Most people know remarkably little about public affairs. Of course, some *are* curious about politics, and a few, a small fraction of the public, are practically obsessed. Differences in the amount and richness of knowledge that people bring to politics are enormous. Converse (1975, 79) referred to such differences as "staggering" and "astronomical," and as we showed earlier, his analysis of belief systems hinges on this point.[9]

So does our analysis of ideological identification. The propensity to claim an ideological identity, the persistence and durability of ideological identification once acquired, the inclination to adjust ideological identification to accommodate changes in the party system, the apparent consequences of ideological identification: all depend on information. It may come as a surprise, in light of all this, that the idea of information is itself a subject of some controversy.

Some criticism is methodological: that information tests, as conventionally deployed, fail to distinguish between incorrect answers and confessions of ignorance (Nadeau and Niemi 1995; Kuklinski et al. 2000; Mondak 2001), fail to award partial credit to partially correct answers (Mondak 2001; Krosnick et al. 2008), fail to require everyone to answer every question (Mondak 2001), fail to measure knowledge equivalently across groups (Pietryka and MacIntosh 2013), and fail to specify what citizens *should* know (Krosnick, Visser, and Harder 2010).[10]

It would be foolish to presume that the measurement of knowledge could not be improved, and more foolish still to argue that methodological efforts in this vein should not continue. But we find it hard to imagine that improvements in measurement would lead us to conclude that the average citizen is well informed about public affairs and that differences in the command of political information in a mass public are negligible. Converse's pithy formula for the distribution of political knowledge in mass publics—low mean, high variance—is very likely to hold into the indefinite future.

A more fundamental challenge to the place of information in our understanding of politics comes in the form of questioning what it is that people must know to carry out the obligations of democratic citizenship. Do citizens really need to know who happens to be the chief justice of the US Supreme Court to make sensible political decisions? Almost never, Arthur Lupia says, and we agree (Lupia 2016; Lupia and McCubbins 1998). But this does *not* mean that tests of factual knowledge built on such questions are meaningless and should be abandoned. To argue this position is to misunderstand the purpose of such tests. Their purpose, as we see it, is not to assess whether citizens happen to know those particular things they need to know to carry out the duties of democratic citizenship. Their purpose, rather, is to assess differences in the amount and richness of knowledge citizens bring to issues of politics, and thereby capture general differences in the degree to which citizens are engaged in public life.

It is of course an empirical question whether political information scales actually succeed in doing so. To us the evidence is overwhelming that they do. Based on a half-dozen well-chosen items, simple composite scales provide a robust measure. With such scales, we have learned that the well informed differ from the poorly informed in many consequential ways: the well informed are much more likely to express opinions on real issues; much more likely to possess stable opinions—real opinions, opinions held with conviction; much more likely to express preferences that are ideologically coherent; much more likely to pick up and take into account vital pieces of new information; much more likely to think about candidates and parties in ideological terms; much more likely to think of *themselves* in ideological terms; much more likely to make decisions and form preferences in line with their interests and values; and much more likely to take an active part in politics.[11]

Taken together, these findings represent about as impressive a body of empirical regularities as political science can muster. That most citizens know so little about politics while others know so much is a fundamental fact, indispensable not only to ideology and its absence but to broader understandings of politics in mass societies as well.

Moving On

Since the 1960s, the public opinion field has been engaged in a spirited debate over the ideological capacity of mass publics. That debate is over, or we hope it is.

One enduring lesson to carry forward is an appreciation for the deep divide between elites and publics. We have no objection to the application of ideological categories to the understanding of elite politics. Party systems, electoral competition, executive influence, the legislative enterprise, bureaucratic politics, judicial decisions: in all these cases and more, political actors are motivated, at least in part, by ideological conviction.

Political elites—those whose lives are immersed in politics and who exert disproportionate influence over policy and discourse—are experts on politics. Citizens are not. Going forward we must do our best to avoid what Robert Abelson once called the academician's error:

> Because academics devote (or aspire to devote) so much cognitive activity to formal operations on abstract materials, it is easy for them to fall into the view that such cognitive activity is generally characteristic. A contrasting view would be that concrete processing of episodic and situational materials is often much more compelling. (1976, 36)

For the political analyst, this means resisting the temptation to interpret elections and political movements in ideological terms. Eisenhower was not elected by a revolt of the moderates; Reagan did not become president as a consequence of the electorate's turn to the right; Obama was not swept into office by liberalism ascendant; the Tea Party did not rise in defense of ideological principles. More mundane and less lofty factors were at play: partisanship, unpopular wars, frightening economic conditions, racial resentments (Campbell et al. 1960; Kinder and Dale-Riddle 2012; Parker and Barreto 2013; Rosenstone 1983; Tesler and Sears 2010; Williamson, Skocpol, and Coggin 2011).

If it is time to move on from ideology, where are we to go? Because of the field's preoccupation with the ideology question, we have learned rather more about how citizens do *not* think about politics than how they do. This is an important and hard-earned lesson. As lessons go, however, it is pretty unsatisfying. If ideological reasoning is beyond most citizens' capacity and interest, then how do citizens arrive—when they arrive—at their preferences and decisions on political matters?

No doubt there is more than one smart way to answer this question. In this final section of our final chapter, we suggest the one path that seems especially promising to us. Over the next several pages, we sketch the architecture for a *group-centered* account of public opinion. Public opinion arises, we say, primarily from the attachments and antipathies of group life.[12]

Groups can be enormous (women) or tiny (the neighborhood bridge club). Because of our interest in politics on a national scale, we are naturally drawn much more to the former than the latter. When control of government and the resources and symbols it commands are at stake, then groups based in particularistic features, such as kin or local community, are subordinated to attachments rooted in broader groupings, such as gender, race, and religion (Posner 2005).

These broad social groupings become important for politics especially insofar as they are associated with persistent inequality. In any modern society, individuals vary in wealth, power, and status. Inequality is generated in part by individual differences in talent and enterprise; by sheer luck, good and bad; and, most relevant here, by recurrent social processes whereby different social groups are subject to systematically different treatment. In Charles Tilly's (1998) analysis, differences in advantage that pivot on categorical opposites—black versus white, Muslim versus Jew, male versus female, citizen versus foreigner—are especially likely to endure. According to Tilly, "paired and unequal categories do crucial organizational work, producing marked, durable differences in access to valued resources" (8).

The division of society into paired and unequal categories is reinforced by a deep human predisposition to divide the social world into in-groups and out-groups—into "us" and "them" (Kinder and Kam 2009). William Graham Sumner ([1906] 2002), who gave the name "ethnocentrism" to this tendency, was convinced that ethnocentrism was a universal feature of human society, and perhaps he was right. When referring to outsiders, we come easily to mistrust, fear, and condescension.[13]

Group-centered politics has two sides, then, both us and them. It is partly about in-groups, the mobilization of in-group solidarity. The preeminent example is provided by partisanship. American elections are, first and foremost, affirmations of loyalty to party, and campaigns are, first and foremost, efforts on the part of parties to reinforce and activate their supporters (e.g., Campbell et al. 1960; Bartels 2000, 2002). Another excellent case of in-group politics involves religion. In 1960, virtually every voter knew that John F. Kennedy was Catholic, and Catholics—especially "good" Catholics, those whose lives were organized around their faith—voted overwhelmingly for him (Converse 1966b; Kinder and Dale-Riddle 2012).

Group-centered politics is also about out-groups; about the activation of attitudes toward outsiders. Such attitudes are occasionally sympathetic, but more often they are hostile. Henry Adams, perhaps best known for his posthumously published autobiography, once wrote: "Politics, as a practice, whatever its professions, had always been the systematic organization of hatreds." Adams goes too far (a vehement anti-

Semite, perhaps he was projecting), but he has a point. Scores of studies show that public opinion on matters of politics is group centered in this way: shaped in powerful ways by the attitudes citizens harbor toward the social groups they see as the principal beneficiaries or victims in play. Just as Catholics voted in great and unusual numbers for Kennedy in 1960, Protestants, driven by distrust of Catholics, voted in great and unusual numbers against him (Converse 1966b; Kinder and Dale-Riddle 2012). Support for tightening welfare benefits derives, in part, from hostility toward the poor (Gilens 1996). Resistance to immigration reflects, in part, suspicions that the new immigrants are un-American (Citrin, Reingold, and Green 1990). Opposition to integration of public schools and to affirmative action at work is motivated by racial hostility (Kinder and Sanders 1996; Sniderman, Hagen, Tetlock, and Brady 1991). And so on. Attitude toward out-groups is not the only force driving opinion in these various cases, but it seems always to be present, and of all the forces that shape opinion, it is often the most powerful.

For people who are completely identified with an in-group—the ardent feminist—or who are entirely consumed by hatred of an out-group —the fanatical racist—political views will be organized around this one commitment. But for the rest of us, which aspects of identity and attitude become important—which are activated—depends on political circumstance. As a general matter, group-centered politics requires that citizens see a connection between some political dispute and some visible social grouping. To get group-centered politics up and running, citizens must "be endowed with some cognitions of the group as an entity and with some interstitial 'linking' information indicating why a given party or policy is relevant to the group," as someone named Converse once put it (Converse 1964, 237).

The extent to which citizens are in possession of information linking a particular group with a particular political entity depends in part on their interest and attention, and as we have seen time and again, we should be careful not to overestimate the public's appetite for political information. But it also depends on what is happening in politics: on the nature of the candidates and issues that happen to be salient at the time and on how those candidates and issues are presented and framed. Public opinion, that is to say, is not only a matter of individual judgment informed by the affinities and animosities of social life. For better or for worse, public opinion is beholden as well to politics.

Appendix A
Alternative Measures of Ideological Identification

The standard ANES measure of ideological identification is in widespread use, and, as the reader knows (perhaps only too well), the standard question has been our workhorse. As we demonstrated back in chapter 3, over a series of empirical tests, the standard question performs well. There are good reasons to think that the standard ANES question gets at what we want it to get at.

But the standard question is not what we would have chosen, if we had had our way. We would have preferred a question—a sequence of questions—that corresponds more faithfully than the standard question does to what we take identification to mean. We say that ideological identification entails a close and abiding attachment to a group marked by a systematic political program. Ideological identification is both categorical and dimensional. It is categorical in that ideological groups—most notably in the contemporary American case, liberals and conservatives—are types or kinds. Ideological identification is dimensional in that strength of psychological attachment varies continuously. For liberals and conservatives in full, identification constitutes a central and abiding and powerful aspect of identity. For liberals and conservatives in name only, "ideological identification" is impossible to distinguish from no attachment at all. And there exist all shades in between.

If we had our way, we would redesign the standard question to take these conceptual points into account. First we would want to know whether people think of themselves as liberal or conservative. That is, we would treat liberals and conservatives as types or kinds. And then, separately, we would want to know, for those who thought of themselves in these terms, the intensity of their attachment. (You might notice that formulated in this fashion, our ideal question would turn out to resemble the canonical question for partisanship.)

Suppose we had in hand something close to our ideal measure. What difference would that make to our results and conclusions?

As it happens, ANES has, on several occasions, asked a question that resembles our ideal, first in a 1984 study and then again in 2000.[1] This experiment in question wording allows us to see whether our story might not change were we to have available a question better suited to our conceptual definition.

Even if we did not have in mind a superior measure, it is of course always prudent to see whether results can be replicated across alternative measures. Any single measure is imperfect. As a consequence, "the most persuasive evidence comes through a triangulation of measurement processes. If a proposition can survive the onslaught of a series of imperfect measures, with all their irrelevant error, confidence should be placed in it" (Webb et al. 1966, 3–4).

The purpose of this appendix is to explore how our story might differ if we had proceeded with alternative measures—alternative measures that at least, *a priori*, we had some reason to prefer. As we will see, with a single exception, our story changes not at all. This surprised us, in that we expected results for ideological identification to brighten up somewhat with measures that more closely matched our understanding of identification. Not so. The outcome is in other respects reassuring, in that our results and conclusions turn out to be robust across different measures.

Alternative Measures

As a reminder, the standard ANES question is worded this way:

> We hear a lot of talk these days about liberals and conservatives. Here is a 7-point scale on which the political views that people might hold are arrayed from extremely liberal to extremely conservative. Where would you place yourself on this scale, or haven't you thought much about this?

As interviewers read the question, they hand a card to respondents. Printed on the card is a horizontal scale. The scale marks and labels each of seven options, running from "extremely liberal" on the left through

"moderate, middle of the road" in the center to "extremely conservative" on the right.

In the 1984 ANES, the standard ideological identification question
was supplemented by a version that comes close to what we would have
in mind. The "branching" version of the ideological identification sequence, as we will call it, begins this way:

> In general, when it comes to politics, do you usually think of yourself as a lib-
> eral, a conservative, a moderate, or what?

As such, the question treats liberals and conservatives as types or kinds.
By using the terms "In general" and "usually," the branching question
suggests that respondents should be taking the long view, which we like.
It omits the invitation to admit that ideology is not how they think about
themselves—a mistake in our book.

Respondents who answered "yes, liberal" or "yes, conservative" were
then asked this question:

> Do you think of yourself as a strong [liberal/conservative] or a not very strong
> [liberal/conservative]?

We like this because it gets directly to the strength or intensity of attachment (as against extremity, under the standard question).

Respondents who answered "yes, moderate," "no, never," or "don't
know" were asked this question:

> Do you think of yourself as more like a liberal or more like a conservative?

They could answer "liberal," "conservative," or continue not to
choose. Respondents who initially said they had "absolutely no understanding of terms 'liberal' and 'conservative'" were not asked the follow-
up question.

At the end of the branching sequence, then, respondents are sorted
into one of seven categories: "strong liberal," "not very strong liberal,"
"leans liberal," "moderate," "leans conservative," "not very strong conservative," and "strong conservative." In the 1984 ANES, both versions
of the ideological identification question—both the standard version and
the branching version—appear in the preelection survey and in the postelection survey.

A second test is made possible by the 2000 ANES. There, the branching version of the ideological question was included in addition to the standard question, with one change. In the 2000 ANES, the first round of the branching question included an explicit invitation for respondents to admit that ideological identification was not for them:

> In general, when it comes to politics, do you usually think of yourself as a liberal, a conservative, a moderate, or haven't you thought much about it?

This addition constitutes a clear improvement, we would say. But those who accepted the invitation were nevertheless asked a follow-up question that read, "If you had to choose, would you consider yourself a liberal or a conservative?" This seems to us a mistake: we have provided excellent reasons for taking respondents at their word when they say they haven't thought about it. In the 2000 ANES, respondents were randomly assigned to answer either the standard ideological identification question or the branching question in the preelection survey. In the postelection survey, all respondents were asked the standard question.

Comparing the standard ANES measure of ideological identification against the two variations, we now work through a series of empirical tests, starting with a simple reliability check.

Empirical Tests

Reliability

A measure is said to be reliable insofar as observations are repeatable (Nunnally 1967). In chapter 3 we assessed the reliability of the standard ideological identification measure through the method of retesting over short intervals. In four ANES presidential election studies (1996, 2000, 2004, and 2008), the standard ideological identification question was asked of respondents twice, once in the preelection interview, and once in the postelection interview. Calculating the Pearson correlation coefficient provides an estimate of reliability. As reported in chapter 3, the Pearson r ranges from .71 in 2000 (an especially turbulent and elongated postelection period) to .82 in 2004 (with ideological identification coded into seven categories, from extremely liberal to extremely conservative). Repeating this test with the branching version of the ideological identification question asked in both the preelection and postelection interviews in the 1984 ANES, the Pearson r is just .62. The branching question appears to be *less* reliable, not more.[2]

Identification and Closeness

A second test simply asks how well ideological identification predicts who feels close to conservatives and who feels close to liberals. In chapter 3 we showed that the standard question predicts feelings of closeness well. Liberals are quite likely to say that they feel close to liberals and very unlikely to say they feel close to conservatives. Conservatives display the same tendency, run in reverse.

We repeat this test using the 1984 and 2000 ANES, separately by question format (the standard question versus the branching version). The results, presented in figure A.1, show no difference. (Figure A.1 also provides Pearson correlations for quantitative assessment.) By this test, the standard question and the branching question perform well and, more to the point here, indistinguishably well.

Identification and Ratings of Liberals and Conservatives

In chapter 3 we reported that ideological identification, measured by the standard ANES question, is closely associated with ratings of ideological groups. As we expected, self-identified liberals evaluate liberals warmly and conservatives coolly; self-identified conservatives do the same, again in reverse. The point to add here is that this is so without regard to how ideological identification is measured. These results are summarized in figure A.2. Once again, in a simple test, the standard ANES measure of ideological identification does as well as the branching alternative; if anything, the standard measure does a bit better.

Ideology and Partisanship

As we established in chapter 3, Democrats tend to claim liberalism as their ideological home, while Republicans are inclined, rather more disproportionately, toward conservatism. In chapter 6 we showed that this relationship has strengthened in recent decades. Both these points— that ideology and partisanship are correlated, and that the correlation is increasing—are on full display in figure A.3, and on full display

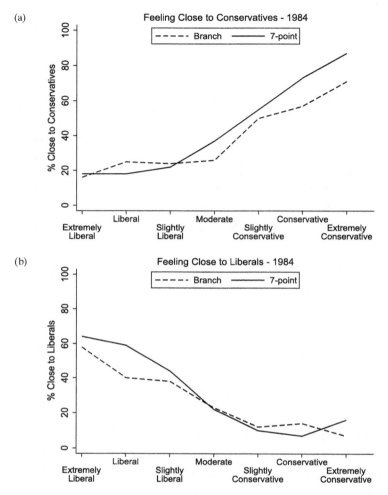

FIGURE A.I **Association between feeling close to conservatives and liberals and ideological identification by question format**

1984 ANES

Closeness to conservatives:	Branching $r = 0.36$	Standard $r = 0.38$
Closeness to liberals:	Branching $r = -0.36$	Standard $r = -0.38$

2000 ANES

Closeness to conservatives:	Branching $r = 0.47$	Standard $r = 0.42$
Closeness to liberals:	Branching $r = -0.47$	Standard $r = -0.44$

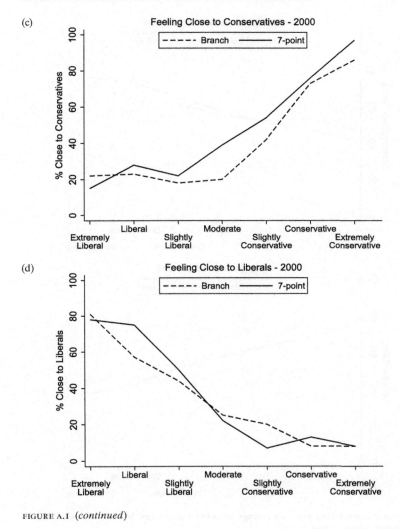

FIGURE A.1 *(continued)*

regardless of how ideological identification is measured. Once again, we can turn up no empirical reason to prefer one measure over another.

Three Simple Lessons Revisited

We began our investigation of ideological identification back in chapter 3 by examining the distribution of answers to the standard ANES

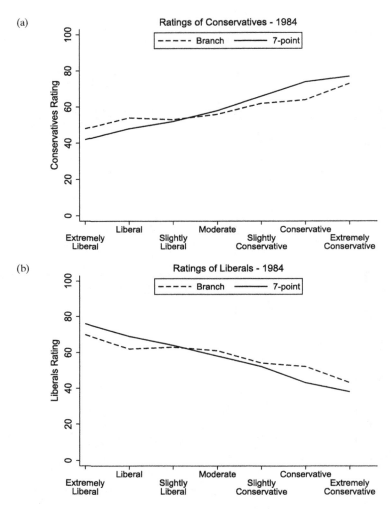

FIGURE A.2 **Association between ratings of conservatives and liberals and ideological identification by question format**

1984 ANES

Conservatives rating:	Branching $r = 0.38$	Standard $r = 0.45$
Liberals rating:	Branching $r = -0.38$	Standard $r = -0.42$

2000 ANES

Conservatives rating:	Branching $r = 0.45$	Standard $r = 0.51$
Liberals rating:	Branching $r = -0.47$	Standard $r = -0.44$

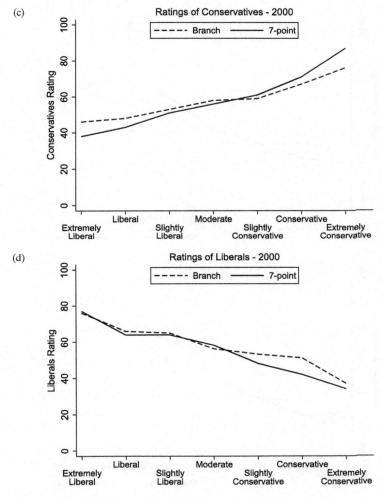

FIGURE A.2 (*continued*)

question. From the distribution we drew three simple lessons. First, ideological identification is not for everyone. When offered the opportunity, many Americans say that they do not think of themselves as liberals or as conservatives. Second, when Americans do claim an ideological identity, large numbers choose moderation. Third, by self-description, conservatives outnumber liberals.

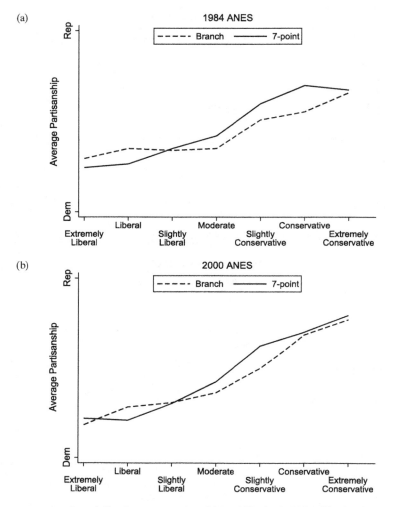

FIGURE A.3 **Association between partisanship and ideological identification by question format**

1984 ANES
Branching: $r = 0.34$
Standard $r = 0.41$
2000 ANES
Branching: $r = 0.51$
Standard: $r = 0.50$

The question we raise here is whether these simple lessons depend on a particular way of measuring ideological identification.

Taking the lessons in reverse order, we can say first of all that the conservative advantage is robust over alternative measures of ideological identification. The standard ANES question produces a conservative advantage; so, too, does the branching alternative. This can be seen in table A.1, which presents the distribution of ideological identification from the 1984 ANES and from the 2000 ANES, separately by question format. (We also split the 2000 ANES sample to separate respondents who were interviewed face-to-face from those interviewed over the telephone.) Regardless of question format, conservatives outnumber liberals, and by roughly the same margin.

TABLE A.1. **Ideological identification in the American electorate by question format (percentage)**

	1984 ANES	
	Standard	Branching
Extremely liberal/strong liberal	1.6	7.4
Liberal/not very strong liberal	7.2	11.4
Slightly liberal/more like a liberal	9.0	11.1
Moderate, middle of the road	23.3	4.0
Slightly conservative/more like a conservative	14.0	20.0
Conservative/not very strong conservative	12.9	16.8
Extremely conservative/strong conservative	1.6	12.7
DK and HTMA/Never, no understanding, and DK	30.2	16.5
N	2,229	2,257

	2000 ANES			
	Face-to-face		Telephone	
	Standard	Branching	Standard	Branching
Extremely liberal/strong liberal	1.6	6.4	1.6	5.1
Liberal/not very strong liberal	5.2	7.9	12.9	9.0
Slightly liberal/more like a ...	9.5	17.1	8.7	13.5
Moderate, middle of the road	25.3	5.5	20.3	7.2
Slightly conservative/more like a ...	12.0	29.4	11.0	24.5
Conservative/not very strong conservative	13.4	9.6	17.4	11.9
Extremely conservative/strong conservative	2.3	11.8	4.5	11.5
DK/HTMA	30.7	12.4	23.6	17.4
N	466	538	400	400

But in other respects, question format makes a substantial difference. For one thing, under branching, far fewer Americans end up being classified as completely nonideological. The proportion of those who say ideology is not for them is cut nearly in half. For another, under branching, the number of moderates shrinks almost to the vanishing point. All things considered, branching seems to produce a different picture of ideology in America.

Different is not necessarily better, of course. We think we should take Americans at their word when they say they do not think of themselves in ideological terms. In chapter 4 we show that such people are distinguished by their lack of interest in politics and especially by their ignorance of political matters. And given what we know about those who, in response to the standard question, claim to be moderates, we are suspicious of a question sequence that pesters those who say they are moderate to confess that, deep down, they really are ideological. Deep down, they really are not.

But let's continue the comparison. In both the 1984 ANES and the 2000 ANES, all respondents were asked for their ideological identification in the standard way and in the branching way. This doubling allows us to make comparisons within individuals. Table A.2 summarizes the results of the simple cross-tabulation of the two question formats, first for 1984 and then for 2000.

There is a lot to take in from table A.2. Here are the three things we think are especially noteworthy. The first of these concerns those who said in response to the standard question that they did not think of themselves in ideological terms. Where did these people land when asked the branching question? A sizable fraction of this group, but far short of a majority, is classified (properly, we would say) as without an ideological identification. But another sizable fraction, between one-quarter and one-half, depending on the exact form of the branching question, end up classified as either leaning left or leaning right—and more the latter than the former, by a two-to-one margin. Similarly, nearly one-half of those who call themselves moderates on the standard question appear as leaning left or as leaning right on the branching question, and once again, conservative-leaning Americans outnumber those who tilt in a liberal direction. Finally, and this seems to us to be an improvement, a substantial fraction of Americans who say they are liberal or conservative on the standard question call themselves *strong* liberals or *strong* conservatives on the branching question. One deficiency with the standard question,

TABLE A.2. **Cross-tabulation between responses to alternative measures of ideological identification (percentage)**

1984 ANES

Branching measure	Liberal 1	2	3	Moderate 4	5	6	Conservative 7	HTMA or DK	
Standard measure									
1	55.6	11.1	8.3	2.8	8.3	0.0	2.8	11.1	100
2	46.6	30.4	8.7	0.6	3.1	4.4	1.9	4.4	100
3	9.0	34.8	34.8	3.0	10.0	4.5	1.5	2.5	100
4	4.8	11.5	16.9	7.5	30.0	14.8	6.0	8.5	100
5	1.0	4.5	2.9	2.2	33.6	38.7	13.4	3.8	100
6	1.4	1.7	1.0	0.4	12.2	26.7	54.5	2.1	100
7	5.6	0.0	0.0	5.6	8.3	8.3	61.1	11.1	100
HTMA or DK	2.8	8.0	9.4	4.6	18.3	12.3	4.0	40.7	100

2000 ANES

Branching measure	Liberal 1	2	3	Moderate 4	5	6	Conservative 7	HTMA or DK	
Standard measure									
1	38.9	0.0	9.0	8.4	14.1	13.2	0.0	16.4	100
2	32.7	26.5	23.4	1.8	7.8	2.5	1.4	4.0	100
3	7.8	36.3	29.7	5.6	11.5	3.9	2.0	3.3	100
4	2.8	11.0	18.9	13.3	27.5	5.4	4.6	16.5	100
5	0.0	5.3	3.5	4.0	43.9	32.9	5.1	5.2	100
6	0.0	0.0	3.1	2.0	22.2	25.1	44.9	2.8	100
7	0.0	0.0	13.2	0.0	9.7	0.0	69.5	7.6	100
HTMA or DK	1.5	0.5	18.0	5.7	34.4	4.1	2.8	32.9	100

from our point of view, is that it refers to location—extreme liberal, extreme conservative—rather than intensity—strong liberal, strong conservative. We would have preferred the latter.

Becoming Ideological

Most Americans claim an ideological identification, but substantial numbers do not, even when taken through the branching question, which pushes them pretty hard to admit to an ideological inclination. In chapter 4, we showed that people are much more likely to take hold of an ideological identification insofar as they are intrigued by politics, possess the intellectual wherewithal to make sense of this difficult subject,

TABLE A.3. **Ideological identification as a consequence of information, involvement, and education by question format (probit coefficients with standard errors in parentheses)**

	1984 ANES		2000 ANES	
	Standard	Branching	Standard	Branching
Political information	1.30 (.16)	1.46 (.19)	.87 (.30)	1.36 (.37)
Political involvement	.43 (.13)	.58 (.15)	.62 (.25)	.65 (.26)
High school graduate	.01 (.08)	.20 (.09)	.74 (.24)	.33 (.23)
Some college	.08 (.11)	.19 (.14)	1.16 (.25)	.23 (.24)
College graduate	.90 (.14)	.71 (.18)	1.35 (.27)	.23 (.28)
Family income	.49 (.13)	.69 (.16)	.41 (.28)	.49 (.32)
Female	−.16 (.07)	−.19 (.08)	−.20 (.15)	.19 (.15)
White	.15 (.09)	.03 (.11)	.35 (.17)	.24 (.17)
Constant	−.97 (.13)	−.51 (.15)	−1.32 (.30)	−.65 (.27)
N	1,957	1,973	751	812

and command a basic working knowledge of how politics works. To what extent must we modify our account when we take up ideological identification as assessed by the branching question?

Very little. Table A.3 presents the results of a probit regression predicting ideological identification measured in the standard way and, separately, by the branching question. Results are broadly similar across the two measures, in both the 1984 ANES and in the 2000 ANES. Political information plays a somewhat stronger part in the prediction of ideological identification under branching; education plays a somewhat weaker role. But the account is essentially the same.

Ideology and the Vote

Table A.4 displays the association between ideological identification and presidential vote in the 1984 and 2000 elections, separately by question format. In each instance, self-described liberals tend to vote for the Democrat, just as self-described conservatives tend to vote for the Republican, and this is so regardless of how ideological identification is measured. There is little to choose between the standard question and the branching alternative.

Table A.5 takes the analysis of voting to the next stage. The table summarizes the results of a multivariate probit regression, based again on the 1984 and 2000 ANES. Neither the 1984 nor the 2000 ANES is a panel study—hence the quotation marks surrounding "Effect" in the

TABLE A.4. **Ideological identification and presidential voting by question format**

1984 ANES

		Extremely/strong liberal	Liberal	Slightly/lean liberal	Moderate	Slightly/lean conservative	Conservative	Extremely/strong conservative
Branching	Mondale	75.0	56.7	65.5	45.8	34.3	25.5	16.3
$r = .39$	Reagan	25.0	43.3	34.5	54.2	65.8	74.5	83.7
Standard	Mondale	91.3	74.6	66.9	45.0	22.3	13.7	23.1
$r = .44$	Reagan	8.7	25.4	33.1	55.0	77.7	86.3	76.9

2000 ANES

		Extremely/strong liberal	Liberal	Slightly/lean liberal	Moderate	Slightly/lean Conservative	Conservative	Extremely/strong conservative
Branching	Gore	92.0	74.3	85.6	54.0	43.8	25.1	13.4
$r = .55$	Bush	8.0	25.7	14.4	46.0	56.2	74.9	86.7
Standard	Gore	100.0	84.8	82.2	59.5	36.8	17.7	4.4
$r = .55$	Bush	0.0	15.2	17.8	40.5	63.2	82.3	95.6

TABLE A.5. "Effect" of ideological identification on presidential voting by question format (probit coefficients with standard errors in parentheses)

	1984 ANES		2000 ANES	
	Branching	Standard	Branching	Standard
Ideological identification	.37 (.08)	.63 (.14)	.48 (.20)	.83 (.25)
Party identification	1.45 (.09)	1.35 (.09)	1.66 (.18)	1.53 (.18)
Views on policy	.68 (.15)	.84 (.17)	.74 (.34)	1.26 (.33)
Economic performance	.80 (.11)	.74 (.12)	−.34 (.19)	−.24 (.17)
Constant	.31 (.06)	.74 (.12)	.03 (.11)	−.11 (.11)
N	1,207	1,046	771	708

title of the table. We are very likely overestimating the effect of ideological identification on the vote, but we can still usefully compare the estimated effects by question format. Here a clear difference does emerge: it appears as if ideological identification is more important when measured in the standard way than when measured by the branching alternative—and by a substantial margin.

But this is mostly appearance. The superiority of the standard measure disappears when we take into account distributional differences. We do so by estimating ideological and partisan voting in a way that takes into account both the impact and size of each type (see chapter 7 for details on this procedure). As shown in table A.6, the importance of ideological voting in presidential elections is modest in absolute terms and dwarfed by the importance of partisanship. This is so for the standard measure. And it is so, in just the same way, for the branching measure.

Ideology and Issue Preference

We turn now to one final set of comparisons. Here we see whether the association between ideological identification and preferences on issues—government spending, employment policy, defense, assistance to African Americans, and abortion—hinges on how ideological identification is measured. It does not. Table A.7 shows that the associations are modest, and this is so regardless how ideological identification is measured. If anything—and this continues a theme that has run through much of our analysis in this appendix—the correlations are a bit brighter by the standard measure of ideological identification (Treier and Hillygus 2009).

TABLE A.6. **Ideological and partisan voting in American presidential elections by question format (weighted average probit coefficients)**

	1984 ANES		2000 ANES	
	Branching	Standard	Branching	Standard
Ideological voting	.19	.17	.27	.25
Partisan voting	1.01	1.00	1.11	1.14

TABLE A.7. **Association between ideological identification and preferences on issues by question format (Pearson r)**

1984 ANES						
	Spending	Jobs	Defense	Blacks	Abortion	Index
Branching	.25	.16	.26	.17	.18	.30
Standard	.27	.16	.31	.22	.23	.36

2000 ANES						
	Spending	Jobs	Defense	Blacks	Abortion	Index
Branching	.28	.20	.26	.21	.32	.45
Standard	.35	.24	.31	.25	.32	.49

Conclusion

The purpose of this appendix has been to explore how our story would have changed had we proceeded with alternative measures of ideological identification. We undertook this analysis partly out of a sense that alternative measures might in fact be superior to the standard measure, and partly out of a more general sense that it is always wise to check results across multiple measures. Measurement, we know, is tricky business.

To our surprise, with a single and benign exception, our story changes not at all. If anything, had we had in hand the branching question, our results would have run even more forcefully against the claim of ideology. Under alternative measures, as under the standard measure, Americans appear to be quite innocent of ideology.

Appendix B

Are Moderates Ideological?

Here we compare moderates to those who rejected ideological terms altogether on three standard measures of ideological sophistication.

Figure B.1 displays the relationship between strength of ideological identification (along the horizontal axis) and command of ideological concepts (along the vertical). Strength of ideological identification is anchored on the low end by those who reject ideological terminology entirely and on the high end by those who claim to be ideologically extreme (either liberal or conservative). More precisely, the scale is coded this way:

Haven't thought about it = 0

Moderate, middle of the road = .25

Liberal or conservative leanings = .50

Liberal or conservative = .75

Extreme liberal or extreme conservative = 1.0

Here we are of course particularly interested in the comparison between those who admit that they haven't thought about ideology (scored 0) and those who claim moderation as their political identity (scored .25).

Command of ideological concepts is represented by the proportion classified as ideological in their commentary on parties and candidates.

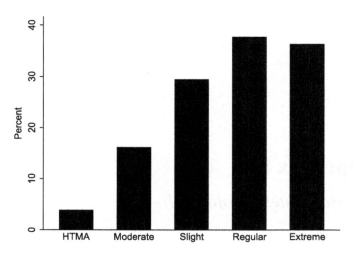

FIGURE B.1 Moderation and command of ideological concepts

Source: 1956–88 ANES Cumulative Data File, merged with Knight's (1987) coding of levels of ideological conceptualization.

We expect this proportion to rise as we progress along the dimension of ideological strength, and this is exactly what figure B.1 shows. Most relevant for current purposes, we see that moderates, though not very likely to make use of ideological terminology in absolute terms, are considerably more likely to do so than are those who say ideology is not for them.

Our second comparison considers the ideological consistency of preferences on policy. Here we simply calculated inter-item correlations (Pearson r), separately for groups defined by their strength of ideological identification. Figure B.2 summarizes the results (the figure presents the absolute value of r). As expected, consistency increases with strength of identification. Among those who failed to claim any ideological identity at all, there is barely any consistency to detect. The median correlation between policy preferences among those who reject ideological terminology is just .10. Things are hardly better for moderates. Among the moderates, the median correlation is just .11.

The notion of non-attitudes provides our third and final test. Figure B.3 presents over-time correlations calculated from the 1972–76 ANES Panel Study. As shown there, preferences on matters of policy are no more stable among the moderates than among those who reject ideological terminology.

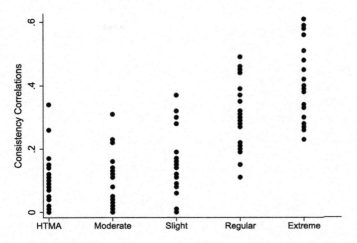

FIGURE B.2 Moderation and preference consistency

Source: ANES Cumulative File.

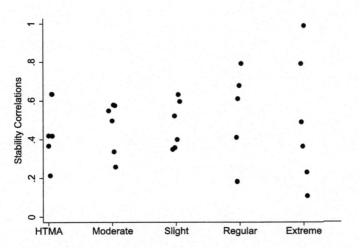

FIGURE B.3 Moderation and preference stability

Source: 1972–76 ANES Panel Study.

In summary, in two of three tests, moderates are indistinguishable from those who remove themselves from ideological analysis. Along with the evidence presented in chapter 4, we see little reason to regard moderation as an ideological category.

Notes

Introduction

1. On these various points, consult Mann and Ornstein 2013, McCarty, Poole, and Rosenthal 2006; Epstein, Parker and Segal 2013; Arceneaux and Johnson 2013; and Mutz 2007.

2. Experts are defined by their ability to organize huge troves of knowledge efficiently and to retrieve relevant aspects of that knowledge rapidly for the task at hand. Expertise—whether the subject is chess or physics or politics—does not come easily. Research in cognitive science suggests that the acquisition of expertise requires both aptitude and *massive* experience (Chase and Simon 1973; Chi, Glaser, and Farr 2014; Novick and Bassok 2005).

3. Converse refers to the notion of ideological innocence once in his 1964 essay:

> the citizen *innocent of "ideology"* is likely to make rather capricious constructions, since the issue is probably one that he has never thought about and will never think about again except when being interviewed (1964, 241, emphasis added).

Working independently and at about the same time, Herbert McClosky (1964, 373) also uses the phrase "innocent of ideology." After comparing the views of delegates to the Democratic and Republican national conventions with the views expressed by a cross section of ordinary Americans, McClosky concluded that ideological innocence fits the American public but not American elites.

4. See, among many examples, Conover and Feldman 1981; Jacoby 1991; Knight 1985; and Levitin and Miller 1979.

5. Figure I.1 summarizes our count of research papers focusing on ideological identification published in top political science journals (*American Political Science Review, American Journal of Political Science, Journal of Politics*, and *Public Opinion Quarterly*) from 1960 to 2015. We relied on Google Scholar full-

text search for "ideological identification" or "ideological self-identification" and excluded book reviews. The figure gives exact counts (filled dots) and a smoothed line through the scatterplot (Lowess algorithm with bandwidth = .8).

6. Of course, there are exceptions. Among them are Conover and Feldman (1981), Kinder (1983), Knight (1985), and Ellis and Stimson (2012), not to mention Converse himself (2007). A few have concluded, both prematurely and erroneously, that the new results on ideological identification simply upend the original claim of innocence (Jost [2006]; Banaji and Heiphetz [2010]). We'll get around to them in our final chapter.

Chapter One

1. For our recapitulation, we rely primarily on the 1964 essay, the paper on non-attitudes presented to the International Congress of Psychology in 1963 and published some years later in a collection edited by Edward Tufte (Converse 1970), and chapters 9 and 10 of *The American Voter* (Campbell et al. 1960).

2. In his 1964 essay, Converse prefers "belief system" to "ideology." Why? Because, he says, the term "ideology" is thoroughly muddied in use. We agree, but this is largely a terminological move, not a substantive one. When Converse refers to a political belief system, we can take him to mean ideology.

3. Ideology has been defined in a variety of ways, but on this point there is virtual consensus (Gerring 1997). Adorno and his collaborators in *The Authoritarian Personality* (1950, 2) define ideology as "an organization of opinions, attitudes, and values." For Herbert McClosky (1964, 362), ideology refers to "systems of belief that are elaborate, integrated, and coherent." Angus Campbell and colleagues (1960, 192), writing in *The American Voter*, describe ideology as "a particularly elaborate, close-woven, and far-reaching structure."

4. Should change come to a central belief, the implications will cascade through the entire system. These are cases of ideological conversion. They occur, but they are rare, and they are a dynamic consequence of structure. In a dynamic sense, structure (or constraint) refers to "the probability that a change in the perceived status (truth, desirability, and so forth) of one idea-element would psychologically require, from the point of view of the actor, some compensating change(s) in the status of idea-elements elsewhere in the configuration" (Converse 1964, 208).

5. Given probability sampling designs and response rates running into the low 80s, Americans participating in the election studies should constitute a faithful sample of the nation as a whole. For the most part they do. On measures of income, education, marital status, and more, the election study samples that Converse analyzed closely resemble the national population. For technical de-

tails on the design of the 1956, 1958, and 1960 studies, consult the ANES web-site, www.electionstudies.org.

6. Instability was rampant on policy beliefs, but not on partisanship. The sta-bility of party identification vastly exceeded the stability of opinion on even the most stable of the policies. The stark contrast between partisanship and policy opinion, is, as Converse noted, "ironic, for in theory of course the party usu-ally has little rationale for its existence save as an instrument to further particu-lar policy preferences. . . . The policy is the end, and the party is the means, and ends are conceived to be more stable and central in belief systems than means." Things, it appears, are actually the other way around: "The party and the affect toward it are more central within the political belief systems of the mass public than are the policy ends that the parties are designed to pursue" (Converse 1964, 240–41).

7. Converse's essay is remembered as a forceful rejection of the notion that mass publics in general, and the American mass public in particular, are teeming with people who reason about politics from ideological principles. This is as it should be. Midway through his attack, however, Converse paused to offer a pos-itive proposal for how citizens might reason about politics, if ideology was be-yond their reach. Perhaps, Converse suggested, citizens organize their opinions on policy according to their attitudes toward the social groups that such policies seem to benefit or harm. This turns out to be a good idea—a *really* good idea. We will come back to it in our final chapter.

Chapter Two

1. For more comprehensive reviews, see Converse 1975, 2000; Kinder 1983, 1998; Kuklinski and Peyton 2007; Sniderman 1993; and the essays collected in the 2006 issue of *Critical Review*. The last includes a reprinting of Converse's original paper, followed by a set of commentaries by a dozen scholars who dif-fer sharply in their assessment of Converse's argument, and concludes with a re-sponse by Converse himself.

"Enough Already about Ideology!" was published the following year under the boring title, "Diversity and Complexity in American Public Opinion" (Kin-der 1983).

2. Jost, a confident and confused critic of ideological innocence, is certain that Converse had no business making general claims about ideology based on evidence from the Eisenhower years: "Converse's conclusions concerning the lack of ideology among ordinary citizens were drawn on the basis of survey data during one of the least politically charged periods in recent American history" (2006, 656). Jost provides no evidence on this point, and he reverses field in his

very next sentence: "But there was always something paradoxical about touting the end of ideology in a decade that witnessed McCarthyism and the 'Red Scare,' a war in Korea to stop the threat of communism, ideological conflict over racial desegregation in American schools, the liberal Hungarian uprising against the Soviet Union, and many other politically charged events" (ibid.). Well, which is it?

3. Nie, Verba, and Petrocik (hereafter NV&P) provided their own test, though their results are not included in table 2.1. Here's why:

NV&P examined citizens' replies to the same candidate and party questions that Converse analyzed. NV&P expected to find ideological thinking increasing over this period, as the ideologically insipid Eisenhower years gave way to the dynamic politics of the 1960s—and on their measure it did. Between 1956 and 1972, the percentage of the public thinking about politics in ideological terms increased steadily and dramatically. NV&P took this as confirmation for the claim that Converse's original conclusion was a product in large part of the ideological neutrality of the times, and that substantial numbers of Americans—perhaps one-third or more—are capable of ideological conceptualization when politics intrudes on private life.

But NV&P worked not from verbatim transcriptions of the original protocols, as had Converse, but from the results of coding carried out by staff at the University of Michigan's Survey Research Center—"Master Codes," as they are known in the trade. Master Codes provide detailed coverage of the content of respondents' replies but with less attention to their quality or sophistication. By relying on Master Codes, NV&P's measure of ideological reasoning is tilted toward vocabulary rather than comprehension. NV&P also followed different criteria. Under their framework, respondents classified as ideologues were required to express either an explicit ideological term (e.g., "liberal") or an implicit ideological term (e.g., "social change"), and to generate elsewhere in their responses to candidates and parties some reference to issues and group benefits.

NV&P conceded that their measure was less sensitive than the measure developed by Converse. It was also far more generous. Recall that Converse discovered just 2.5 percent of the public to be full-fledged ideologues in 1956; in the same year, working from the same questions but following different procedures, NV&P placed nearly five times as many (12.0 percent) in the same category.

Both the 1976 and 1979 editions of *The Changing American Voter* contain errors, acknowledged and corrected in NV&P's note to *The American Political Science Review* published in 1981. Our summary and commentary here reacts to the corrected findings.

NV&P are of course free to measure ideology in any way they please. But there are good reasons to prefer Converse's method. NV&P's measure of ideological reasoning is limited to detecting ideological vocabulary; Converse's measure aims for ideological comprehension. NV&P provide no evidence on the reliability or validity of their coding. In contrast, the Converse measure stands up well to a series of empirical tests. It displays good reliability (Campbell et al. 1960). It is related in the expected way to indicators of political information, formal education, political involvement, and political participation (Converse 1964; Hagner and Pierce 1982). And finally, ideological thinking, as assessed by Converse's method, is consequential: compared to the rest of the public, Americans in possession of an ideological point of view are much more likely to vote according to their class interests (Converse 1964) and much more likely to display consistency in their views on policy (Jacoby 1995).

4. A second feature of the political environment emphasized by NV&P has to do with the political agenda. They argue that the issues that burst onto the national scene shortly after Converse completed his essay—civil rights, Vietnam, urban unrest—"penetrated" the private lives of ordinary people to an unusual degree. As a consequence, they say, Americans in growing numbers began to think about the political world in ideological ways.

Perhaps they are correct, though how this would take place—how the penetration of issues into everyday life generates more ideological thinking—is left unspecified by NV&P and remains mysterious to us.

5. The figures on education come from the National Center for Education Statistics, 2012.

6. How can this result be reconciled with the significant rise in the use of ideological concepts in 1964 and 1968 displayed in figure 2.1? We suggest that the increase reflects a facility on the part of a segment of the public to pick up, at least temporarily, the terms that ideologically charged campaigns make prominent. Using ideological vocabulary does not guarantee that ideological ideas are understood. Parroting campaign rhetoric, if that is what we see here, should not be confused with ideological thinking (Field and Anderson 1969; Pierce 1970; Levitin and Miller 1979; Smith 1989).

7. Goldwater readily acknowledged that his books were ghostwritten. But we assume, as Hofstadter (1965) did, that Goldwater read his books carefully before he signed them and that they faithfully represented his views. On Goldwater's rise, see Perlstein's excellent *Before the Storm* (2001).

8. The evidence for party polarization is abundant. It shows up in roll-call voting in Congress; party platforms; presidential candidates' stump speeches; appointments; and more (e.g., Adams 1997; Carmines and Stimson 1989; McCarty, Poole, and Rosenthal 2006; Rohde 1991; Sanbonmatsu 2002; Wolbrecht 2000).

9. Our analysis is based on the multilevel model developed by Baldassarri and Gelman (2008). Our results differ somewhat from theirs. A close look at their analysis turns up a problem, at least from the point of view of our project. Baldassarri and Gelman include in their category of issues a mix of things: preferences on policies, but also general views on equality, attitudes on race, and

views on changes in moral standards. We remove these; when we do, the trend estimate is cut in half.

10. The Pearson correlation (1972–76) for busing is .54; for abortion, .62. The median Pearson correlation (1972–76) for the rest of the policy questions is under .40. For party identification, the four-year Pearson correlation (1972–1976) is .81.

11. What makes busing and abortion exceptional is not obvious, though we suspect it has to do with the intersection of politics and morality: when policy touches on the public's sense of right and wrong, real preferences are more likely to result (Graham, Haidt, and Nosek 2009; Ryan 2014; Stoker 1992).

12. Much the same contrast shows up in an examination of the French electorate and candidates for the National Assembly (Converse and Pierce 1986). Once again, the views of the general public showed little constraint, while the candidates vying for the public's support lined up consistently either in favor of integration of Europe or against it.

13. Erikson (1979), analyzing the same 1956–60 election study panel with assumptions similar to Achen's, reports very similar results. Analyzing other panels, so do Inglehart (1985) and Judd and Milburn (1980). Brody (1986) modifies Converse's original black-and-white model to allow for meaningful change, and finds less evidence of non-attitudes.

14. Achen (1975) and Erikson (1979) find little support for the predictability of opinion stability, but they fail to consider political information as a predictor (Converse 2000).

15. In the most recent challenge to the non-attitude thesis, Ansolabehere, Rodden, and Snyder (2008) show that when opinions are averaged over multiple questions from the same policy domain, the observed stability of the composite preference climbs to respectable levels. The over-time correlations reported by Ansolabehere, Rodden, and Snyder approach but do not quite reach the observed correlation for party identification over the same period, measured by a single item. The Ansolabehere team treats this as an achievement: "This is an important result, because the relatively high level of stability found for party identification is often taken as evidence that party identification is something real, solid, and meaningful in public opinion" (220).

Our reaction is different. We think it more impressive that it requires many questions to generate a measure of preference on economic policy that approaches in its stability what a single question can do for party identification. This suggests to us that partisanship is "real, solid, and meaningful" in a way that preferences on economic policy are not.

16. Consistent with this interpretation are the repeated demonstrations that substantial fractions of the American electorate can be enticed to volunteer opinions on utterly obscure or even *fictitious* legislative proposals (e.g., Bishop et al. 1980; Bishop, Tuchfarber, and Oldendick 1986; Schuman and Presser 1980).

17. Converse says only this: "independent measures of political information, education, and political involvement all showed sharp and monotonic declines as one passed downward through the levels [of conceptualization] in the order suggested. Furthermore, these correlations were strong enough so that each maintained some residual life when the other two items were controlled, despite the strong underlying relationship between education, information, and involvement" (1964, 217–18).

Insofar as information shows up in the literature taking off from Converse's work, it appears in research on the non-attitude puzzle.

18. Zaller has compared the performance of political knowledge against a variety of standard measures of attention and interest—including education, media exposure self-report, participation in politics, and professed interest in politics. Over an extensive series of empirical tests, political knowledge emerges as the decisive winner (Zaller 1990, 1992; Luskin 1987; Price and Zaller 1993).

We are aware of the ongoing tiff over the conceptualization, measurement, and analysis of political information (e.g., Lupia 2006, 2016; Prior and Lupia 2008; Levendusky 2011; Mondak 2001; Converse 2000; Luskin and Bullock 2011). We'll get to this debate, but not until our final chapter.

19. Here's another way to see this association. The results below are derived from a probit analysis predicting use of ideological concepts (scored 0,1) from political information (based on multiple item scales, scored 0 to 1):

TABLE 2.5. **Predicting use of ideological terms from political information (probit coefficients with standard errors in parentheses)**

	1964	2000
Political information	1.65 (.12)	1.17 (.13)
Constant	−1.56 (.08)	−1.52 (.09)

Source: 1964 and 2000 ANES.

20. Here are the results from a probit analysis predicting understanding of ideological concepts (scored 0,1) from political information (based on multiple item scales, scored 0 to 1):

TABLE 2.6. **Predicting understanding of ideological terms from political information (probit coefficients with standard errors in parentheses)**

	1960	1964
Political information	1.17 (.14)	1.36 (.12)
Constant	−1.57 (.10)	−1.70 (.08)

Source: 1960 and 1964 ANES.

21. We have already cited evidence of the relationship between information and stability as part of our review of the non-attitude claim earlier in the chapter. The results we are about to present here are consistent with those cited earlier.

22. Information and ideology are intimately connected, but are they connected *causally*? Converse implies that they are. His most comprehensive discussion of the relationship between the two comes in a section of his 1964 essay called "*Consequences* of Declining Information for Belief Systems" (our emphasis).

We cannot settle the causal question definitively, but we can make some headway in that direction. As we have just demonstrated, the relationship between information and ideology is strong on all four indicators of ideological thinking. This remains so when we repeat each analysis, this time taking into account involvement and education in addition to information. Compared to the poorly informed, the well informed are much more likely to use ideological categories in their political justifications, to display an adequate understanding of ideological categories, to organize their beliefs along ideological lines, and to persevere in their opinions in the face of changing political winds. This evidence does not prove a causal connection, but it is consistent with the claim that command of information enables ideological thinking.

Chapter Three

1. Our conception of ideological identification bears a strong resemblance to that put forward by Conover and Feldman (1981) in their excellent and pioneering analysis. Conover and Feldman treat ideological identification "as a statement of group consciousness—a declaration of group loyalty" (623). They say further that ideological identification should be thought about the way party identification is; that ideological identification, like party identification, "reflects a 'psychological identification' to a particular group" (624).

We endorse this position, with two emendations. First, we prefer the language of loyalty to the language of consciousness. The latter presumes an unrealistically high standard—one we think few people would meet—and loyalty can do the work that ideological identification is widely assumed to do. And second, the parallel to party identification is fine and we intend to offer an extended comparison between party identification and ideological identification here, but the parallel is not perfect, and we see this immediately when we ask the question: to what group, exactly, do ideological identifiers pledge their allegiance? The question is easy to answer for party identification; it is far less obvious in the case of ideological identification.

One more (definitional) thing. Conover and Feldman argue (following Kerlinger 1967, 1984) that liberalism and conservatism, as popularly understood,

"constitute relatively distinct attitude systems" (620). Liberalism and conservatism are not necessarily polar opposites: "liberals and conservatives view the political world not from different sides of the same coin, but rather, if you will,
from the perspective of entirely different currencies" (624). We agree—more
precisely, we think that a proper definition of ideological identification should
allow for the possibility that liberalism and conservatism are distinct types; that
they are not necessarily mirror images; that they are not end-points on a single
continuum.

2. In one of his fireside chats to the nation, Roosevelt explained his use of the
term "liberal":

> Those of us in America who hold to this [liberal] school of thought,
> insist that these new remedies can be adopted and successfully main-
> tained in this country under our present form of government if we use
> government as an instrument of cooperation to provide these reme-
> dies. We believe that we can solve our problems through continuing ef-
> fort, through democratic processes instead of Fascism or Communism.
> We are opposed to the kind of moratorium on reform which, in effect,
> is reaction itself.
>
> Be it clearly understood, however, that when I use the word "lib-
> eral," I mean the believer in progressive principles of democratic, rep-
> resentative government and not the wild man who, in effect, leans in
> the direction of Communism, for that is just as dangerous as Fascism.
> —Franklin D. Roosevelt, "Fireside Chat," June 24, 1938, quoted in
> Gerhard Peters and John T. Woolley, *The American Presidency Proj-
> ect*, http://www.presidency.ucsb.edu/ws/?pid=15662.

3. For the purpose of this test, we coded ideological identification into three
categories: liberal, moderate, and conservative. If we repeat the test and code
ideological identification into seven categories, from extremely liberal to extremely conservative, the Pearson correlations increase a bit: under this coding,
they range from 0.71 (in 2000) to 0.82 (in 2004).

4. The results in figure 3.1 are based on combining results from eight con-
secutive election studies between 1972 and 2000, each of which included liberals and conservatives in the group closeness inventory. Notice the kink in the
relationship: self-identified liberals are more likely to say they feel close to liberals than are self-identified extreme liberals, and the same is so for conservatives,
though in the latter case the difference is tiny.

5. Here's the exact question:

> I'd like to get your feelings toward some of our political leaders and
> other people who are in the news these days. I will use something we
> call the feeling thermometer and here is how it works:
>
> I'll read the name of a person and I'd like you to rate that person

using the feeling thermometer. Ratings between 50 degrees and 100 degrees mean that you feel favorable and warm toward the person. Ratings between 0 degrees and 50 degrees mean that you don't feel favorable toward the person and that you don't care too much for that person. You would rate the person at the 50 degree mark if you don't feel particularly warm or cold toward the person. If we come to a person whose name you don't recognize, you don't need to rate that person. Just tell me and we'll move on to the next one.

Our first person is [for example] Bill Clinton. How would you rate him using the thermometer?

And still using the thermometer how would you rate the following: [next comes a list of groups, including "liberals" and "conservatives."]

The results in figure 3.2 are based on combining presidential-year ANES results between 1972 (when the standard ideological identification question first appeared) and 2012.

6. An adequate measure, yes—but not perfect. In appendix A we discuss and analyze alternative measures.

7. McGann (2014) has recently proposed an alternative method, based on item response theory.

8. From at least one point of view, this conservative advantage is odd. At the same time that a majority of Americans claim a conservative identification, majorities also support the liberal alternative on many policy debates. On average, Americans favor more government spending on education; they want government to try harder to protect the environment; they place higher priority on maintaining programs and services than they do on balancing the budget; and so forth. Ellis and Stimson call this misalignment a paradox, show that it is "an enduring feature of American public opinion" (2012, 98) and dedicate a large part of their stimulating book to explaining it.

9. For party identification conceived of in this way, see, in addition to *The American Voter* (Campbell et al. 1960), writings by Bartels (2000, 2002) and Green, Palmquist, and Schickler (2002). The best-known alternative is set out by Fiorina (1977, 1981).

10. Here is the canonical question in full:

Generally speaking, do you usually think of yourself as a Republican, a Democrat, an Independent, or what?

[If Republican]: Would you call yourself a strong Republican or not a very strong Republican?

[If Democrat]: Would you call yourself a strong Democrat or not a very strong Democrat?

[If Independent or No Preference]: Do you think of yourself as closer to the Republican or to the Democratic Party?

Some of the difference we report in the text between ideological identification and party identification is no doubt explained by differences in question wording. In particular, the ideology question includes an explicit invitation to say no; the party question does not. We investigate the difference that such wordings make to our results—those reported here and over the succeeding chapters—in appendix A.

11. Some of this difference may be caused by question wording: "strong" (partisans) versus "extreme" (ideologues)—although Knight (1987) finds that replacing "extreme" with "very" in the standard ideological identification question is inconsequential.

12. The striking fact is not that ideological identification and party identification are correlated, but that the correlation between the two has increased substantially since the mid-1970s. We will describe this change and do our best to explain it in chapter 6.

Chapter Four

1. Unfortunately, no ideological identification question was included as part of the original 1965 interview. (The ANES version of the question had not yet been invented; it appeared for the first time in the 1972 installment of the election study series.)

2. Figure 4.1 also reveals that, on balance, the class of 1965 tilts slightly in the liberal direction. For the class of 1965, the average score registered on the seven-point scale in 1973 was 3.81, a bit to the left of the ideological center (4.0); for the general public, as assessed by the 1972 ANES, the average score was 4.14, a bit to the right of dead center.

3. Cronbach's *alpha* is .77. On the measurement of information in this fashion, see Zaller 1990, 1992.

4. Ellis and Stimson (2012) suggest that some Americans come to think of themselves as conservative in politics because they follow conservative religious teachings.

5. We are drawing here on Burns, Schlozman, and Verba 2001; Luskin 1987, 1990; Rosenstone and Hansen 1993; and Verba, Schlozman, and Brady 1995.

The concept of political involvement was developed in *The American Voter* (Campbell et al. 1960). For important empirical applications, see, in addition to *The American Voter*, Almond and Verba 1963; Neuman 1986; Prior 2011; Verba and Nie 1972; and Verba, Schlozman, and Brady 1995. Respondents were asked in the 1965 interview how closely they followed government and public affairs and whether they paid attention to political news on television, in newspapers, and on the radio. Our measure of political involvement averages answers across the four questions, and is scored 0 (low) to 1 (high). It has mean of .70, standard deviation of .23, and Cronbach's *alpha* of .54.

6. If we restrict the analysis to the young (Americans under thirty at the time of the survey), the results are virtually identical to those displayed in table 4.2.

Until now, our analysis has relied on years of formal schooling as a measure of skill. An innovation introduced into the 2012 ANES allows us to do better on this score. For the first time, the 2012 ANES included a measure of verbal ability, in the form of a ten-item, multiple-choice vocabulary test. Each item consists of a prompt word and five response choices (plus a "don't know" option). Respondents are asked to select the option that comes closest to the meaning of the prompt. Origins of the test go back to the development of intelligence testing in psychology in the early decades of the twentieth century. In the 1970s, the National Opinion Research Center at the University of Chicago developed a short-form version of a verbal ability test and included it in the General Social Survey (Malhotra, Krosnick, and Haertel 2007).

We treat verbal ability as an aspect of crystalized intelligence. By "intelligence," we mean "a very general mental capability that, among other things, involves the ability to reason, plan, solve problems, think abstractly, comprehend complex ideas, learn quickly, and learn from experience" (Gottfredson 1997, 13). By "crystallized intelligence," we mean the organized storehouse of knowledge about the nature of the world—including politics. Within this framework, the ANES measure of verbal ability represents one component of crystallized intelligence. The pressing question for us here is whether adding a more direct and better measure of ability will alter our understanding of who becomes ideological and who does not. Here are the results:

TABLE 4.7. **Information, involvement, and skill as sources of ideological identification (probit coefficients with standard errors in parentheses)**

Political information	1.04 (.23)
Political involvement	.94 (.22)
Skill	.68 (.21)
High school graduate	.04 (.13)
Associate degree	−.06 (.17)
College graduate	.39 (.16)
Postgraduate degree	.14 (.20)
Constant	−1.08 (.16)
N	1,902

Source: 2012 ANES.

These results strengthen the case we have been building. Becoming ideological is a consequence of information, involvement, and skill.

7. Time is coded 0 to 1, where 0 = interviewed on the day before the elec-

tion and 1 = interviewed on the day after Labor Day. Here are the results for the young (those thirty and under):

TABLE 4.8. **Time to Election Day and likelihood of ideological identification among the young (probit coefficients with standard errors in parentheses)**

Time (days to election/67)	.24 (.14)
Political information	1.50 (.16)
Political involvement	.54 (.12)
Some college	.52 (.07)
College graduate	.73 (.12)
Constant	−.76 (.11)
N	2,241

Source: ANES 1976–2008 (pooled).

We repeated the analysis summarized in the text, taking up each election separately. A suggestion of the expected effect appears in one case and one case only, in 2000. We also ran through the entire analysis one more time, after first excluding respondents who were interviewed either in the first week after the election (eager, easy to reach) or in the final week, immediately before the election (reluctant, hard to reach). Results are the same: as the election nears, the rate of ideological identification slightly declines.

8. The correlation between age and strength of partisanship does not necessarily reflect the effects of aging. It could be aging, but it could also be the product of generational change: in this case, older cohorts entering politics under more highly charged circumstances than younger cohorts, with all cohorts hanging onto their partisan attachments throughout life. A generational account is plausible (Burnham 1970). With cross-sectional data collected within a limited period of time, distinguishing between aging and generational change is impossible. This is known as the cohort conundrum (Converse 1976, 16–24; Mason et al. 1973).

9. Impressive, even more so, because figure 4.2 is restricted to adult citizens and thereby fails to take into account the increasing identification known to occur earlier on, through childhood and adolescence (Converse 1969).

10. Essentially the same pattern appears if we treat "moderate" as nonideological (that is, coded as 0).

Older Americans are less well educated than the young, and as we've just learned, education is a potent predictor of who identifies ideologically and who does not. When we add education into the analysis, the association between age and identification diminishes. Elderly Americans are still less likely to claim an ideological identity than the young, but the difference is cut roughly in half. In contrast, adding education to age in the prediction of partisan strength has no material consequence.

Notice that there are implications of these results for what we should observe among the class of 1965. High school seniors were first interviewed in the spring of 1965, as graduation approached. The same people were questioned three more times and, on each occasion, as we know, were asked whether they thought of themselves in ideological terms: in 1973, once more in 1982, and on one final occasion in 1997. Based on the ANES results, we expect to see an increase in the likelihood that Americans will claim an ideological identification over this period. As Americans move from early adulthood to their middle ages, they should be more likely to claim an ideological identity. And they are: from 87.7 percent in 1973 to 96.9 percent in 1997. (Keep in mind that the sample excludes those in the cohort who dropped out of the education system before graduating from high school and that the percentages are based on study participants who completed all four interviews.)

11. These results are presented in appendix B.

Taken altogether, our findings on moderation resemble those reported by Converse and Pierce (1986) in their study of French voters. Converse and Pierce find, as we do, large numbers of the public attracted to the ideological midpoint. In the French case, the middle is overrun by citizens not much interested in politics, unable to say what distinguishes the left from the right, and confused over where to place French political parties along an ideological continuum. Insofar as political conflict in France takes ideological form, those who choose the ideological middle should be regarded, in Converse and Pierce's estimation, as "noncombatants" (128, 129).

We also investigated *types* of moderates: distinguishing between those who, in a branching version of the standard question, chose "moderate" in response to the first question and then, when pushed gently in a second question, said they felt closer to liberals, felt closer to conservatives, or remained "committed" to moderation. The branching version of the standard question was included in the 1984 and 2000 ANES. On both occasions, "pure" moderates were vastly outnumbered by those who reported that they leaned in an ideological direction (4.1 percent compared to 27.0 percent in 1984; 5.0 percent compared to 18.0 percent in 2000). To our surprise, moderates who leaned to the left or to the right were not that different from pure moderates: not on information, education, political interest, or use of ideological concepts. We were surprised because the results are radically different when it comes to partisanship: independents who lean Democratic or lean Republican are much more engaged in political life than are pure independents (Keith et al. 1992).

12. Converse and Markus (1979) make this point—that the sample base for calculating the stability of ideological identification is markedly smaller and better informed than the base for calculating the stability of party identification.

13. Here's the model:

Ideological Identification$_{t+1}$ = a_0 + B_1Ideological Identification$_t$
+ B_2Information$_t$ + B_3[Information$_t$ × Ideological Identification$_t$] + e

14. Three additional tests also show that the greater stability of party identification over ideological identification holds in online and telephone surveys, and holds as well across variations of the standard ideological identification measure.

In the 2008–9 ANES Panel Study, respondents were recruited by telephone and participated in a series of Internet surveys beginning in January 2008 and ending in September 2009. Five observations of ideological identification were taken: in January, February, June, September, and October. The question used to elicit ideological identification did not include the polite prompt to say "not for me" and was presented in a branching format.

In the 1989 ANES Pilot Study, respondents were interviewed by telephone, and the standard ideological question was replaced by a fully labeled branching format.

Finally, we also analyzed the national panel study carried out in 2006, 2008, and 2010 by the General Social Survey.

In all three instances, the familiar result appears: partisanship is more stable than ideological identification.

Chapter Five

1. Keynes's famous sentence, emphasis intact, appears in *The Tract of Monetary Reform*. Keynes was writing out of frustration with his fellow economists, in particular those who, faced with impending economic calamity, counseled only patience: wait long enough, they would say, and things will be fine. The passage continues: "Economists set themselves too easy, too useless a task if in tempestuous seasons they can only tell us that when the storm is long past the ocean is flat again" (80). Whether Keynes proceeded to prescribe the right remedy for economic affliction is of course debatable, but it is hard to argue with his premise.

2. For the purpose of this comparison, Americans who said that ideological identification was not for them are coded to the midpoint, along with moderates.

3. Kurtosis (k) is calculated thus:

$$k = \{[\text{Sum } (X - x_{mean})^4/N]/s^4)\} - 3$$

One disadvantage of kurtosis is its sensitivity to scale effects. This poses no trouble for our analysis, since we are interested in how kurtosis changes over time (if it does) for a single variable—ideological identification—measured in identical fashion (ruling out scale effects).

4. Our analysis of ideological identification on the General Social Survey series reveals the same thing.

5. If the number of extreme liberals and extreme conservatives doubled every forty years, as it did, roughly, between 1972 and 2012, it would take more than a century for the American electorate to resemble the ideologically polarized (and hypothetical) electorate portrayed in figure 5.1.

6. Following Baldassarri and Gelman 2008, the model is multilevel with varying intercepts and slopes. The model allows the average correlation (given by the intercept) and the time trend (slope) to vary by issue. Formally,

$$r_{it} = \beta_0 + \beta_1 t + \varepsilon_{it}$$

where r_{it} is the correlation between issue i and ideological identification in the year t (in decades).

7. Our results are consistent with those reported by DiMaggio, Evans, and Bryson (1996) but differ somewhat from those reported by Baldassarri and Gelman (2008). As we noted back in chapter 2, Baldassarri and Gelman include in their category of issues a mix of things: preferences on policies, but also general views on equality, attitudes on race, and views on changes in moral standards. We remove these. They report a coefficient estimate for the time parameter (t) for the correlation between ideology and opinion to be .04 (standard error of .01); for the correlation between partisanship and opinion to be .05 (standard error of .01).

8. As such, figure 5.3 amounts to a replication and extension of one of the principal results presented by Iyengar, Sood, and Lelkes (2012).

9. From the 2012 ANES, on the 0-to-100-point thermometer scale, Democrats' rating of Republicans is 31.6, Republicans' rating of Democrats is 34.5, and the public's rating of Congress is 47.0, of illegal immigrants, 40.0, and of atheists, 39.0.

10. We can start the ideology series earlier than the corresponding series for partisanship. Democrats and Republicans did not become part of the ANES thermometer rating battery until 1980.

11. To the best of our knowledge, Green, Palmquist and Schickler (2002) were the first to notice this trend.

12. The increase in consistency between partisanship and ideological identification since the 1970s is more apparent among whites than among blacks, among men than among women, among older Americans than among younger ones, and among the rich than among the poor.

13. Increasing consistency could be a result of an entirely different process: namely, generational replacement. Under generational replacement, older cohorts, whose attachments to party and to ideology were formed in a period when the two parties were less ideologically distinct than they are today, are being gradually replaced by younger cohorts, who are coming of age in a period of party polarization. Fortunately, it is straightforward to determine how much of

the increasing consistency between party identification and ideological identification observed in the ANES from 1972 to 2012 is caused by generational replacement and how much by individual change (Firebaugh 1989). To do so, we
pool the ANES presidential election studies and estimate the effect of time and
cohort (year of birth) on ideological-partisan consistency. With time and cohort
effects estimated, it is a simple matter to calculate how much of the change is a
product of generational replacement or individual change. The model is written
this way:

$$y_{it} = \beta_0 + \beta_1 \text{Time}_{it} + \beta_2 \text{Cohort}_{it} + \varepsilon$$

where

$$y_{it} = \text{Ideological-partisan consistency for the}$$
$$\text{i}^{\text{th}} \text{ respondent in the t}^{\text{th}} \text{ survey;}$$

$$\text{Time}_{it} = \text{Year of measurement of the i}^{\text{th}} \text{ respondent in the t}^{\text{th}} \text{ survey;}$$

$$\text{Cohort}_{it} = \text{Birth year of the i}^{\text{th}} \text{ respondent in the t}^{\text{th}} \text{ survey.}$$

The contribution made by generational replacement is given by:

$$\beta_2[C_T - C_1]$$

where

$$C_T = \text{Average birth year for the sample in the final survey}$$

$$C_1 = \text{Average birth year for the sample in the first survey}$$

While the contribution made by individual change is:

$$\beta_1[YR_T - YR_1]$$

where

$$YR_T = \text{Year of the final survey}$$

$$YR_1 = \text{Year of the first survey}$$

Results show that the increase in the association between partisanship and ideological identification since the 1970s is caused *entirely* by individual change.
Generational replacement does not figure into it.

    14. In equation form:

$$y_{it} = \beta_0 + \beta_1 \text{Party Polarization}_{t-1} + \beta_2 \text{Information}_{it}$$
$$+ \beta_3[\text{Party Polarization}_{t-1} \times \text{Information}_{it}] + \varepsilon$$

$$y_{it} = \text{Ideological-partisan consistency for respondent i at time t}$$

$$\text{Party Polarization}_{t-1} = \text{Ideological distance between}$$

the Democratic congressional party and the
Republican congressional party at time t−1

Information$_{it}$ = Interviewer rating of respondent i at time t.

15. Our model accounts for most of the observed aggregate change in "ideological partisanship." Holding information constant at its mean, we predicted scores on ideological partisanship for minimum and maximum observed values of party polarization. The model predicts an ideological partisanship score of .187 under sample observed minimum polarization and a score of .323 under sample observed maximum polarization. Between 1972 and 2012, actual ideological partisanship from .146 to .386. Explained change is [(.323 − .187)/(.386 − .146)] = 56.7 percent.

16. Our conclusion is consistent with what others have found to be the case when examining the public's views on government policy. Most Americans take moderate positions on most matters of policy, and they are about as moderate in their opinions today as they were decades ago (DiMaggio, Evans, and Bryson 1996; Hetherington 2009; Fiorina and Abrams 2008; Fiorina, Abrams, and Pope 2011). For a dissenting view, see Abramowitz 2010.

17. Sniderman and Stiglitz take us to task (in a northern California sort of way) for being blind to this apparently essential fact:

> Habits die slowly, though. For a research program that aims to provide a theory of ideology as separate and unrelated to party, see Kinder and Kalmoe (2010). From our perspective, to examine ideology independent of party idetification [sic] approximates making steak Bercy without white wine and shallots (2012, 94).

We concede we may need to brush up on our culinary skills. Evidently, preparing steak Bercy without white wine and shallots is an unpardonable act. (In our own defense: one of us is vegetarian, the other gave up his chef's apron after a tragic accident.) That one concession aside, we stand by our insistence that ideology and party are conceptually and empirically distinct.

Chapter Six

1. This is the way democratic politics is supposed to work. Does it work this way? Compare Stimson, MacKuen, and Erikson's analysis (1995) with that of Achen and Bartels (2016).

2. This percentage may seem small. That is because voters are more likely to identify ideologically than nonvoters. In the ANES, combining studies from 1972 to 2008, 79.5 percent of presidential voters claim an identification (if we include "moderate"), compared to 60.2 percent of nonvoters.

3. In equation form, our vote model is written this way:

$$\text{Vote}_{i,t} = \beta_0 + \beta_1 \text{Ideological Identification}_{i,t-1} + \beta_2 \text{Partisanship}_{i,t-1}$$
$$+ \beta_3 \text{Economic Performance}_{i,t} + \beta_4 \text{Views on Policy}_{i,t-1} + \varepsilon$$

$\text{Vote}_{i,t}$ is respondent i's reported presidential vote, coded 1 for the incumbent party's candidate and 0 for the challenging party's candidate (only Democratic and Republican votes are counted). $\text{Partisanship}_{i,t-1}$ is based on the canonical question, coded from −1 (strong Democrat) to +1 (strong Republican). $\text{Economic Performance}_{i,t} = -1$ if economic conditions have gotten much worse (in i's judgment), 0 if economic conditions have not changed, and $= +1$ if economic conditions have gotten much better. $\text{Views on Policy}_{i,t-1}$ is based on i's average response to a set of topical issues: −1 means extreme right, 0 means neither right nor left, and +1 means extreme left. And our key variable, Ideological Identification$_{i,t-1}$, is scored from −1 (extremely liberal) through 0 (moderate) to +1 (extremely conservative), with those who claimed no ideological identification treated as moderates.

4. Also relevant here is the fact that when it comes to presidential voting, moderates and those who decline ideological identification are indistinguishable. We estimated a version of the vote model where ideological identification was represented by four categorical groups: liberals, conservative, those who declined ideological terminology, and moderates. In this analysis, moderates serve as the omitted reference group. The results indicate that when partisanship, views on policy, and assessments of the economy are taken into account, moderates and those who refuse to describe themselves ideologically vote the same way—more evidence that moderation does not represent an ideological stance, and therefore more evidence weighing against ideological voting.

5. The modified vote model is written this way:

$$\text{Vote}_{i,t} = \beta_0 + \beta_1 \text{Extreme Ideological Identification}_{i,t-1} + \beta_2 \text{Average}$$
$$\text{Ideological Identification}_{i,t-1} + \beta_3 \text{Slight Ideological Identification}_{i,t-1}$$
$$+ \beta_4 \text{Strong Partisans}_{i,t-1} + \beta_5 \text{Weak Partisans}_{i,t-1} + \beta_6 \text{Leaning Partisans}_{i,t-1}$$
$$+ \beta_7 \text{Economic Performance}_{i,t} + \beta_8 \text{Views on Policy}_{i,t-1} + \varepsilon$$

In this specification, the intercept (β_0) reflects the baseline vote: that is, the vote cast by those who are neither partisans nor ideologues, who see no change in the economy, and who are at the exact center of disputes over policy. The coefficients for extreme, average, and slight ideological identification reflect the degree to which the choices of voters with these types of ideological commitments depart from the baseline. And likewise for strong, weak, and leaning partisans.

6. In formal terms, the augmented model can be written this way:

$$\text{Vote}_{i,t} = \beta_0 + \beta_1 \text{Ideological Identification}_{i,t-1} + \beta_2 \text{Partisanship}_{i,t-1}$$
$$+ \beta_3 \text{Economic Performance}_{i,t} + \beta_4 \text{Views on Policy}_{i,t-1} + \beta_5 \text{Political}$$

$$\text{Information}_{i, t-1}\, \beta_6[\text{Ideological Identification}_{i, t-1} \times \text{Information}_{i, t-1}]$$
$$+ \beta_7[\text{Partisanship}_{i, t-1} \times \text{Information}_{i, t-1}] + \beta_8[\text{Economic Performance}_{i, t}$$
$$\times \text{Information}_{i, t-1}] + \beta_9[\text{Views on Policy}_{i, t-1} \times \text{Information}_{i, t-1}] + \varepsilon$$

where the "information" is coded -1 (very low) to $+1$ (very high) and all other variables are measured and scored as before. To measure information, we rely on interviewer ratings. At the conclusion of each interview, ANES interviewers are asked to classify each respondent's "general level of information about politics and public affairs" into one of five categories: very low, fairly low, average, fairly high, and very high. This simple rating turns out to be a useful if imperfect measure of information (Zaller 1985, 1992; Bartels 1996; Jacoby 2014), and we take advantage of it here.

7. What about affect? The question here is whether the political consequences of ideological identification depend on the extent to which ideological categories are affectively charged. Motivated reasoning does *not* require citizens to possess a deep understanding of liberalism or conservatism. The logic requires only that citizens have feelings toward liberalism or conservatism. Affect (really, strength of affect) is what is important, not depth of understanding. Under this view, the potency of ideological identification should depend on the degree to which people have real—non-neutral—feelings toward either liberals or conservatives or both. What really matters is the strength of the affective tag attached to ideological terms. Ideological identification should be more consequential among Americans who feel warm toward their own ideological group and cool toward the ideological opposition; among Americans who feel roughly the same toward the two, ideological identification should be inconsequential.

To test this hypothesis, we added two new terms to our original vote model: Strength of Ideological Affect and [Strength of Ideological Affect × Ideological Identification], where Strength of Ideological Affect = |Rating of Liberals – Rating of Conservatives|. By the affective strength hypothesis, we expect to find a significant interaction, in which ideological identification becomes more important to the vote as strength of ideological affect increases. We estimated this augmented vote model in four presidential elections and found support for the interaction hypothesis in one.

8. Insofar as it was possible to do, we took a look at ideological voting in presidential primary elections. In presidential primaries, partisanship is irrelevant (or largely irrelevant), and voters tend to be better informed. So perhaps ideological identification would become more important. We looked at the 1980 ANES Panel Study. That year, Carter was challenged by Ted Kennedy, the iconic liberal; on the Republican side, Reagan, the true conservative, was challenged primarily by George H. Bush. The analysis is hampered by small numbers. That said, in neither case do we detect a significant effect of ideological identification.

9. Whether this is how things actually work in the American case is a matter

of some dispute. On the responsiveness of the US national government to public opinion, see, among others, Achen and Bartels (2016), Miller and Stokes (1963), Bartels (1991, 2008), Erikson, MacKuen, and Stimson (2002), Gilens (2012), and Lenz (2013).

10. In chapter 5, we calculated the correlation between ideological identification and preference on every policy question present on the ANES from 1972 to 2012. The average correlation (Pearson r) was .23.

11. In equation form:

$$y^* = x'\beta + \varepsilon$$

$$y_t^* = \beta_0 + \beta_1 \text{Ideological Identification}_{i,\,t-1}$$
$$+ \beta_2 \text{Partisanship}_{i,\,t-1} + \beta_3 \text{Belief in Limited Government}_{i,\,t-1}$$
$$+ \beta_4 \text{Belief in Equal Opportunity}_{i,\,t-1} + \varepsilon$$

$$\Pr(y = m) = \Pr(\tau_{m-1} < y^* < \tau_m) = \Phi(\tau_m - x'\beta) - \Phi(\tau_{m-1} - x'\beta)$$

In the expressions above, y refers to opinion on a particular policy. The term y^* represents the unobserved latent variable in each case. That is, we assume that the opinion expressed on any particular question arises from a latent, continuous opinion, and that our survey questions segment this continuum at a series of ordered thresholds (y^* falls into one of m categories). Views on policy are assessed at time t and predispositions, including ideological identification, are assessed at time $t\text{-}1$.

In our analysis, opinion variables are coded from −1 to +1, such that higher values indicate the conservative option: more spending on defense, cut spending on welfare, no on abortion, and so on (those who say don't know or they haven't thought about the issue are coded to the middle of the scale, at 0). Ideological Identification is scored from −1 (extremely liberal) through 0 (moderate) to +1 (extremely conservative), with those who claimed no ideological identification coded as missing. Partisanship is based on the canonical question, coded from −1 (strong Democrat) to +1 (strong Republican). Limited government is assessed by a three-item scale developed by Markus (2001), scored to range from −1 to 1 (where 1 represents belief in a government limited in scope and power). Equal opportunity is assessed by a two-item scale (see Feldman 1988), scored to range from −1 to 1 (where 1 represents belief in the importance of equal opportunity).

In the analysis of the 2008–9 ANES Panel Study, the model includes only measures of ideological identification and partisanship.

12. See Nelson and Kinder (1996); Kinder (1998). We'll have more to say about group-centrism in our final chapter.

13. This is how Ellis and Stimson describe the change:

> In the transition year from Kennedy to Johnson, 1963–1964, the ranks of self-identified liberals declined by 1.5 points. That is larger than typical year to year movements, but not so large as to be remarkable.

From 1964, while LBJ was winning landslide reelection, to 1965, there was another drop of 1.4. After 1965, when the 89th Congress set about passing everything in Johnson's "Great Society" package, the drop was more remarkable, another 2.4 points—on top of the previous 2.9. And then in 1966 came a really big drop, 5.2 points, the largest one year movement in the history of the series. (2012, 64)

14. The two equations are written this way:

$$\text{Opinion}_{i,June} = \beta_0 + \beta_1\text{Opinion}_{i,January} + \beta_2\text{Ideological Identification}_{i,January} + \beta_3\text{Party Identification}_{i,January} + \varepsilon$$

$$\text{Opinion}_{i,September} = \beta_0 + \beta_1\text{Opinion}_{i,June} + \beta_2\text{Ideological Identification}_{i,June} + \beta_3\text{Party Identification}_{i,June} + \varepsilon$$

On the policy questions, those who said either that they had not thought about the issue or that they did not know what their opinion was, are coded to the middle (0); ideological identification is scored from −1 (extremely liberal) through 0 (moderate) to +1 (extremely conservative), with those who claimed no ideological identification coded as missing; and partisanship is based on the canonical question, coded from −1 (strong Democrat) to +1 (strong Republican).

15. On this point, see Fiorina (1981); Hibbs (2000); Kinder, Adams, and Gronke (1989); Kramer (1983); and Markus (1988).

16. Economic conditions are measured by change over the past year in real disposable income per capita. According to Douglas Hibbs, "Growth of real disposable income per capita is probably the broadest single aggregate measure of changes in voters' economic well-being, in as much as it includes income from all market sources, is adjusted for inflation, taxes, government transfer payments and population growth, and tends to move with changes in unemployment" (2000, 149). Between the third quarter of 1975 and the third quarter of 1976, real disposable income per capita grew by 2.26 percent; from the third quarter of 1995 to the third quarter of 1996, it grew by 2.13 percent.

17. To be precise: effect of ideological identification (b = −.001, ns in 1976; b = .066, ns in 1996); effect of party identification (b = .310, significant in 1976; b = .126, significant in 1996).

18. Change in the national economy in all years but 1976; there, the question refers to change in "business conditions."

19. In this setup, judgment of the national economy is scored −1 if the respondent said the economy was worsening, 0 if staying the same, and +1 if improving; actual economic change is change in real disposable income per capita over the previous year; and information is the interviewer's rating of each respondent's level of information, coded −1 to +1.

20. Perhaps liberals and conservatives do differ—the relevant coefficient sits

on the borderline of statistical significance—but in any case the difference is slight.

21. Figures are in constant (2009) dollars. Here's the exact wording of the question:

> Would you say that the size of the yearly budget deficit increased, decreased, or stayed about the same during Clinton's time as President?
> Would you say it has increased/decreased a lot or a little?

22. Here's the exact question, which has appeared in every ANES presidential election study starting in 1988 except 1996:

> Would you say that over the past year, the level of unemployment in the country has gotten better, stayed about the same, or gotten worse?
> Would you say much better/worse or somewhat better/worse?

23. Where assessment of unemployment is the person's judgment of change in unemployment over the preceding year, coded −1 if much worse, −.5 if somewhat worse, +.5 if better, and +1 if much better, and ideological identification and party identification as per usual.

24. The story is different for partisanship. Jennings and Markus (1984) show that partisanship responds *sluggishly* to participation in elections. Simulation results arising from their dynamic model imply that an appreciable change in partisanship requires an unbroken series of contrary votes—a possible path, but an improbable one.

25. This is the model in equation form:

$$\text{Ideological Identification}_{i,t} = \beta_0 + \beta_1 \text{Income}_{i,t} + \beta_2 \text{Union}$$
$$\text{Member}_{i,t} + \beta_3 \text{Race}_{i,t} + \beta_4 \text{Gender}_{i,t} + \beta_5 \text{Education}_{i,t}$$
$$+ \beta_6 \text{Age}_{i,t} + \beta_7 \text{Region}_{i,t} + \beta_8 \text{Religion}_{i,t} + \varepsilon$$

where ideological identification is scored from −1 (extremely liberal) through 0 (moderate) to +1 (extremely conservative), with those who claimed no ideological identification treated as missing. Income refers to relative family income. Union member is scored 1 if respondent or some member of respondent's household is a union member, 0 otherwise. Race is scored 1 if black, 0 otherwise. Gender is scored 1 if woman, 0 otherwise. Education, a control variable, is a set of binary variables: less than high school graduate, high school graduate, some college, college degree, postcollege, with high school graduate serving as the excluded reference group. Age is given in years. Region is a set of binary variables corresponding to official census regions (Northeast is excluded reference). Religion is a set of binary variables: atheist or secular, Jewish, Catholic, liberal Protestant, conservative Protestant, mainstream Protestant, and other (a control variable), with mainstream Protestant the excluded reference.

26. Support for the generational hypothesis includes observations that those

active in the protest politics of the 1960s were indelibly altered by their experiences (Jennings 1987) and that Americans remember best those events that took place when they were just entering political life (Schuman, Belli, and Bischoping 1997; Schuman and Rieger 1992; Schuman and Scott 1989).

27. For a detailed and stirring account of this period of American history, see Branch 1988.

28. Based on responses to these questions, we created an index of reaction to the racial crisis. We scored each item to range from 0 (liberal) to 1 (conservative), with each response weighted equally. For the index as a whole, mean = .478, standard deviation = .169 and coefficient *alpha* = .666.

29. Here is the model written in equation form:

$$\text{Ideological Identification}_{i,1997} = \beta_0 + \beta_1 \text{Reaction to the Racial}$$
$$\text{Crisis}_{i,1965,1973} + \beta_2 \text{Parental Class}_{i,1965} + \beta_3 \text{Religion}_{i,1965} + \beta_4 \text{Region}_{i,1965}$$
$$+ \beta_5 \text{Race}_{i,1965} + \beta_6 \text{Gender}_{i,1965} + \varepsilon$$

where ideological identification is scored from −1 (extremely liberal) through 0 (moderate) to +1 (extremely conservative), with those who claimed no ideological identification treated as missing. Political Information is an index based on respondent's answer to six information test items in the 1965 interview and the same six administered in the 1973 interview, scored 0 to 1 (high information). Parental class is represented by a composite measure, scored 0 to 1, based on four equally weighted indicators, all taken from interviews with parents in 1965: head of household's occupation, head of household's education, head of household's spouse's education, and family income (Cronbach's *alpha* = .80). As for religion, our analysis distinguishes among mainline Protestant, evangelical Protestant, Catholic, Jewish, secular, and a small residual category as well. The distinction between evangelical and mainline Protestant is made on the basis of belief in biblical authority. When it comes to region, our analysis distinguishes among South, West, Northeast (the excluded category), and North Central. Race is coded 1 if African American, 0 otherwise. Gender is coded 1 if female, 0 otherwise.

Effects are estimated with Generalized Least Squares, treating families as nested within schools and with variances adjusted for clustering (following Jennings, Stoker, and Bowers 2009).

Chapter Seven

1. As of August 16, 2016, Jost's essay was cited 773 times (according to Google Scholar); an earlier paper setting out a psychological account of ideology published in *Psychological Bulletin* was cited 2,330 times (Jost et al. 2003).

2. Does Jost have anything useful to say on ideology? Yes, absolutely. In sev-

eral essays, Jost summarizes a substantial literature documenting systematic (if modest) relationships between ideology on one hand and temperament and lifestyle on the other (e.g., Jost, Federico, and Napier 2009; Jost, Nosek, and Gosling 2008).

3. Ellis and Stimson are of course free to call answers to ideology self-description questions whatever they wish. They wish to call such answers symbolic ideology, and they define it in terms that are nearly indistinguishable from the operational procedures used to measure it. Symbolic ideology, they say, is "a representation of how citizens think about themselves: whether they consider their views to be liberal, conservative, moderate, or something else" (11).

4. When we look outside the United States, ideological terminology shifts from liberal and conservative to left and right. We assume that the two sets of terms are functionally equivalent (Fuchs and Klingemann 1990).

5. If anything, the literature on ideological identification is more extensive outside the United States than inside. It is curious and disappointing that studies of ideological identification in the United States seem so unconcerned with ideological identification in other parts of the world.

A left-right self-placement question has become a fixture on virtually all the major cross-national surveys. Here's one version of the question, as it appears on the 2010 Americas Barometer:

> Nowadays, when we speak of political leanings, we talk of those on the left and those on the right. In other words, some people sympathize more with the left and others with the right. According to the meaning that the terms "left" and "right" have for you, and thinking of your own political leanings, where would you place yourself on this scale?

Here's another (from the European Community Survey):

> In political matters people talk of the "Left" and the "Right." How would you place your views on this scale?

Notice that the left-right question typically omits the invitation to refuse that is part of the ANES question.

6. Comparisons are inexact because of differences in question format. On one hand, the left-right question has more values (10 rather than 7); on the other hand, the endpoints are labeled "left" and "right" rather than "extreme liberal" and "extreme conservative." And the left-right question does not include a nudge to say: not for me.

Moderation may be a product of affluence. Left-right extremism is negatively associated with economic development. Relatively high levels of ideological extremism are observed in Mexico, Ukraine, Brazil, Albania, and Kyrgyzstan.

As for why some citizens claim the left while others claim the right, the literature offers two primary explanations (as we discussed in chapter 6). The first points to social structure; the second to divisions over prominent issues (e.g., Dalton 2010; deVries, Hakhverdian, and Lancee 2013; Inglehart and Klingemann 1976; Inglehart 1990; Zechmeister and Corral 2012; Sani and Sartori 1983). In either instance, identification is conceived of as a consequence of citizens' reactions to the major conflicts dividing their society. In this respect at least, the view from Europe and Latin America seems ahead of the understanding of ideological identification holding sway in the United States.

7. Converse and Pierce (1986) never use the language of identification. Instead, they say "personal location" or "personal position" or "self-location." The avoidance of the term "identification" seems deliberate. As one of the authors of *The American Voter,* Converse was more than familiar with the theory and language of identification; he and his colleague Pierce choose not to deploy such theory and language in this case. Perhaps they thought it would have been theoretically presumptuous to do so.

8. As we would expect, the pattern changes for more sophisticated segments of the public. Among Americans with some college education, ideological identification moves roughly in tandem with movement in partisanship. Among the sophisticated, shifts in macropartisanship and shifts in macroideology go roughly hand in hand. Movement toward the Democrats is accompanied by movement toward liberalism; likewise for Republicans and conservatism (Box-Steffensmeier and De Boef 2001).

9. On this same point, see Delli Carpini and Keeter (1996) and Weiss et al. (2001), among many others.

Knowledge levels are lower even than we think. In the best of surveys, some of those selected to be part of the sample refuse to participate; some break off the interview shortly after starting; others can never be found. John Brehm (1993) has shown that those who fall out of samples are the sorts of people who do poorly on knowledge tests. In addition, response rates to both household and telephone surveys have been falling steadily for at least two decades. This is true for the ANES, the General Social Survey, the Survey of Consumer Attitudes, the Bureau of Labor Statistics Household Surveys—it is true everywhere (Tourangeau and Plewes 2013). Nonresponse is increasing, and if weighting fails to fully correct for it, then the margin by which we are overestimating what the public knows of politics is likely increasing, too.

10. There are good arguments here, but the practical implications that follow are unclear. Some research finds that conventional practice leads to underestimation of the public's level of knowledge (Mondak 2001; Mondak and Davis 2001; Krosnick et al. 2008); other research concludes that that alterations in standard practice produce trivial gains in knowledge or no gains at all (Sturgis, Allum, and Smith 2008; Luskin and Bullock 2011).

If knowledge tests are modified to follow, as the current critics would have it, best practices, the importance of political knowledge actually increases. Properly assessed, knowledge is even more consequential than we have been saying (Mondak 2001; Mondak and Anderson 2004).

Finally, when citizens are paid for correct answers or when they are given ample time to research answers to questions about politics, they do better (Prior and Lupia 2008). But the improvements are surprisingly small. And while Prior and Lupia's experiment demonstrates that citizens are capable of doing (somewhat) better under special circumstances, we should remember that estimates of the public's knowledge typically come from surveys carried out in and around national elections, when conditions seem most propitious for performance on knowledge tests. In these contexts, citizens are being bombarded with political communication, interest and discussion are peaking, and parties and interest groups are mobilizing (Luskin and Bullock 2011).

11. On these points see, among others: Sturgis and Smith 2010; Mondak 2001; Price and Zaller 1993; Gilens 2001; Fiske and Kinder 1981; Bartels 1988; Delli Carpini and Keeter 1996; Kinder and Kam 2009; Zaller 1992; Iyengar 1990; Verba, Schlozman, and Brady 1995; Popkin and Dimock 1999; Burns, Schlozman, and Verba 2001.

Command of political knowledge is correlated with things that also matter to politics, such as interest, ability, and attention to news. When mass publics are partitioned by information, they are also being partitioned by these other factors. If information effects are estimated without taking into account interest, ability, attention, and so on, biased estimates caused by omitted variables may be the result (Levendusky 2011).

12. This section of the chapter draws liberally from Kinder 1998, Kinder and Kam 2009, and Kinder and Dale-Riddle 2012.

13. For evidence on this point, see Brewer and Campbell 1976; Tajfel et al. 1971; Brewer and Brown 1998; and Kinder and Kam 2009. For an argument that ethnocentrism constitutes an evolutionary adaptation, see Lumsden and Wilson 1981; Sober and Wilson 1998; and Wilson and Wilson 2007.

The assumption of group motivation is bolstered indirectly by the surprising unimportance of *self-interest*. When it comes to explaining American public opinion, the assumption of fundamentally selfish citizens doesn't carry us very far (e.g., Sears et al. 1980; Citrin and Green 1990; Green 1992).

Appendix A

1. The 1986 ANES Time Series Study also included the branching format, as did several ANES off-year pilot studies and the 2008–9 ANES Panel. We focus here on the two presidential year surveys, which include both face-to-face and telephone interviews.

2. Our results are consistent with those reported by Knight (1987).

References

Abelson, Robert P. 1959. Modes of resolution of belief dilemmas. *Journal of Conflict Resolution* 3:343–52.

———. 1968. Psychological implication. In *Theories of cognitive consistency: A sourcebook*, edited by Robert P. Abelson, Elliot Aronson, William J. McGuire, Theodore M. Newcomb, Milton J. Rosenberg, and Percy H. Tannenbaum, 112–39. Chicago: Rand McNally.

———. 1976. A script theory of understanding, attitude, and behavior. *Cognition and social behavior*. Hillsdale, NJ: Erlbaum.

———. 1986. Beliefs are like possessions. *Journal for the Theory of Social Behavior* 16 (3): 223–50.

Abercrombie, Nicholas, Stephen Hill, and Bryan S. Turner. 1980. *The dominant ideology thesis*. London: Allen and Unwin.

Abramowitz, Alan I. 2010. *The disappearing center: Engaged citizens, polarization, and American democracy*. New Haven, CT: Yale University Press.

Achen, Christopher H. 1975. Mass political attitudes and the survey response. *American Political Science Review* 69:1218–31.

———. 1983. Toward theories of data: The state of political methodology. In *Political science: The state of the discipline*, edited by Ada W. Finifter, 69–93. Washington, DC: American Political Science Association.

Achen, Christopher H., and Larry M. Bartels. 2016. *Democracy for realists*. Princeton, NJ: Princeton University Press.

Adams, Greg D. 1997. Abortion: Evidence of an issue evolution. *American Journal of Political Science* 41 (3): 718–37.

Adorno, Theodor W., Else Frenkel-Brunswik, Daniel J. Levinson, and R. Nevitt Sanford. 1950. *The authoritarian personality*. New York: Harper and Row.

Almond, Gabriel A., and Sidney Verba. 1963. *The civic culture: Political attitudes and democracy in five nations*. Princeton, NJ: Princeton University Press.

Ansolabehere, Stephen, Nathan Rodden, and James M. Snyder Jr. 2008. The strength of issues: Using multiple measures to gauge preference stability, ideological constraint, and issue voting. *American Political Science Review* 102 (2): 215–32.

Arceneaux, Kevin, and Martin Johnson. 2013. *Changing minds or changing channels? Partisan news in an age of choice.* Chicago: University of Chicago Press.

Baldassarri, Delia, and Andrew Gelman. 2008. Partisans without constraint: Political polarization and trends in American public opinion. *American Journal of Sociology* 114 (2): 408–46.

Baker, Peter. 2013. Obama offers liberal vision. *New York Times*, January 21, 2013.

Banaji, Mahzarin R., and Larisa A. Heiphetz. 2010. Attitudes. In *Handbook of social psychology*, edited by D. T. Gilbert and S. T. Fiske, 353–93. Hoboken, NJ: John Wiley & Sons.

Bartels, Larry M. 1988. *Presidential primaries and the dynamics of public choice.* Princeton, NJ: Princeton University Press.

——. 1991. Constituency opinion and congressional policy making: The Reagan defense buildup. *American Political Science Review* 85 (2): 457–74.

——. 1996. Uninformed votes: Information effects in presidential elections. *American Journal of Political Science* 40:194–230.

——. 2000. Partisanship and voting behavior, 1952–1996. *American Journal of Political Science* 44:35–50.

——. 2002. Beyond the running tally: Partisan bias in political perceptions. *Political Behavior* 24:117–50.

——. 2008. *Unequal democracy: The political economy of the new gilded age.* Princeton, NJ: Princeton University Press.

Bem, Daryl J. 1965. An experimental analysis of self-persuasion. *Journal of Experimental Social Psychology* 1:199–218.

——. 1972. Self-perception theory. *Advances in Experimental Social Psychology* 6:1–62.

Bennett, Stephen Earl. 1988. "Know-nothings" revisited: The meaning of political ignorance today. *Social Science Quarterly* 69 (2): 476–90.

——. 1989. Trends in Americans' political information, 1967–1987. *American Politics Quarterly* 17 (4): 422–35.

Benoit, Kenneth, and Michael Laver. 2006. *Party policy in modern democracies.* New York: Routledge.

Berinsky, Adam J. 2009. *In time of war.* Chicago: University of Chicago Press.

Bishop, George F., Robert W. Oldendick, Alfred J. Tuchfarber, and Stephen E. Bennett. 1980. Pseudo-opinions on public affairs. *Public Opinion Quarterly* 44 (2): 198–209.

Bishop, George F., Alfred J. Tuchfarber, and Robert W. Oldendick. 1986. Opinion on fictitious issues: The pressure to answer survey questions. *Public Opinion Quarterly* 50 (2): 240–50.

Bobbio, Norberto. 1996. *Left and right: The significance of a political distinction.* Translated by Allan Cameron. Chicago: University of Chicago Press.

Box-Steffensmeier, Janet, and Suzanna De Boef. 2001. Macropartisanship and macroideology in the sophisticated electorate. *Journal of Politics* 63 (1): 232–48.

Box-Steffensmeier, Janet, Kathleen Knight, and Lee Sigelman. 1998. The interplay of macropartisanship and macroideology: A time series analysis. *Journal of Politics* 60:1031–49.

Branch, Taylor. 1988. *Parting the waters.* New York: Simon and Schuster.

Brehm, John. 1993. *The phantom respondents: Opinion surveys and political representation.* Ann Arbor: University of Michigan Press.

Brewer, Marilyn B., and Rupert J. Brown. 1998. Intergroup relations. In *Handbook of social psychology*, 4th ed., edited by Daniel Gilbert, Susan T. Fiske, and Gardner Lindzey, 554–94. Boston: McGraw-Hill.

Brewer, Marilyn B., and Donald T. Campbell. 1976. *Ethnocentrism and intergroup attitudes.* New York: Wiley.

Brody, Charles J. 1986. Things are rarely black and white: Admitting gray into the Converse model of attitude stability. *American Journal of Sociology* 92 (3): 657–77.

Budge, Ian, Hans-Dieter Klingemann, Andrea Volkens, Judith Bara, and Eric Tanenbaum. 2001. *Mapping policy preferences: Estimates for parties, electors, and governments, 1945–1998.* Vol. 1. New York: Oxford University Press.

Budge, Ian, David Robertson, and Derek Hearl, eds. 1987. *Ideology, strategy and party change: Spatial analyses of post-war election programmes in 19 democracies.* New York: Cambridge University Press.

Burnham, Walter Dean. 1970. *Critical elections and the mainsprings of American politics.* New York: Norton.

Burns, Nancy, Kay Lehman Schlozman, and Sidney Verba. 2001. *The private roots of public action.* Cambridge, MA: Harvard University Press.

Butler, David, and Donald Stokes. 1969. *Political change in Britain: Forces shaping electoral choice.* New York: St. Martin's Press.

Campbell, Angus, Philip E. Converse, Warren E. Miller, and Donald E. Stokes. 1960. *The American voter.* New York: Wiley.

Carmines, Edward G., and James A. Stimson. 1989. *Issue evolution: Race and the transformation of American politics.* Princeton, NJ: Princeton University Press.

Castles, Francis G., and Peter Mair. 1984. Left-right political scales: Some 'expert' judgments. *European Journal of Political Research* 12:73–88.

Chase, William G., and Herbert A. Simon. 1973. Perception in chess. *Cognitive psychology* 4 (1): 55–81.

Chi, Michelene T. H., Robert Glaser, and Marshall J. Farr. 2014. *The nature of expertise*. New York: Psychology Press.

Citrin, Jack, and Donald P. Green. 1990. The self-interest motive in American public opinion. *Research in Micropolitics* 3:1–28.

Citrin, Jack, Beth Reingold, and Donald P. Green. 1990. The "Official English" movement and the symbolic politics of language in the United States. *Western Political Quarterly* 43 (3): 535–49.

Conover, Pamela Johnston, and Stanley Feldman. 1981. The origins and meanings of liberal/conservative self-identifications. *American Journal of Political Science* 25:617–45.

Converse, Philip E. 1964. The nature of belief systems in mass publics. In *Ideology and discontent*, edited by D. E. Apter, 206–61. New York: Free Press.

———. 1966a. The concept of a normal vote. In *Elections and the political order*, edited by Angus Campbell, Philip E. Converse, Donald Stokes, and Warren E. Miller, 9–39. New York: Wiley.

———. 1966b. Religion and politics: the 1960 election. In *Elections and the political order*, edited by Angus Campbell, Philip E. Converse, Donald Stokes, and Warren E. Miller, 96–124. New York: Wiley.

———. 1969. Of time and partisan stability. *Comparative Political Studies* 2 (2): 139–71.

———. 1970. Attitudes and non-attitudes: Continuation of a dialogue. In *Analysis of social problems*, edited by Edward R. Tufte, 168–89. Reading, MA: Addison-Wesley.

———. 1975. Public opinion and voting behavior. In *Policies and policymaking*, edited by Fred I. Greenstein and Nelson W. Polsby, 75–169. Handbook of political science 6. Reading, MA: Addison-Wesley.

———. 1976. *The dynamics of party support: Cohort-analyzing party identification*. Beverly Hills, CA: Sage.

———. 2000. Assessing the capacity of mass electorates. *Annual Review of Political Science* 3:331–53.

———. 2006. Reply: Democratic theory and electoral reality. *Critical Review* 18 (1–3): 297–330.

———. 2007. Perspectives on mass belief systems and communication. In *The Oxford handbook of political behavior*, edited by Russell J. Dalton and Hans-Dieter Klingemann, 144–58. New York: Oxford University Press.

Converse, Philip E., and Gregory B. Markus. 1979. Plus ça change . . . : The new CPS election study panel. *American Political Science Review* 73:32–49.

Converse, Philip E., and Roy Pierce. 1985. Measuring partisanship. *Political Methodology* 11(3/4): 143–66.

———. 1986. *Political representation in France*. Cambridge, MA: Belknap Press of Harvard University Press.

Cover, Albert D., and David R. Mayhew. 1977. Congressional dynamics and the decline of competitive congressional elections. In *Congress reconsidered*, edited by Lawrence C. Dodd and Bruce I. Oppenheimer, 54–72. Washington, DC: Congressional Quarterly Press.

Dahl, Robert. 1956. *A preface to democracy*. Chicago: University of Chicago Press.

Dalton, Russell J. 2010. Ideology, partisanship, and democratic development. In *Comparing democracies: Elections and voting in the 21st century*, 3rd ed., edited by Lawrence LeDuc, Richard Niemi, and Pippa Norris, 143–65. London: SAGE Publications Ltd.

Delli Carpini, Michael, and Scott Keeter. 1996. *What Americans know about politics and why it matters*. New Haven, CT: Yale University Press.

Destutt de Tracy, A. 1801. *Éléments d'Ideologie*. Paris: Didot.

deVries, Catherine E., Armen Hakhverdian, and Bram Lancee. 2013. The dynamics of voters' left/right identification: The role of economic and cultural attitudes. *Political Science Research & Methods* 1 (2): 223–38.

DiMaggio, Paul, John Evans, and Bethany Bryson. 1996. Have Americans' social attitudes become more polarized? *American Journal of Sociology* 102 (3): 690–755.

Downs, Anthony. 1957. *An economic theory of democracy*. New York: Harper.

Dworkin, Ronald W. 2006. *Is democracy possible here? Principles for a new political debate*. Princeton, NJ: Princeton University Press.

Ellis, Christopher, and James A. Stimson. 2009. Symbolic ideology in the American electorate. *Electoral Studies* 28:388–402.

———. 2012. *Ideology in America*. New York: Cambridge University Press.

Elster, Jon. 1985. *Making sense of Marx*. New York: Cambridge University Press.

Epstein, Lee, Christopher M. Parker, and Jeffrey A. Segal. 2013. Do justices defend the speech they hate? In-group bias, opportunism, and the first amendment. Paper presented at the annual meeting of the American Political Science Association.

Erikson, Robert S. 1979. The SRC panel data and mass political attitudes. *British Journal of Political Science* 9 (1): 89–114.

Erikson, Robert S., Michael B. MacKuen, and James A. Stimson. 2002. *The macro polity*. New York: Cambridge University Press.

Feldman, Stanley. 1988. Structure and consistency in public opinion: The role of core beliefs and values. *American Journal of Political Science* 32 (2): 416–40.

———. 1989. Measuring issue preferences: The problem of response instability. *Political Analysis* 1(1): 25–60.

———. 2003. Values, ideology, and the structure of political attitudes. In *Oxford handbook of political psychology*, edited by David O. Sears, Leonie Huddy, and Robert Jervis, 477–508. New York: Oxford University Press.

Festinger, Leon. 1957. *A theory of cognitive dissonance.* Stanford: Stanford University Press.

Field, John O., and Ronald E. Anderson. 1969. Ideology in the public's conceptualization of the 1964 election. *Public Opinion Quarterly* 33 (3): 380–98.

Fiorina, Morris P. 1977. An outline for a model of party choice. *American Journal of Political Science* 21:601–25.

———. 1981. *Retrospective voting in American national elections.* New Haven, CT: Yale University Press.

Fiorina, Morris P., and Samuel Abrams. 2008. Political polarization in the American public. *Annual Review of Political Science* 11:563–88.

Fiorina, Morris P., Samuel J. Abrams, and Jeremy C. Pope. 2011. *Culture war? The myth of a polarized America.* New York: Pearson Longman Press.

Firebaugh, Glenn. 1989. *Analyzing repeated surveys.* Sage University Paper Series in Quantitative Applications in the Social Sciences, No. 07-115. Thousand Oaks, CA: Sage.

Fiske, Susan T., and Donald R. Kinder. 1981. Involvement, expertise, and schema use: Evidence from political cognition. In *Personality, cognition, and social interaction*, edited by Nancy Cantor and John F. Kihlstrom, 171–90. Hillsdale, NJ: Erlbaum.

Free, Lloyd A., and Hadley Cantril. 1967. *The political beliefs of Americans: A study of public opinion.* New Brunswick, NJ: Rutgers University Press.

Freeden, Michael. 2003. *Ideology: A very short introduction.* New York: Oxford University Press.

Fuchs, Dieter, and Hans-Dieter Klingemann. 1990. The left-right schema. In *Continuities in political action*, by M. Kent Jennings et al., 203–34. Berlin: Walter de Gruyter.

Gaines, Brian J., James H. Kuklinski, Paul J. Quirk, Buddy Peyton, and Jay Verkuilen. 2007. Same facts, different interpretations: Partisan motivation and opinion on Iraq. *Journal of Politics* 69 (4): 957–74.

Gauchet, Marcel. 1992. La droite et la gauche. In *Les lieux de mémoire*, edited by Pierre Nora, vol. 3, *Les France.* Paris: Gallimard.

Geertz, Clifford. 1973. Ideology as a cultural system. In *The interpretation of cultures: Selected essays*, edited by Clifford Geertz, 193–233. New York: Basic Books.

Gerber, Alan, and Donald Green. 2000. The effects of canvassing, telephone calls, and direct mail on voter turnout: A field experiment. *American Political Science Review* 94 (3): 653–63.

Gerber, Alan S., Gregory A. Huber, and Ebonya Washington. 2010. Party affiliation, partisanship, and political beliefs: A field experiment. *American Political Science Review* 104 (4): 720–44.

Gerring, John. 1997. Ideology: A definitional analysis. *Political Research Quarterly* 50 (4): 957–94.

———. 1998. *Party ideologies in America, 1828–1996*. New York: Cambridge University Press.

Gilens, Martin. 1996. "Race coding" and white opposition to welfare. *American Political Science Review* 90 (3): 593–604.

———. 2001. Political ignorance and collective policy preferences. *American Political Science Review* 95 (2): 379–96.

———. 2012. *Affluence and influence*. Princeton, NJ: Princeton University Press.

Goldwater, Barry. 1960. *Conscience of a conservative*. Shepherdsville, KY: Victor.

Goren, Paul. 2001. Core principles and policy reasoning in mass publics: A test of two theories. *British Journal of Political Science* 31:159–77.

Gottfredson, Linda S. 1997. Mainstream science on intelligence: An editorial with 52 signatories, history, and bibliography. *Intelligence* 24 (1): 13–23.

Graham, Jesse, Jonathan Haidt, and Brian A. Nosek. 2009. Liberals and conservatives rely on different sets of moral foundations. *Personality Processes and Individual Differences* 96 (5): 1029–46.

Green, Donald P. 1992. The price elasticity of mass preferences. *American Political Science Review* 86 (1): 128–48.

Green, Donald P., and Alan S. Gerber. 2008. *Get out the vote: How to increase voter turnout*. Washington, DC: Brookings Institution Press.

Green, Donald, Bradley Palmquist, and Eric Schickler. 2002. *Partisan hearts and minds*. New Haven, CT: Yale University Press.

Hagner, Paul R., and John C. Pierce. 1982. Correlative characteristics of levels of conceptualization in the American public, 1956–76. *Journal of Politics* 44 (3): 779–807.

Hetherington, Marc. 2001. Resurgent mass partisanship: The role of elite polarization. *American Political Science Review* 95 (3): 619–31.

———. 2009. Putting polarization in perspective. *British Journal of Political Science* 39 (2): 413–48.

Hetherington, Marc, and Thomas Rudolph. 2015. *Why Washington won't work: Polarization, political trust, and the governing crisis*. Chicago: University of Chicago Press.

Hibbs Jr., Douglas A. 2000. Bread and peace voting in U.S. presidential elections. *Public Choice* 104:149–80.

Highton, Benjamin. 2009. Revisiting the relationship between educational attainment and political sophistication. *Journal of Politics* 71 (4): 1564–76.

Hofstadter, Richard. 1965. *The paranoid style in American politics*. New York: Knopf.

Hooghe, Liesbet, Gary Marks, and Carole J. Wilson 2002. Does left/right structure party positions on European integration? *Comparative Political Studies* 35 (8): 965–89.

Huber, John. 1989. Values and partisanship in left-right orientations: Measuring ideology. *European Journal of Political Research* 17 (5): 599–621.

Huber, John, and Ronald Inglehart. 1995. Expert interpretations of party space and party locations in 42 societies. *Party Politics* 1 (1): 73–111.

Hunter, James Davison. 1992. *Culture wars: The struggle to control the family, art, education, law, and politics in America.* New York: Basic Books.

———. 1994. *Before the shooting begins: Searching for democracy in America's culture war.* New York: Simon & Schuster.

Hunter, James Davison, and Alan Wolfe. 2006. *Is there a culture war? A dialogue on values and American public life.* Washington, DC: Brookings Institution Press.

Inglehart, Ronald. 1985. Aggregate stability and individual-level flux in mass belief systems: The level of analysis paradox. *American Political Science Review* 79 (1): 97–116.

———. 1990. Values, ideology, and cognitive mobilization in new social movements. In *Challenging the political order*, edited by R. Dalton and M. Kuechler, 43–66. Cambridge: Polity Press.

Inglehart, Ronald, and Hans-Dieter Klingemann. 1976. Party identification, ideological preference, and the left-right dimension among Western mass publics. In *Party identification and beyond*, edited by Ian Budge, Ivor Crewe, and Dennis Farlie. London: Wiley.

Iyengar, Shanto. 1990. Shortcuts to political knowledge: Selective attention and the accessibility bias. In *Information and the democratic process*, edited by John Ferejohn and James Kuklinski, 160–85. Urbana: University of Illinois Press.

Iyengar, Shanto, and Donald R. Kinder. 1987. *News that matters: Television and American opinion.* Chicago: University of Chicago Press.

Iyengar, Shanto, Guarav Sood, and Yptach Lelkes. 2012. Affect, not ideology: A social identity perspective on polarization. *Public Opinion Quarterly* 76 (3): 405–31.

Iyengar, Shanto, and Sean J. Westwood. 2014. Fear and loathing across party lines: New evidence on group polarization. *American Journal of Political Science* 59 (3): 690–707.

Jacobson, Gary C. 2008. *A divider, not a uniter: George W. Bush and the American people: The 2006 election and beyond.* New York: Pearson Longman.

Jacobs, Lawrence R., and Robert Y. Shapiro. 1994. Issues, candidate image, and priming: The use of private polls in Kennedy's 1960 presidential campaign. *American Political Science Review* 88 (3): 527–40.

Jacoby, William G. 1991. Ideological identification and issue attitudes. *American Journal of Political Science* 35:178–205.

———. 1995. The structure of ideological thinking in the American electorate. *American Journal of Political Science* 39:314–35.

———. 2014. Is there a culture war? Conflicting value structures in American public opinion. *American Political Science Review* 108:754–71.

Jennings, M. Kent. 1987. Residues of a movement: The aging of the American protest generation. *American Political Science Review* 81 (2): 367–82.

———. 1992. Ideology among mass publics and political elites. *Public Opinion Quarterly* 56:419–41.

Jennings, M. Kent, and Gregory B. Markus. 1984. Partisan orientations over the long haul: Results from the three-wave political socialization panel study. *American Political Science Review* 78:1000–1018.

Jennings, M. Kent, Laura Stoker, and Jake Bowers. 2009. Politics across generations: Family transmission reexamined. *Journal of Politics* 71:782–99.

Jessee, Stephen A. 2012. *Ideology and spatial voting in American elections*. New York: Cambridge University Press.

Jost, John T. 2006. The end of the end of ideology. *American Psychologist* 61: 651–70.

Jost, John T., Christopher M. Federico, and Jaime L. Napier. 2009. Political ideology: Its structure, functions, and elective affinities. *Annual Review of Psychology* 60:307–37.

Jost, John T., Jack Glaser, Arie W. Kruglanski, and Frank J. Sulloway. 2003. Political conservatism as motivated social cognition. *Psychological Bulletin* 129 (3): 339–75.

Jost, John T., Brian A. Nosek, and Samuel D. Gosling. 2008. Ideology: Its resurgence in social, personality, and political psychology. *Perspectives on Psychological Science* 3:126–36.

Judd, Charles M., and Michael A. Milburn. 1980. The structure of attitude systems in the general public: Comparisons of a structural equation model. *American Sociological Review* 45:627–43.

Keith, Bruce E., David B. Magleby, Candice J. Nelson, Elizabeth Orr, Mark C. Westlye, and Raymond E. Wolfinger. 1992. *The myth of the independent voter*. Berkeley: University of California Press.

Kennedy, David. 1999. *Freedom from fear*. New York: Oxford University Press.

Kerlinger, Fred N. 1967. Social attitudes and their criterial referents: A structural theory. *Psychological Review* 74 (2): 110–22.

———. 1984. *Liberalism and conservatism: The nature and structure of social attitudes*. Vol. 1. Hillsdale, NJ: Lawrence Erlbaum.

Keynes, John Maynard. 1924. *A tract of monetary reform*. New York: MacMillan.

Kinder, Donald R. 1983. Diversity and complexity in American public opinion. In *Political science: The state of the discipline*, edited by Ada Finifter, 391–401. Washington, DC: American Political Science Association.

———. 1998. Opinion and action in the realm of politics. In *Handbook of social psychology*, 4th ed., edited by D. Gilbert, S. Fiske, and G. Lindsey, 778–867. Boston: McGraw Hill.

Kinder, Donald R., Gordon S. Adams, and Paul W. Gronke. 1989. Economics and politics in the 1984 American presidential election. *American Journal of Political Science* 33 (2): 491–515.

Kinder, Donald R., and Allison Dale-Riddle. 2012. *The end of race?* New Haven, CT: Yale University Press.

Kinder, Donald R., and Cindy Kam. 2009. *Us against them: Ethnocentric foundations of American opinion.* Chicago: University of Chicago Press.

Kinder, Donald R., and D. Roderick Kiewiet. 1981. Sociotropic politics: The American case. *British Journal of Political Science* 11 (2): 129–61.

Kinder, Donald R., and Lynn M. Sanders. 1996. *Divided by color: Racial politics and democratic ideals.* Chicago: University of Chicago Press.

Kinder, Donald R., and David O. Sears. 1981. Prejudice and politics: Symbolic racism versus racial threats to the good life. *Journal of Personality and Social Psychology* 40 (3): 414–31.

Klingemann, Hans D. 1979. Measuring ideological conceptualizations. In *Political action*, by S. Barnes et al., 279–303. Beverly Hills, CA: Sage Publications.

Knight, Kathleen. 1985. Ideology in the 1980 election: Ideological sophistication does matter. *Journal of Politics* 47:828–53.

———. 1987. *Measurement of liberal/conservative identification.* American National Election Study Technical Report. Ann Arbor: Center for Political Studies, University of Michigan.

Kramer, Gerald H. 1971. Short-term fluctuations in U.S. voting behavior, 1896–1964. *American Political Science Review* 65 (1): 131–43.

———. 1983. The ecological fallacy revisited: Aggregate- versus individual-level findings on economics and elections, and sociotropic voting. *American Political Science Review* 77 (1): 92–111.

Krosnick, Jon A., and Matthew K. Berent. 1993. Comparisons of party identification and policy preferences: The impact of survey question format. *American Journal of Political Science* 37: 941–64.

Krosnick, Jon A., and Donald R. Kinder. 1990. Altering the foundations of support for the president through priming. *American Political Science Review* 84 (2): 497–512.

Krosnick, Jon A., Arthur Lupia, Matthew DeBell, and Darrell Donakowski. 2008. *Problems with ANES questions measuring political knowledge.* American National Election Study Technical Report. Ann Arbor: Center for Political Studies, University of Michigan.

Krosnick, Jon A., Penny S. Visser, and Joshua Harder. 2010. The psychological underpinnings of political behavior. In *Handbook of social psychology*, 5th ed., edited by Susan T. Fiske, Daniel T. Gilbert, and Gardner Lindzey, 2:1288–1342. New York: Wiley.

Kuklinski, James H., and Buddy Peyton. 2007. Belief systems and political decision-making. In *The Oxford handbook of political behavior*, edited by

Russell J. Dalton and Hans-Dieter Klingemann, 45–64. New York: Oxford University Press.

Kuklinski, James H., Paul J. Quirk, Jennifer Jerit, David Schweider, and Robert F. Rich. 2000. Misinformation and the currency of democratic citizenship. *Journal of Politics* 62 (3): 790–816.

Lakoff, Sanford. 2011. *Ten political ideas that have shaped the modern world.* New York: Rowman & Littlefield.

Lane, Robert E. 1962. *Political ideology.* New York: Free Press of Glencoe.

———. 1969. *Political thinking and consciousness: The private life of the political mind.* Markham Publishing.

———. 1973. Patterns of political belief. In *Handbook of political psychology*, edited by Jeanne N. Knutson. San Francisco: Jossey-Bass.

Laponce, J. A. 1981. *Left and right: The topography of political perceptions.* Toronto: University of Toronto Press.

Laver, Michael, and Ian Budge. 1992. Measuring policy distances and modelling coalition formation. In *Party policy and government coalitions*, edited by Michael Laver and Ian Budge, 15–40. Basingstoke, UK: Macmillan.

Lazarsfeld, Paul, Bernard Berelson, and Hazel Gaudet. 1948. *The people's choice.* 2nd ed. New York: Columbia University Press.

Lenz, Gabriel. 2013. *Follow the leader? How voters respond to politicians' policies and performance.* Chicago: University of Chicago Press.

Levendusky, Matthew. 2009. *The partisan sort.* Chicago: University of Chicago Press.

———. 2011. Rethinking the role of political information. *Public Opinion Quarterly* 75 (1): 42–64.

Levin, Yuval. 2014. *The great debate: Edmund Burke, Thomas Paine, and the Birth of Right and Left.* New York: Basic Books.

Levitin, Teresa A., and Warren E. Miller. 1979. Ideological interpretations of presidential elections. *American Political Science Review* 73 (3): 751–71.

Lewis-Beck, Michael, William G. Jacoby, Helmut Norpoth, and Herbert F. Weisberg. 2008. *The American voter revisited.* Ann Arbor: University of Michigan Press.

Lippmann, Walter. 1925. *The phantom public.* New York: Harcourt, Brace.

Lipset, Seymour Martin. 1967. *The first new nation.* New York: Anchor Books.

Lumsden, Charles J., and Edward O. Wilson. 1981. *Genes, mind, and culture: The coevolutionary process.* Cambridge, MA: Harvard University Press.

Lupia, Arthur. 2006. How elitism undermines the study of voter competence. *Critical Review* 18(1–3): 217–32.

———. 2016. *Uninformed: Why people know so little about politics and what we can do about it.* New York: Oxford University Press.

Lupia, Arthur, and Mathew McCubbins. 1998. *The democratic dilemma: Can citizens learn what they need to know.* New York: Cambridge University Press.

Luskin, Robert C. 1987. Measuring political sophistication. *American Journal of Political Science* 31 (4): 856–99.

———. 1990. Explaining political sophistication. *Political Behavior* 12 (4): 331–61.

Luskin, Robert C., and John G. Bullock. 2011. "Don't know" means "don't know": DK responses and the public's level of political knowledge. *Journal of Politics* 73 (2): 547–57.

Malhotra, Neil, Jon A. Krosnick, and Edward Haertel. 2007. *The psychometric properties of the GSS Wordsum vocabulary test.* GSS Methodological Report. National Opinion Research Center, University of Chicago.

Mann, Thomas E., and Norman J. Ornstein. 2013. *It's even worse than it looks: How the American constitutional system collided with the new politics of extremism.* New York: Basic Books.

Mann, Thomas E., and Raymond E. Wolfinger. 1980. Candidates and parties in congressional elections. *American Political Science Review* 74 (3): 617–32.

Mannheim, Karl. [1928] 1952. The problem of generations. In *Essays on the sociology of knowledge,* edited by P. Kecskemeti, 276–332. London: Routledge and Kegan Paul.

Markus, Gregory B. 1982. Political attitudes during an election year: A report on the 1980 NES panel study. *American Political Science Review* 76:538–60.

———. 1988. The impact of personal and national economic conditions on presidential voting, 1956–1988. *American Journal of Political Science* 36 (3): 829–34.

———. 2001. American individualism reconsidered. In *Citizens and politics: Perspectives from political psychology,* edited by James H. Kuklinski, 401–32. New York: Cambridge University Press.

Markus, Gregory B., and Philip E. Converse. 1979. A dynamic simultaneous equation model of electoral choice. *American Political Science Review* 73 (4): 1055–70.

Mason, Karen O., William M. Mason, H. H. Winsborough, and W. Kenneth Poole. 1973. Some methodological issues in cohort analysis of archival data. *American Sociological Review* 38 (2): 242–58.

McCann, James A. 1997. Electoral choices and core value change: The 1992 presidential campaign. *American Journal of Politics* 41 (2): 564–83.

McCarty, Nolan, Keith T. Poole, and Howard Rosenthal. 2006. *Polarized America: The dance of ideology and unequal riches.* Cambridge, MA: MIT Press.

McClosky, Herbert. 1964. Consensus and ideology in American politics. *American Political Science Review* 58 (2): 361–82.

McGann, Anthony J. 2014. Estimating the political center from aggregate data: An item response theory alternative to the Stimson dyad ratios algorithm. *Political Analysis* 22 (1): 115–29.

Mendelberg, Tali. 2001. *The race card*. Princeton, NJ: Princeton University Press.

Miller, Warren E., and Donald E. Stokes. 1963. Constituency influence in Congress. *American Political Science Review* 57:45–56.

Mondak, Jeffery J. 2001. Developing valid knowledge scales. *American Journal of Political Science* 45 (1): 224–38.

Mondak, Jeffery J., and Mary R. Anderson. 2004. The knowledge gap: A reexamination of gender-based differences in political knowledge. *Journal of Politics* 66 (2): 492–512.

Mondak, Jeffery J., and Belinda Creel Davis. 2001. Asked and answered: Knowledge levels when we will not take "don't know" for an answer. *Political Behavior* 23 (3): 199–224.

Mutz, Diana C. 2007. Effects of "in-your-face" television discourse on perceptions of a legitimate opposition. *American Political Science Review* 101 (4): 621–35.

Myrdal, Gunnar. 1944. *An American dilemma: The Negro problem and modern democracy*. New York: Transaction Publishers.

Nadeau, Richard, and Richard G. Niemi. 1995. Educated guesses: The process of answering factual knowledge questions in surveys. *Public Opinion Quarterly* 59 (3): 323–46.

Nelson, Thomas E., and Donald R. Kinder. 1996. Issue frames and group-centrism in American public opinion. *Journal of Politics* 58:1055–78.

Neuman, W. Russell. 1986. *The paradox of mass politics*. Cambridge, MA: Harvard University Press.

Nie, Norman H., and Kristi Anderson. 1974. Mass belief systems revisited: Political change and attitude structure. *Journal of Politics* 36:540–90.

Nie, Norman H., Sidney Verba, and John R. Petrocik. 1976. *The changing American voter*. Cambridge, MA: Harvard University Press.

———. 1981. Reply to Abramson and Smith. *American Political Science Review* 75:149–52.

Noel, Hans. 2013. *Political ideologies and political parties in America*. New York: Cambridge University Press.

Noel, Alain, and Jean-Phillippe Therien. 2008. *Left and right in global politics*. New York: Cambridge University Press.

Novick, Laura R., and Miriam Bassok. 2005. Problem solving. In *The Cambridge handbook of thinking and reasoning*, edited by Keith Holyoak and Robert G. Morrison, 321–50. New York: Cambridge University Press.

Nunnally, Jum. 1967. *Psychometric theory*. New York: McGraw-Hill.

Page, Benjamin. 1978. *Choices and echoes in presidential elections: Rational man and electoral democracy*. Chicago: University of Chicago Press.

Parker, Christopher S., and Matt A. Barreto. 2013. *Change they can't believe in:*

The Tea Party and reactionary politics in America. Princeton, NJ: Princeton University Press.

Perlstein, Rick. 2001. *Before the storm.* New York: Hill and Wang.

Pew Research Center. 2007. *Political knowledge of current affairs little changed by news and information revolutions.* Washington, DC.

Pierce, John C. 1970. Party identification and the changing role of ideology in American politics. *Midwest Journal of Political Science* 14 (1): 25–42.

Pietryka, Matthew T., and Randall C. MacIntosh. 2013. An analysis of ANES items and their use in construction of political knowledge scales. *Political Analysis* 21 (4): 407–29.

Poole, Keith T. 1998. Recovering a basic space from a set of issue scales. *American Journal of Political Science* 42 (3): 954–93.

Poole, Keith T., and Howard L. Rosenthal. 1984. The polarization of American politics. *Journal of Politics* 46 (4): 1061–79.

Popkin, Samuel E., and Michael A. Dimock. 1999. Political knowledge and citizen competence. In *Citizen competence and democratic institutions,* edited by Stephen L. Elkin and Karol Edward Soltan, 117–46. University Park: Pennsylvania State University Press.

Posner, Daniel N. 2005. *Institutions and ethnic politics in Africa.* New York: Cambridge University Press.

Price, Vincent, and Zaller, John. 1993. Who gets the news? Alternative measures of news reception and their implications for research. *Public Opinion Quarterly* 57:133–64.

Prior, Markus. 2011. You've either got it or you don't? The stability of political interest over the life cycle. *The Journal of Politics* 72 (3): 747–66.

Prior, Markus, and Arthur Lupia. 2008. Money, time, and political knowledge: Distinguishing quick recall and political learning skills. *American Journal of Political Science* 52 (1): 169–83.

Putnam, Robert D., Robert Leonardi, and Raffaella Y. Nanetti. 1979. Attitude stability among Italian elites. *American Journal of Political Science* 23: 463–94.

Rohde, David W. 1991. *Parties and leaders in the post-reform House.* Chicago: University of Chicago Press.

Rotunda, Ronald D. 1986. *The politics of language: Liberalism as word and symbol.* Iowa City: University of Iowa Press.

Rosenstone, Steven J. 1983. *Forecasting presidential elections.* New Haven, CT: Yale University Press.

Rosenstone, Steven J., and John Mark Hansen. 1993. *Mobilization, participation and democracy in America.* New York: Macmillan.

Ryan, Timothy J. 2014. Reconsidering moral issues in politics. *Journal of Politics* 76 (2): 380–97.

Safire, William. 2008. *Safire's political dictionary*. New York: Oxford University Press.

Sanbonmatsu, Kira. 2002. *Democrats, Republicans and the politics of women's place*. Ann Arbor: University of Michigan Press.

Sani, Giacomo, and Giovanni Sartori. 1983. Polarization, fragmentation and competition in Western democracies. In *Western European party systems: Continuity and change*, edited by Hans Daalder and Peter Mair, 307–40. Beverly Hills: Sage.

Sartori, Giovanni. 1969. Politics, ideology, and belief systems. *American Political Science Review* 63 (2): 398–411.

Schattschneider, E. E. 1942. *Party government*. New York: Farrar & Rinehart.

Schlesinger, Arthur M. 1986. *The cycles of American history*. Boston: Houghton Mifflin Harcourt.

Schuman, Howard, Robert F. Belli, and Katerine Bischoping. 1997. The generational basis of historical knowledge. In *Collective memory of political events: Social psychological perspectives*, edited by James W. Pennebaker, Dario Paez, and Bernard Rime. Mahwah, NJ: Lawrence Erlbaum.

Schuman, Howard, and Stanley Presser. 1980. *Questions and answers in attitude surveys: Experiments on question form, wording, and context*. New York: Academic Press.

Schuman, Howard, and Cheryl Rieger. 1992. Historical analogies, generational effects, and attitudes toward war. *American Sociological Review* 57 (3): 315–26.

Schuman, Howard, and Jacqueline Scott. 1989. Generations and collective memories. *American Sociological Review* 54 (3): 359–81.

Schumpeter, Joseph A. 1942. *Capitalism, socialism, and democracy*. New York: Harper and Row.

Sears, David O. 1993. Symbolic politics: A socio-psychological theory. In *Explorations in political psychology*, edited by Shanto Iyengar and William J. McGuire, 113–49. Durham, NC: Duke University Press.

Sears, David O., P. J. Henry, and Rick Kosterman. 2000. Egalitarian values and contemporary racial politics. In *Racialized politics: The debate about racism in America*, edited by David O. Sears, Jim Sidanius, and Lawrence Bobo, 75–117. Chicago: University of Chicago Press.

Sears, David O., Richard Lau, Tom R. Tyler, and Harris, M. Allen Jr. 1980. Self-interest vs. symbolic politics in policy attitudes and presidential voting. *American Political Science Review* 74 (3): 670–84.

Sears, David O., and Nicholas A. Valentino. 1997. Politics matters: Political events as catalysts for preadult socialization. *American Political Science Review* 91 (1): 45–65.

Shils, Edward. 1958. Ideology and civility: On the politics of the intellectual. *Sewanee Review* 66:450–80.

Smith, E. R. 1989. *The unchanging American voter*. Berkeley: University of California Press.

Sniderman, Paul M. 1993. The new look in public opinion research. In *The state of the discipline*, edited by Ada Finifter, 219–46. Washington, DC: American Political Science Association.

Sniderman, Paul M., Richard A. Brody, and James H. Kuklinski. 1984. Policy reasoning and political values: The problem of racial equality. *American Journal of Political Science* 28 (1): 75–94.

Sniderman, Paul M., Richard A. Brody, and Philip E. Tetlock. 1991. *Reasoning and choice: Explorations in political psychology*. Cambridge: Cambridge University Press.

Sniderman, Paul M., Michael G. Hagen, Philip E. Tetlock, and Henry E. Brady. 1991. Reasoning chains. In *Reasoning and choice: Explorations in political psychology*, edited by Paul M. Sniderman, Richard A. Brody, and Philip E. Tetlock, 70–92. Cambridge: Cambridge University Press.

Sniderman, Paul M., and Edward H. Stiglitz. 2012. *The reputational premium*. Princeton, NJ: Princeton University Press.

Sober, Elliott, and David Sloan Wilson. 1998. *Unto others: The evolution and psychology of unselfish behavior*. Cambridge, MA: Harvard University Press.

Stimson, James A. 1991. *Public opinion in America: Moods, cycles, and swings*. Boulder, CO: Westview.

Stimson, James A., Michael B. MacKuen, and Robert S. Erikson. 1995. Dynamic representation. *American Political Science Review* 89: 543–65.

Stoker, Laura. 1992. Interests and ethics in politics. *American Political Science Review* 86 (2): 369–80.

Stokes, Donald E. 1966. Party loyalty and the likelihood of deviating elections. In *Elections and the political order*, edited by Angus Campbell, Philip E. Converse, Warren E. Miller, and Donald E. Stokes, 125–35. New York: Wiley.

Stokes, Donald E., and Warren E. Miller. 1962. Party government and the saliency of Congress. *Public Opinion Quarterly* 26 (4): 531–46.

Sturgis, Patrick, Nick Allum, and Patten Smith. 2008. An experiment on the measurement of political knowledge in surveys. *Public Opinion Quarterly* 72 (1): 90–102.

Sturgis, Patrick, and Patten Smith. 2010. Fictitious issues revisited: Political interest, knowledge and the generation of nonattitudes. *Political Studies* 58: 66–84.

Sullivan, John L., James E. Pierson, and George E. Marcus. 1978. Ideological constraint in the mass public: A methodological critique and some new findings. *American Journal of Political Science* 22 (2): 233–49.

Sumner, William Graham. [1906] 2002. *Folkways: A study of mores, manners, customs, and morals*. Mineola, NY: Dover Publications.

Tajfel, Henri, Michael G. Billig, Robert P. Bundy, and Claude Flament. 1971. Social categorization and intergroup behavior. *European Journal of Social Psychology* 1 (2): 149–78.

Tesler, Michael. 2012. The spillover of racialization into health care: How President Obama polarized public opinion by racial attitudes and race. *American Journal of Political Science* 56:690–704.

——. 2015. Priming predispositions and changing policy positions: An account of when mass opinion is primed or changed. *American Journal of Political Science* 59 (4): 806–24.

Tesler, Michael, and David O. Sears. 2010. *Obama's race*. Chicago: University of Chicago Press.

Tilly, Charles. 1998. *Durable inequality*. Berkeley: University of California Press.

Tourangeau, Roger, and Thomas J. Plewes, eds. 2013. *Nonresponse in social science surveys: A research agenda*. Washington, DC: National Academies Press.

Treier, Shawn, and D. Sunshine Hillygus. 2009. The nature of political ideology in the contemporary electorate. *Public Opinion Quarterly* 73 (4): 679–703.

Tversky, Amos, and Daniel Kahneman. 1973. Availability: A heuristic for judging frequency and probability. *Cognitive Psychology* 5:207–32.

Valentino, Nicholas A., Vincent L. Hutchings, and Ismael White. 2002. Cues that matter: How political ads prime racial attitudes during campaigns. *American Political Science Review* 96 (1): 75–90.

Verba, Sidney, and Norman H. Nie. 1972. *Participation in America. Political democracy and social equality*. New York: Harper and Row.

Verba, Sidney, and Gary R. Orren. 1985. *Equality in America*. Cambridge, MA: Harvard University Press.

Verba, Sidney, Kay L. Schlozman, and Henry E. Brady. 1995. *Voice and equality: Civic voluntarism in American politics*. Cambridge, MA: Harvard University Press.

Webb, Eugene J., Donald T. Campbell, Richard D. Schwartz, and Lee Sechrest. 1966. *Unobtrusive measures*. Chicago: Rand McNally.

Weiss, Andrew, Anthony Lutkus, Wendy Grigg, and Richard G. Niemi. 2001. The next generation of citizens: NAEP trends in civics—1988–1998. NCES 2000-494. Washington, DC: U.S. Department of Education, National Center for Education Statistics.

Williamson, Vanessa, Theda Skocpol, and John Coggin. 2011. The Tea Party and the remaking of Republican conservatism. *Perspectives on Politics* 9 (1): 25–43.

Wilson, David S., and Edward O. Wilson. 2007. Rethinking the theoretical foundation of sociobiology. *The Quarterly Review of Biology* 82 (4): 327–48.

Wolbrecht, Christina L. 2000. *The politics of women's rights: Parties, positions, and change*. Princeton, NJ: Princeton University Press.

Zaller, John. 1985. *Pre-testing information items on the 1985 NES Pilot Survey.*
Report to the Board of Overseers. Ann Arbor: National Election Study.

——. 1990. Political awareness, elite opinion leadership, and the mass survey
response. *Social Cognition* 8 (1): 125–53.

——. 1992. *The nature and origin of mass opinion.* Cambridge: Cambridge University Press.

Zaller, John, and Stanley Feldman. 1992. A simple theory of the survey response: Answering questions versus revealing preferences. *American Journal
of Political Science* 36:579–618.

Zechmeister, Elizabeth J., and Margarita Corral. 2012. Individual and contextual constraints on ideological labels in Latin America. *Comparative Political Studies* 46 (6): 675–701.

Index

CHICAGO STUDIES IN AMERICAN POLITICS

A series edited by
BENJAMIN I. PAGE, SUSAN HERBST, LAWRENCE R. JACOBS, AND ADAM J. BERINSKY

CPSIA information can be obtained
at www.ICGtesting.com
Printed in the USA
LVOW03s1131230118
563339LV00005B/9/P

9 780226 452456